Temple Israel Congregation
of Ottawa

DONATED BY

Zelda Freedman

In Honour of the Fiftieth Anniversary of

Sheila and Mort Baslaw

The Torah's Seventy Faces

Commentaries on the Weekly Sidrah

Compiled by
Simcha Raz

Edited with an Introduction by
Rabbi Dov Peretz Elkins

authorHOUSE™

1663 LIBERTY DRIVE, SUITE 200
BLOOMINGTON, INDIANA 47403
(800) 839-8640
WWW.AUTHORHOUSE.COM

First published by AuthorHouse 07/21/05

ISBN: 1-4208-5930-7 (sc)

Printed in the United States of America
Bloomington, Indiana

This book is printed on acid-free paper.

Preface

by Simcha Raz

The weekly Torah portions have served throughout history as a treasure for teaching and preaching, for law and lore, for discussion and dialog. In each portion, one finds viewpoints and background which elevate the soul, give a sense of awe and wonder, spark encouragement in times of crisis, and motivate creativity and human action. It is no wonder that, over the course of generations, wells of wisdom have sprung from the depths of these weekly lections, from which we can sustain our spirit and slake our thirst, each person according to need and temperament. Pearls of wisdom, ethical lessons, parables, wise proverbs, and tales of parents and children: it is all there.

*

Our task in this collection of commentaries was to assemble a selection of these treasures, and to present to the reader choice nuggets from these hewn stones. Among the selections are sources from ancient rabbis, Talmudic scholars, and masters of the Midrash, as well as teachers from all periods of our history – biblical commentators, Hasidic saints, pious educators and purveyors of ethical tales. The commentaries touch on a plethora of subjects, including relations among people, with our Maker, and with ourselves. In all this, we come to know that our holy Torah has never known boundaries. In every generation, the "people of the book" invested their thoughts, attitudes, and beliefs, recognizing that within these chapters of the Torah are embedded not only pathways that reach to the distant past, but also forms of expression for the harried present and for dreams of the future.

*

Several sections of these commentaries were broadcast Sabbath eves on Israeli Radio over the course of three years at the initiative of Rebetzin Shulamit Melamed. The warm response by many listeners hastened my desire to expand the material, to complete the project, and to set it into the form of this book. My hope and prayer is that it will spark the interest of a broader audience and enhance their appreciation of our sacred heritage.

Simcha Raz

B"H, United Jerusalem, 27 Iyyar, 5758 (1998)
On the Yahrzeit of my Teacher, my Father, Rabbi Chaim Rakover, z"l.

Introduction to One Volume English Edition

Much of the material found in this book has already been published in my five volume Hebrew series called, *Shiv'im Panim LaTorah,* "The Seventy Faces of the Torah."

Several additional chapters first published in a volume called "Darchei Noam – Ways of Pleasantness," have been reprinted here as well. They were originally commissioned by Rabbi Yerachmiel Barilka, of the Jewish National Fund, and translated by staff members at the JNF.

It was a great honor when my friend Rabbi Dov Peretz Elkins agreed to combine all of the writings and edit them, with the help of the Almighty, for the benefit of the general public and the Jewish people.

Simcha Raz

Editor's Introduction

Several decades ago while browsing through one of my favorite book-stores in Jerusalem I discovered a Hebrew book called *Siah Aggadah*, by Simcha Raz, which is a wonderful collection of profound and stimulating thoughts on Parashat HaShavua. I used it for several years in my weekly preparation for sermons and teaching in my congregation. During another, later visit to Israel I found yet another fascinating book by the same author, *Pitgamay Hasidim, Hasidic Sayings*. I love quotations, short thoughts and aphorisms, and found this collection to be an extraordinary selection of such pithy words of advice. So I decided to try to track down Simcha Raz, and see if he were interested in having me translate the book into English, and share it with a wider audience. I wrote the publisher, who put me in touch with Rabbi Raz, and that began a friendship which has lasted over a decade now.

My son Jonathan, a writer who lives in Tel Aviv, and I translated *Pitgamay Hasidim*, and called it *Hasidic Wisdom*, since the sayings were from Hasidic masters. It was published by Jason Aronson in 1997, and is still in print (though Jason Aronson was absorbed into a large publishing house, Rowman Littlefield, in 2004). Over the years, Simcha Raz and I discussed the possibility of bringing some of his other wonderful books to the English-speaking public, and finally settled on his five-volume compendium, *Shivim Panim LaTorah*, which is the present book. It has been reduced because many of the commentaries in the original are somewhat geared toward a Hebrew-speaking audience.

Many of Simcha Raz's other books are now available in English, and I encourage anyone who finds any book by this author to grab it. He is a master anthologist, a gifted writer and teacher, and a person conversant with all of Jewish literature, with an eye to select the things that people love to read. His ability to pick the right passages and put them into inspiring and informative collections is an uncanny talent. His work has been recognized far and wide, and it is an honor to be associated with his prolific collections. It is also an honor to have him as a friend, mentor, teacher and co-worker.

I want to thank my research and editorial assistant Irit Printz, who helped put this volume into shape when my busy ministry distracted me from finishing it on time. She has done a superb job of working along with me in making the book reader-friendly.

Origin of the Title

The title of this collection of commentaries on the parshiyot of the Torah comes from the Midrash, Bemidbar Rabbah 13:15,16. The Midrash points out that a silver "mizrak" or bowl, was offered by each of the N'siim (Heads of the Tribes) at the Hanukkat Hamizbeah, the Dedication of the Altar, as a symbol of Torah that has been likened to wine (since it is customary to drink wine in a Mizrak). The Midrash asks why did the Mizrak weigh 70 shekels (b'shekel hakodesh)? And the answer is, "k'shem sh'yayin heshbono shivim, kakh yesh shivim panim baTorah." - just as the "gematria" [numerology] of yayin is 70, so are there 70 ways of expounding the Torah. In short, there is a multiplicity of interpretations for each verse of the Torah. The Torah is a spiritual fountain of inspiration that lends itself to endless commentaries, explanations and embellishments. Thus, this collection.

It is my hope that Simcha Raz's work in collecting these stimulating and informative commentaries will illuminate the words of our sacred Torah and make them better understood and even more inspiring to many students of our holy Tradition.

Dov Peretz Elkins

DPE@JewishGrowth.org
www.JewishGrowth.org
May, 2005
Yom Ha-atzmaut, 5765

Table of Contents

Genesis

Exodus

Leviticus

Numbers

Deuteronomy

<u>Genesis</u>

Parashat Bereshit

In the beginning, God created the Heaven and the Earth. (Gen. 1:1)

Continuous renewal

Rabbi Levi Yitzhak of Berdichev used to say that in our daily prayers we recite: "who forms the light and creates the darkness" – in the present tense – and not "who formed the light and created the darkness" as one would expect. This is our practice because the processes of creation and formation are continuous and from the time of the work of creation until now, and from now until the end of time, it has not ceased for even one moment. Each day God, with infinite goodness, renews the work of creation and regulates the luminaries, and causes the world to rejoice.

Rabbi Aharon of Karlin added: Just as God almighty renews the work of creation each day, so one has to establish a new interpretation each day. A person who does not progress – regresses. A person who does not have something new each day – has nothing old either.

God divided the light from the darkness... And there was evening and there was morning, the first day... [And God] divided the waters which were under the firmament from the waters which were above the firmament... and there was evening and there was morning, the second day. (Gen. 1:4-8)

Dispute

Midrash states: Why was "that it was good" not written in connection with the second day of the creation of the world? Rabbi Hanina said: Because on it a schism (a division) was created- the waters were divided for the creation of the firmament- as it is said, "let it divide the waters from the waters" (Gen. 1:6). Rabbi Tabyomi said: "that it was good" was not written regarding the second day because of a schism which, after all, was brought about for the greater stability and orderliness of the world (since dry land was thus revealed and rain was made possible). How much more, then, should this apply to divisions which lead to greater disorder in the world?

If "that it was good" was not said regarding the second day because division is mentioned on that day, then the question has to be raised – What about the first day? On the first day it is written that "God divided the light from the darkness", yet "that it was good" is written regarding the first day! What was the first day's division? It was between light and dark. Nothing could be better than that light and dark should be distinct and divided from each other, and not all mixed up together. That is why it is appropriate for "that it was good" to be said about the first day.

On the second day, however, the division is between two similar things, between siblings, between friends. It is a division between water and water, which are differentiated and divided into 'upper' and 'lower'. Such a division is difficult for the world, and it is not possible to say about it "that it was good".

God said: Let us created humanity in our image. (Gen. 1:26)

Me and you

To whom was this statement made? The Baal Shem Tov taught: This statement was made to Adam himself. The Creator said to Adam: Please come, Me and you together "we will make humanity". Please try to be a human being. If a person does not try to be human, no power in the world can help him become one.

So God created Adam in his image, in the image of God created He him; man and woman God created them. (Gen. 1:27)

Against imitation

Rabbi Menahem Mendel of Kotzk used to say about this verse: One should safeguard one's image and uniqueness, and not imitate others in deed or in thought. For Adam was created "in his image" – in Adam's own personal image, and only subsequently "in the image of God".

In the image of God

Creation reaches its peak of purpose with the creation of humanity in the image of God. Here, the Torah sets the place of humanity in the world, and the value of the human creature – about whom King David sang "for you have made people a little lower than angels" (Ps. 8:6). This necessitates an attitude of respect towards every person.

And why were Adam and Eve created alone? To teach you that whosoever destroys a single soul, scripture accounts it as if the whole world was destroyed. (Sanhedrin 37a)

God formed Adam of the dust of the earth, and blew into his nostrils the breath of life. (Gen. 2:7)

Wherever you go

The Creator created humanity from higher elements and from lower elements. Rabbi Israel Salant (founder of the musar movement) used to say: In matters concerning you yourself – your body, your soul– you may sometimes liken yourself to higher things, which are non-physical, and can ignore physical pleasure and needs. But in matters concerning others, you shall surely remember that people are created from lowly elements – "man was created from the dust of the earth and his end will be the dust of the earth, and by the sweat of his brow shall he have bread" – people have physical needs!

God planted a garden eastward in Eden; and God placed there Adam whom he had created. (Gen. 2:8)

Heartfelt joy

Once, in a dream, Rabbi Moshe Teitelbaum of Ohel sought to enter the Garden of Eden of the holy tanaim (the sages of the Mishnahic period). He was told that he would have to immerse himself in Miriam's well. He came to a high mountain with a deep well in it and exclaimed: "who can ascend such a mountain and how shall I stand in a holy place?"

(Ps. 24:3). He heard a cry: Angels will carry you up there and they will immerse you and will not harm you. The angels came, raised him up and lowered him down, immersing him. From there, they brought him to the Garden of Eden of the tanaim. He saw them sitting, with their crowns on their heads, studying Torah. He was astounded: was this all there was to the Garden of Eden? He saw no trees laden with fruits, no canopy of splendor, no fireworks, no angels, no miraculous wonders. He did not hear the sound of singing, the chirping of birds, the song of angels, or the playing of violins. He called out with soulful yearning: Is this all that there is to the Garden of Eden? He heard a heavenly voice proclaim: Moshe, son of Hanna, do you think that the holy tanaim are within the Garden of Eden? If so, you are sorely mistaken, for the Garden of Eden is within the tanaim! Rabbi Moshe asked: Why do I not see streams of joy around them? The voice answered him: Because the streams of joy do not flow around the tanaim, but within them. Then Rabbi Moshe awoke, elated with an intense joy.

Cleaving to the Divine Presence

The Chief Rabbi of Israel, Rabbi Avraham Yitzhak Kook, participated in the celebration when Magdiel was established. Trees were planted as part of the celebration, and they honored Rav Kook with planting the first sapling. The Rabbi threw down the spade they gave him, and began to dig the hole with his own bare hands. Rabbi Ze'ev Gold, who was also at the event, looked at him and saw that the Rav's face was burning like a torch. He was excited and trembling, and he was planting the sapling in the ground with awe and fear. Rabbi Gold asked: "Such great excitement, what is the reason for it? With God's help, hundreds of such trees are being planted in Israel". Rav Kook responded: "When I was holding the young sapling in my hand, I remembered a midrash: From the time of the world's creation, God has been occupied with nothing other than the first planting. You, as well, when you enter Israel, do not occupy yourselves with anything other than planting the first planting (Lev. Rabbah 25). At the moment that I held the sapling in my hand to put it in the ground, I remembered this midrash and I felt that I was cleaving to the Divine Presence, and a great fear overcame me.

God called out to Adam and said: Where are you? (Gen. 3:9)

A call for all times

When Rabbi Shneur Zalman of Ladi was imprisoned in the Petersburg prison, the royal ministers used to visit him in his cell. One of the ministers, who was knowledgeable in the Old Testament, asked him: the Creator calls Adam who was hiding among the trees and asks him "Where are you?" Didn't the Creator know where Adam was hiding?

Rabbi Shneur Zalman replied: "Where are you?" was not a question, but rather a summons to awaken. Where are you, Adam, in your world? This and that many days and years of your lifetime have already passed and what have you achieved in your world? This is a summons that God almighty sends to each person at all times and ages.

"Where are you?" is a sublime ethical calling no less important than a religious calling. A person's conscience is the voice of God. This summoning was not made only to Adam, and was not only heard in the Garden of Eden. That voice of God walks always in the garden of the world and is ready for every person at all times.

So God drove Adam out. (Gen. 3:24)

Happiness of the heart

The Baal Shem Tov asked: Who was it that expelled Adam and Eve from the Garden of Eden? Did an angel expel them? Did God? Yonatan Ben Uziel explained: "and Adam became troubled". In any case, people, when troubled, cannot be in the Garden of Eden. In the first days of Creation, when everything was still new and spring fresh, Adam and Eve's heart was open to the brilliance of the world. Everything that they saw, they praised the Creator "the very good" God gave the world. However, after the 'original sin', when they were no longer satisfied with what had been prepared for them, and a sense of need for things that were not intended for them grew, many troubles overcame them, preventing them from seeing the splendor of the world. Thus the gates of Eden were closed behind them.

So it came to pass, when they were in the field, that Cain rose up against his brother Abel and slew him. Then God said to Cain: Where is Abel your brother? But he said: I know not; Am I my brother's keeper? (Gen. 4:8-9).

A murderer's reaction

Adam and Eve brought mortality into the world, and Cain, their first-born, brought murder into it. Adam and Eve were corrupted by the serpent. But, in Cain's case, the cause was internal: "And God paid attention to Abel and his offering, but to Cain and his offering God paid no heed. And Cain was very angry" (Gen. 4:4-5). The flames of jealousy raged in Cain's heart and the world became too small to contain both of them. Adam and Eve, the first sinners, were embarrassed by their sin and hid from God. But Cain, the murderer, did not know the meaning of shame. On the contrary. When God asked "where is Able your brother?", Cain answered impertinently: "I do not know; Am I my brother's keeper?" This was his direct response after the crime. Not a shadow of embarrassment, not a hint of regret.

Moreover, the sages tell us that Cain not only did not recognize his sin, but even dared to cast aspersions against his Creator and to deflect the responsibility for the crime onto God: What Cain said was: "Am I my brother's keeper? You are the keeper of all creatures and You ask him of me?!" To what is this similar? To a thief who stole some vessels during the night and was not caught at the time. In the morning, the guard caught him and asked: "Why did you steal the vessels?" The thief replied: "I am a thief, and I have been true to my calling. You are a guard. Why were you not true to your calling?" This, too, is how Cain spoke: I killed him. You created in me the evil inclination. You safeguard everything but You let me kill him? It is really You who killed him, for had You accepted my offering, as you accepted his, I would not have been jealous of him.

Parashat Noah

These are the generations of Noah; Noah was a just man and perfect in his generations, and Noah walked with God. (Gen. 6:9)

From step to step

Rabbeynu Bahya taught us: The verse enumerates three sublime steps. Which Noah attained. First, he was a "righteous man" – avoiding injustice in all his actions. From there he ascended and attained, through his actions, a higher level: "perfect in his generations". He not only acted justly, but was perfect in his integrity, perfect in his heart. And from there, he went on to the highest step: "and Noah walked with God". He communed with the Creator: the step that only a select few attain.

A leader according to the times

Would it not have sufficed for Scripture to have stated that Noah was a righteous and perfect man? Why was it necessary to add "in his generations"? Rashi commented: "Some of our rabbis explain this as being in his praise: Had he lived in a generation of righteous people, he would have been even more righteous. Others, however, explain it as being to his discredit: In comparison with those of his own generation, he was righteous, but had he lived in the generation of Avraham, he would have been of no importance".

The Torah testifies about Noah that he was both righteous and perfect. Is it really possible that some interpret it to his discredit? But, there is also a difficulty with those of our rabbis who explain it to his credit. What more could one be than perfectly righteous? A "person" and "righteous" and "perfect" – and what else?

One can learn from here that sometimes it is not enough to be perfectly righteous. In a generation in which "the earth was filled with lawlessness" (Gen. 6:11), in a generation of corruption and deceit, it is not the most righteous thing for a person to look only to himself, to shut himself away in a Noah's ark and say: "I have saved my own soul". What such a person should do is act to rectify the injustices and to reduce the failures of the generation.

God said to Noah, The end of all flesh has come before me; for the earth is filled with violence through them. (Gen. 6:13)

Not forever

The Kli Yakar says: "The end of all flesh" – this is the day of death. Said the Holy One: The day of death came before Me with the complaint that no-one remembered him. Were they to recall him and remember "the end of all flesh" on earth, they would not run hither and thither to grow rich at the expense of others, to extort the poor and the needy. Were they to remember, the earth would not be filled with violence. If only they were to take it to their hearts that strength does not last forever and that capital is not permanent...

Person to person

Noah was chosen by the Creator to continue humanity's existence at a time when the decree was made to end the world and all it contained. According to Pirke Avot (chapter 5), the ten generations from Adam until Noah were sinners and evildoers. Only after these many generations, which were marked by constant sinning was the decree made to bring the flood into the world.

Our Sages of blessed memory taught that despite the fact that the generation of the Flood sinned and committed evil deeds against God, God's decision to destroy them was based solely on their behavior towards each other. The Talmud states: "Rabbi Yohanan said – Let us examine the seriousness of stealing. The generation of the Flood transgressed in every manner possible, engaging in all possible transgressions. Yet the judgment against them was not sealed until they engaged in theft" (Sanhedrin 108a).

A window (tzohar) shall you make in the ark. (Gen. 6:16)

A shelter

What is the nature of this "tzohar"? Rabbi Abba the son of Kahana said: It means a skylight. Rabbi Levi said: A precious stone [which provides light on its own]. Rabbi Pinhas said in Rabbi Levi's name: During the whole twelve months that Noah was in the Ark, he did not require the light of the sun by day, nor the light of the moon by night. Rather, he had a polished gem – which he hung up. When the gem was dim, Noah knew it was day, and when it shone, he knew that it was night. (Gen. Rabbah 31:11)

Rabbi Yair Hayyim Bekhrach commented on this midrash: This is how a person with possessions behaves. If the gem seems dim, without intrinsic value, this is a sign that it is "daytime" – that things are being seen in their correct perspective and the correct path is being followed. But, if the gem is shining brightly, this is a sign that it is "nighttime" – that the person is floundering in the dark and has lost the correct way of life.

For people's inclinations are evil from youth. (Gen. 8:21)

Sin lies at the door

Rabbi Israel of Koznitz used to say: Everybody has in them something of Cain, and something of Abel, something from the generation of the Flood, and something from the Tower generation. Jealousy and hatred are from Cain, sycophancy and inaction are from Abel. Desire and lust are from the generation of the Flood, pride and pursuit of honor are from the Tower generation. Thus, those who care for their own soul should make an effort to increase their good inclination over the bad, to implant in their heart good qualities and expel from it qualities that are not good.

Rabbi Nahman of Bratzlav used to say: There is no such thing as a person who does not contain a mixture of the four sons who are mentioned in the Passover Haggadah. Everyone has something of the wise son, the wicked son, the simple son, and the one who does not know how to ask. Happy is the person who knows how to place the wise son at the head to govern all four of them.

Whoever sheds man's blood, by man shall his blood be shed. (Gen. 9:6)

Causing embarrassment

The Hafetz Hayyim connects this verse to the following Talmudic teaching: "He who publicly shames his neighbor is as though he shed blood" (Baba Metzia 58b). He explains that whoever causes the blood of another person to drain away within, who insults that person publicly and thereby causes the natural whiteness of the face to be replaced by a blush of embarrassment "by man shall his blood be shed" – he is considered as though he had really shed blood and is severely punished. On this matter, the sages taught us that "It is better for a person be thrown into a fiery furnace than to put another person to shame in public" (Berakhot 34b).

The whole earth was of one language, and of one speech. (Gen. 11:1)

Against Dispute

We learn in the Midrash: The generation of the Flood was steeped in robbery… therefore not a remnant of them was left. But the generation of the Tower loved each other – as it is written: "And the whole earth was of one language". This is why a remnant of them was left. (Gen. Rabbah 38:6)

Rabbi said: Great is peace, for even if Israel were to practice idolatry but maintained peace among themselves, the Holy One would say "I have no dominion over them". And so we learn that peace is great and that dispute is hated. So long as unity prevailed among the generation of the Tower, it was impossible to punish them. As the Zohar (1:76a) put it: "From here we learn that quarrelsome people soon come to grief. For we see here that as long as the peoples of the world lived in harmony, being of one mind and one will, even though they rebelled against the Holy One, the supernal judgment could not touch them. But as soon as they were divided, "Adonai scattered them abroad" (Gen. 11:8).

They said, Come, let us build us a city and a tower, whose top may reach to heaven; and let us make us a name. (Gen. 11: 4)

Jealousy, covetousness, and pursuit of honor

Rabbi Israel of Koznitz used to say: "A person should keep distant from all bad qualities, the results of which will be severe for that person sooner or later. But more than any other, distance should be kept from three bad qualities: jealousy, covetousness, and the pursuit of honor. These, according to Rabbi Eleazar HaKappar, "put a person out of this world" (Pirke Avot 5:21) – that is, shorten a person's life.

Rabbi Koznitz continued: See how these three despicable qualities began to show themselves immediately in the world? Cain, the son of Adam and Eve, murdered his brother, Abel, out of jealousy, as it is written: "And Adonai had respect for Abel and for his offering. But for Cain and for his offering Adonai did not have respect" (Gen. 4:4-5). The Torah testifies that the generation of the Flood was steeped in robbery, as it is written: "And God looked upon the earth, and, behold, it was corrupt; for all flesh had corrupted its way upon the earth" (Gen. 6:12). The sin of those of the generation of the Flood stemmed from their chasing after honor, as it is written: "let us make us a name" (Gen. 11:4).

Not from fear

Gathered together in Noah's ark were people and beasts, animals, and birds, snakes and scorpions, and every creeping thing of the earth all dwelling together peacefully. They did no harm to one another, they did not attack each other. If this is so, what is so remarkable about the prophecy of the End of Days "and the wolf will dwell with the lamb"? After all, this had already occurred in the time of Noah.

However, there will be a great change at the End of Days. The time of the Flood was a time of calamity. The common danger of death was hovered over all of them equally. Therefore, it was natural that the beasts and the animals would unite and make peace among themselves during such a time.

So too, even with regard to people, there is a possibility that political parties will unite and make peace among themselves and will create a unified front for the purpose of defense and security. Yet, the vision of the prophet "and the wolf will dwell with the lamb" was made only regarding the End of Days – days of peace and tranquility. It is important to note that the coming together of humanity will be brought about not through terror and fear, but through the expansion of wisdom, the increase of insight, and the purification of character.

The positive side of the evil inclination

Every attribute and talent a person possesses may be used in either a positive or a negative manner. This is also true regarding a person's inclinations. Our Sages saw a positive aspect even in the evil inclination. The Midrash states: "Rabbi Shmuel ben Nahman said – 'And it was good', this is the good inclination; 'And it was very good', this is the evil inclination. So the evil inclination is very good? How strange! But without the evil inclination, man would not build a house and would not marry a woman and would not sire children and would not involve himself in work and commerce". (Gen. Rabbah 9)

What would the world look like without the evil inclination? The answer is given in the Talmud (Yoma 69b): "When they killed the evil inclination towards idolatry they said: 'since it is now a time of Divine favor, let us pray for the evil inclination towards immorality to be subdued before us. They prayed, and it was delivered into their hand. A prophet told them: See, if you kill the evil inclination, the world will become desolate. They captured it for three days. During that time, they sought a fresh laid egg throughout all of Israel in order to cure a sick person but none was found (because without the evil inclination, the hens would not mate with the roosters and would not lay eggs). They said: "What shall we do? Shall we kill the evil inclination? The world would become desolate!"

There is no evil without good and it is possible to use even the evil inclination in a positive manner. It is because of this that people were given insight – so they will know how to discern between good and evil, between positive and negative outcomes. These things were given and imprinted in the hearts of people for all time.

Parashat Lekh Lekha

Adonai had said to Abram: Get out from your country, and from your family, and from your father's house, to a land that I will show you. (Gen. 12:1)

"Go forth"

With this portion of Lekh Lekha, the Torah begins the story of the nation's ancestry: Avraham, Sarah, Yitzhak, Rivkah, Yaakov, Leah, and Rahel. These stories are imprinted with a string of difficult trials in which hour ancestors try to prove they are fit to be chosen by God to disseminate the belief in the uniqueness of the Creator of the World among those dwelling in the land.

According to our sages, Avraham was tested on ten occasions – from the call to go forth to the command to sacrifice his son Yitzhak. The sages noted that, in both the first trial and the last trial, Avraham is told "Lekh Lekha" (go). In the first trial, he is asked to leave his country, and in the last trial he is asked to go to Mount Moriah.

Meet yourself

Rabbi Shmuel of Succatchov used to say that the call "Lekh Lekha" was not meant only for the first Hebrew (Avraham), but for all who were created in the image of God, meaning that one should take the path that is appropriate for one's character. "Lekh Lekha" – go to yourself, be what you are.

Trust and perfect faith

Avraham was commanded to leave his country, his native land, and his father's house. He was told nothing about the nature of the land to which he was destined to go, "whether it is fat or lean, whether there is wood in it, or not" (Num. 13:20). The only thing he was told was that it will be "a land that I will show you". Avraham did not know where he was going, but only whom he was following. This action embodied the trust and perfect faith of Avraham. Of subsequent generations it was said: "I remember you, the devotion of your youth... when you went after me in the wilderness, in a land that was not sown" (Jer. 2:2).

Reward for each step

The Magid of Dubno used to say: There are two possible reasons for a person to go from one place to another. Either he has a reason to go to a particular place, or he has to flee from where he was. The fugitive's only interest is fleeing from where he is. Every step he takes fulfills this goal. The more steps he takes, the further away he will be. But for the person who tries to reach a particular place, his goal is achieved only when he reaches his destination.

God commanded Avraham to leave his home for two reasons. God wanted Avraham to distance himself from his native land and to forget it. God also wanted him to reach the Land of Israel, for, once there, Avraham could be influenced by the Divine Holy spirit. This is the meaning of the verse: "Get out from your country" – that he should leave his native Land; "to a land that I will show you" – that he should reach the Land of Israel.

We read in the Midrash: "Why did God not reveal the destination immediately? In order to make it more beloved in his eyes, and to reward him for every step he took" (Gen. Rabbah 39:9). Had God revealed to Avraham that the intention was that he should arrive at a particular place, then Avraham would not have fulfilled the Divine command until he actually arrived there. But, since God said to him "Get out from your country", the very distancing from his native land was a goal per se. In this way, he could be rewarded for every step, because every step is a mitzvah in its own right.

Adonai appeared to Abram, and said, To your seed will I give this land. (Gen. 12:7)

I wish I had a portion in the Land

At the age of seventy five, Avraham left his country and went to the land of Canaan. What made him do this? The Midrash states: Rabbi Levi said: When traveling in Aram Naharyim, Avraham saw the inhabitants eating and drinking and acting irresponsibly. He said: I wish not to have a portion in this land. Since he arrived on the border of Israel and he saw them weeding at the time of weeding, and hocing at the time of hoeing, he said: "I wish I had a portion in that Land". Then God said to him: "To your seed will I give this land". (Gen. Rabbah 39)

Abram said to Lot, Let there be no strife...between me and you...for we are brothers. (Gen. 13:8)

My brother is hitting me

Gold once asked Iron: Why do you make so much noise when you are hit? I, too, am hit but remain almost silent. You, replied the iron, are hit by a stranger and so your sufferings are not that great, but I am hit by my brother, that is why the pain is so great, and the disgrace so large...

Lift up now your eyes, and look from the place where you are to the north, and to the south, and to the east, and to the west. (Gen. 13:14)

Look and see

God said to Moshe: "Get up to the top of Pisgah, and lift up your eyes" (Deut. 3:27). This tells us that the Land of Israel necessitates a lifting of the eyes. Everyone merits seeing its virtue and glory. One who lowers the eyes – said Rabbi Meir Simhah of Bavinsk – sees the Land of Israel as a geographic location, a country like any other country. But one who raises the eyes up envisions the Land of Israel as the Land of Heaven, a land higher than all other countries in its virtue and spirit.

For all the land which you see, to you will I give it, and to your seed forever. (Gen. 13:15)

The vision and the inheritance

Later in this chapter we read: "Arise, walk through the land in its length and in its breadth; for I will give it to you" (Gen. 13:17). In this second promise, Avraham is not assured that the land will be given to his seed forever, as he was the first time.

Rabbi Yaakov Dushinsky, who served as president of the Rabbinical court in Capetown, South Africa, offered the following explanation: What the eyes of parents see – the vision, the faith, the cognition – can be passed on to the children. The merit of the parents is available for the children, as is the right to the world outlook and the spiritual aspirations of their ancestors. But what the ancestors acquired and conquered with the sweat of their brow, by their swords and their bows, the children are obliged to hold onto and assure with an alert defense and exceptional and constant safeguarding.

A spiritual inheritance is an eternal inheritance. The yearning for the land, the love of the land, these were bequeathed to our children in the course of thousands of years. "I will give [the Land] to you" – Only to you. If your children want it, they will have to walk through it, and put down roots in it, and defend it, and till it, and safeguard it anew in each generation.

That I will not take from a thread to a sandal strap, and that I will not take any thing that is yours, lest you should say, I have made Abram rich. (Gen. 14:23)

You shall live a life of poverty

Rabbi David Cohen Hanazir relates: I have never asked for any material benefit from Rabbi Avraham Yitzhak Kook. The spiritual treasures and the Torah with which he plentifully endowed me were sufficient for me. On one occasion, I went to him and asked for a match to light a candle for the yeshivah. The Rabbi was greatly pleased that he had an opportunity to do me some favor. He hurriedly got up and invited me into his room and this is what he said: "You should know, my son, that I have nothing of my own, and all that you see in this house is not mine. I did not build the house. The broken chair you are sitting on is not mine, and even this gown that I am wearing – it is not mine either". And this is how Rabbi Kook lived to his last day. And when he died, he left no inheritance. In his will, there was just one legacy – a request from members of his family that they settle his debts.

Look now toward heaven, and count the stars ... so shall your seed be. (Gen. 15:5)

Heaven is the limit

Rabbi Shapira, head of the Hakhmei Lublin yeshivah, said: The Holy One called to Avraham: "Look now toward heaven, and count the stars". And just as you are looking up to the heavens and are counting the stars, even though you well know that mortal humans cannot count the many, many stars in the heavens, "so shall your seed be" – nothing shall be too wonderful or too out of reach for your seed. They will strive ever upwards, rising up above human nature. With them, desire shall not be measured by their ability, for their ability will soar to the heavens and will sometimes attain the unlimited willpower that is in them.

He believed in Adonai; and God counted it to him for righteousness. (Gen. 15:6)

Seventy facets of the Torah

One is belief – despite the Torah's many paths. Every path is good if it suits the emotional character of the believer. The yearning for Godliness is so multi-faceted that it cannot find its expression in only one way.

After the death of Rebbe Elimelekh of Lizhensk, his students looked for another righteous teacher to replace him. They came to Lublin, to the Visionary of Lublin. When they saw that the Visionary's way of worshipping God was not the one to which they were accustomed with their rebbi, they were about to leave Lublin to look for another righteous person. However, when they entered the Visionary's room in order to receive a blessing before parting, he told them: "The Torah has seventy facets, but to do God's work there are four hundred facets. After all, what value would there be to God if there was only one way to worship the Holy One?

The Baal Shem Tov taught: God wants to be worshipped in all possible ways, but a person must choose the way itself, and cleave to it mightily. A long hallway leads to the inner hall wherein resides the Creator, and many gates are chiseled throughout the hallway. The hallway is open to everyone, but every gate within opens with a key that fits the character of the person passing the threshold. There is a gate that is opened with joy and another that is opened with a tear; there is a gate that is opened with the strength of praise and glorification and another that is opened with prayer and confession; there is a gate that is opened with love, and another that is opened with awe. The righteous teacher gave his students the task of examining themselves to discover toward which path each of them is drawn.

Judaism is not even deterred by the doubts of the soul. Its teacher found a positive side to the doubts. Thus said the Rebbe of Bratzlav: "… The scream itself is an aspect of belief. Even though doubts, heresy, and great questions enter the mind, it is obvious that the person's heart contains a spark of belief. Were this not the case, there would be no scream at all".

An undeserved gift

Rebbe Moshe of Kovrin said: The belief in God was planted in and inscribed on the heart of Avraham. However, he did not think that belief came to him of his own power. Rather, "and he counted it to him for righteousness" – he thought that the Creator of the world had rewarded him with righteousness and kindness, and that the Creator had planted his belief in the Divine uniqueness in his heart

Parashat Vayera

Father of the Nation

After the Torah relates the history of the first nineteen generations of humanity, it offers its audience an extensive description of the life of Avraham and devotes three entire portions to it. It is noteworthy that the Torah is not concerned with Avraham's history outside of Canaan, but rather, it begins to relate his history from the time he comes to the land that is destined for his offspring. At that time, Avraham "was five and seventy years old" (Gen. 12:4). Since Avraham lived to be one hundred and seventy five, we know nothing about almost half of his life!

Adonai appeared to him by the terebinths of Mamre, as he sat in the tent door in the heat of the day. (Gen. 18:1)

Guests

Rashi explains: he sat at the tent door to see if there is a wayfarer that he could bring into his home.

For the poor, who had become accustomed to receiving bread of charity and who were not embarrassed by it, there was no need to wait; they would find the way themselves. However, often there was among them a "wayfarer", a poor person who would approach the door and then back away and then approach again. Each time he would change his mind and back away going the way he came. He did not have the courage to enter and stretch out his hand. A wayfarer of this type must be waited for at the entrance...

It was a hot dry day, the kind of day when people would close themselves into their homes against the boiling sun. However, Avraham sat at the tent door, anticipating guests who might happen to pass by his home despite there being no chance of finding anybody outside on such a hot day.

We read in the Talmud: Rabbi Hama Bar Hanina said: "That same day, the third day after Avraham's circumcision, God took the sun from its case and made it shine with intense heat so that no guests should bother this righteous man [while he was sick]". Avraham sent his servant Eliezer outside to look for guests. Eliezer went out but did not find anyone. Avraham said: 'I do not believe you', and went out to see for himself. (Bava Metzia 86b)

What a unique man was Avraham, who on the third day after his circumcision, still suffering painfully, was dismayed that he had no guests! He could not hide inside his home and live focused on himself only. He could not sit in his home without guests for even one day. Ill as he was, he rose from his sickbed and went outside to search for wayfarers.

When God saw that Avraham was so disheartened that no wayfarer came to his door, God commanded the angels to appear before Avraham in the form of men. Avraham was so happy to see these guests that, even though they appeared to him to be Arabs who bowed down to the dust of their feet (Kiddusin 32b), he nonetheless ran toward them, bowed down low before them and asked them to come to his home.

I will place God before me at all times

It happened once that Rabbi Barukh of Kosov was chastising his friends, and said to them: "In all your ways, know God" (Prov. 3:6) - This is a very important rule in Hasidism. Each person must always remember, at every moment, that one stands, sits and lies before the Ruler of all Rulers, the Blessed Holy One, that one must not divert attention from the Creator for even one minute.

One of the listeners replied: "Our master, I am so totally immersed in my business. How is it possible for me to avoid diverting attention for even a short time from the worship of the Blessed One?

Rabbi Barukh replied: Scripture says – "God appeared at Elonay Mamray, and he was sitting at the door of his tent". What does it matter where God appeared to Avraham – at Elonay Mamray, or somewhere else? The Torah teaches us that even at a moment when Avraham was dwelling in the gentile neighborhood of Elonay Mamray, even when he was immersed in mundane matters, sitting at his tent, waiting to welcome guests, even then he fulfilled what is written in Scripture, "I shall place God before me at all times" (Ps. 16:8).

You too, my son, concluded Rabbi Barukh, just as you are able to think thoughts of business when you stand in prayer or are involved in Torah study, so can you examine your soul when you are busy with worldly matters.

The Deeds of the Ancestors Become the Torah of the Children

Avraham taught us the importance of Hakhnasat Orhim - Welcoming Guests. This mitzvah should be pursued even to the point that the guests would be sitting inside the house, so that they would feel perfectly at home, and the host would sit outside, "at the door of the tent". This was what the Community of Jerusalem did with Pilgrims to Jerusalem on the Festivals. So we learn in Avot D'Rabbi Natan (chapter 35), "Guests would relax inside the house, and the hosts would be outside".

One of the frequenters at the home of the sainted Jerusalem Rabbi Aryeh Levin told the following story: "It happened once that I visited him in the evening to discuss some matters with him. I found his door locked. I was told that the Rav was teaching a class in Daf Yomi (the daily page of Talmud). An hour later I returned. This time they told me that the Rav had gone to a Religious Celebration (Simhat Mitzvah). I returned two hours later, and still did not find him. I was told that this time the Rav had gone to comfort the bereaved. I returned still later, and I found two other people waiting for him at the door. I was aware that the Rav would visit the small building near the edge of the street. I asked people nearby that when the Rav arrives to please signal me so that I could have a few private words with him.

The Rav arrived very late at night, walking slowly, and offered a greeting of shalom to the guests waiting for him. I asked if he would step inside with me so I could chat with him in private, and if the other two guests would be kind enough to wait outside for a moment. Nevertheless the Rav invited them inside. I was rather surprised at that. After we all enter his room, he sat them down on his bed, asked their forgiveness, went outside with me and said: "The two of us can talk outside, so why should we make the guests wait outside?"

The Story of a Thief

A thief was locked up in the criminal jail in Jerusalem, did his time and was released at evening time. After roaming far from Jerusalem, without a penny in his pocket, he went to the home of Rabbi Aryeh Levin whom he knew from the Rabbi's visit to the jail, in order to ask for a handout. Rabbi Levin and his wife received him as an honored guest. They furnished him with a large sum of money, and did not permit him to leave until he had a sumptuous meal. At the end of the meal Reb Aryeh said to him, "I am grateful to you for visiting us. Because of you I serendipitously fulfilled two mitzvot: Hakhnasat Orhim (Welcoming Guests) and Gemilut Hasadim (Doing Acts of Kindness), but, if you please, the hour is late, and why should you travel during night hours? Honor us and stay here overnight". Reb Aryeh prepared a guest bed, and blessed him with good night.

At the rising of the sun, Reb Aryeh awoke to attend morning prayers, and he noticed that this honored guest had stolen his treasured kiddush cup, and his silver candlesticks had disappeared! He awakened his wife and told her what had happened, and said: "I forgive this thief completely so that he will not be punished because of me". Then he added: "Let's make a pact between us that this sorrowful incident will not create a precedent, and will not prevent us from hosting other thieves in our home in the future...".

He looked and he saw three men standing nearby. As soon as he saw them, he ran from the entrance of the tent to greet them. (Gen. 18:2)

With a Full Heart

Scripture says "He saw" twice in this verse. What does this teach us? The first "He saw" indicates that they were important men, men of stature, but after he looked more carefully, "He saw" that they were simple wanderers, Bedouin. Nevertheless, "he ran to greet them" in order to fulfill the mitzvah of Hakhnasat Orhim.

The story is told of a distinguished and handsome chap who was hosted at the home of the Magid of Trisk. The host thought him to be a fine scholar, and an important person. He served him the finest delectable foods, and offered the finest drinks available, and he went to every length to serve him properly, and did not fail to prepare his bed every single night.

It soon became apparent that this 'distinguished scholar' was anything but, and was a deceitful, crafty knave. The Magid's family and friends were deeply troubled for their father and teacher who erred regarding this unworthy creature. The Rav noticed this reaction and told them: do not be upset. When the Blessed Holy One wanted to bring merit to Avraham with the great mitzvah of Hakhnasat Orhim, God did not bring to him men of great stature, in fact, they were not even human beings who eat, drink and sleep - but God brought before him angels who fooled him and pretended to be eating and drinking, and Avraham brought them food and drink for naught. Why did God do this? In order to teach the descendents of Avraham for all future generations that if a person does a mitzvah, well and good. It should be done with a full heart, and a willing soul, with no expectation of reward, or regard for who might benefit from it.

For I know him, that he will command his children ... to do justice. (Gen. 18:19)

Deeds of loving-kindness

The "grandfather" of Slobodka, Rebbe Natan Tzvi Finkel, used to say: The Torah accentuated the kind deeds of our Father Avraham, and his kind heart which was filled with loved and compassion for all who were created in God's image. Yet the Torah passes over in total silence the deep faith Avraham had in his Creator. This is somewhat strange, since Avraham was the very first who, at age thirteen, recognized his Creator; who realized that Adonai is God, and there is none else. Avraham was sentenced to death for his faith, taught all humanity the concept of the Unity of Divinity, and brought souls to God and to Torah. And yet all the praise heaped on Avraham is for his acts of goodness, and not for the depth of his faith. From this we learn that it was Avraham's Loving-kindness which was the highest principle in his character.

A World of Kindness

Rabbi Natan Tzvi Finkel used to say: The Torah emphasizes Avraham's numerous deeds of kindness, and tells us that his heart was filled with love and compassion for all of creation. Yet, it is totally silent regarding his belief in, and knowledge of, God. This, despite Avraham being the first person who recognized that "Adonai is God and there are none beside him" – and he was only three at the time!

Avraham was sentenced to burn for his belief, taught all of humanity the unity of God and brought people to a belief in God and His Torah. Yet, all of the praise for Avraham relates only to his charitable deeds and not to his greatness of faith. From this we learn that charity is the first and foremost principle in Avraham's personality.

Avraham drew near, and said: Will you destroy the righteous with the wicked? (Gen. 18:23)

Removing Evil from Israel

Avraham was the paragon of charity. His enemy was the city of Sodom whose evil ways contradicted all of his customs. One would have thought that, upon hearing of Sodom's upcoming destruction, Avraham would have been pleased. Nevertheless, Avraham was not happy and prayed that the judgment be cancelled. Why? Had Avraham been happy or pleased at the fall of Sodom, that, in itself, would constitute a bit of Sodom-like evil. Avraham's desire wasn't that Sodom shouldn't exist – rather, he wished that 'Sodomism' should not exist, that evil should be erased from the world and not the evildoers.

The Righteousness of the Righteous

Rebbe Nahman of Bratzlav used to say: When people talk about a righteous person – a truly God fearing person – thoughts of repentance and the desire to be close to the Almighty begin to stir because each Jew is always filled with the desire to be close to God. Afterwards, however, they say: who can be like that righteous man? After all, he had a holy soul from his youth. It is as if the righteousness of the righteous comes only from the holy soul that they were born with. Actually, this is not so. The righteous remain so only by applying themselves diligently to the work of God over days and years, growing greater and becoming stronger through time, and not letting themselves fall under any circumstances. We can all be like them.

He said, I will not destroy it for the sake of the ten. (Gen. 18:32)

Don't be a fool

Rabbi Menahem Mendel of Kotzk used to say: In order to save Sodom from being destroyed, at least ten righteous men were needed. However, in order to destroy the world and everything in it – one fool is enough.

Go to the Land of Moriah. (Gen. 22:2)

Dedication

Rabbi Hayyim of Zanz taught: Two mountains were chosen: Mount Sinai, on which the Torah was given to the People of Israel, and Mount Moriah, on which Avraham bound his son Yitzhak, and on which the Chosen House, the Holy Temple, was built. Now is it not puzzling? Why was the Chosen House not built on Mount Sinai, on which the Giving of the Torah occurred? The answer is that the mountain on which a member of the Household of Israel stretched out a neck for the slaughter, is holy to God. On it the Holy Spirit, and the Torah, was truly revealed.

Parashat Hayyei Sarah

Sarah was a hundred and twenty seven years old: these were the years of Sarah's life. (Gen. 23:1)

Constant Perfection

Rashi comments: The words "Sarah's life" are repeated to indicate to us that all the years were equally good. The Sfat Emet wrote about this: The way of people is that, as they grow older, they become wiser, better their ways and improve their deeds, change their bad and flawed qualities and conduct to which they had become accustomed. That being so, only their last days are lived in fitting perfection. But our matriarch, Sarah, all the days of her life were without fault and blemish. Although she surely excelled in her old age, this was only due to an overflowing and accumulation of her good deeds and not because of any changes or rejection of her deeds in her youth. She ascended from one level to another, but she had no blemish in her that required correction, and that is what Rashi intended when he commented that "all were equally good"....

One should bless the bad as well as the good

"The years of Sarah's life were equally good" – is it really possible to say that all of Sarah's life were good? Did she not have any bad years? Were some of her years not full of sorrow, suffering, tribulation, and all sorts of anguish? exile after exile during famines in the land; the deeds of Pharaoh and that of Avimelekh; years of infertility and barrenness, and – finally – there was the binding of her son Yitzhak. Can one really say, "the years of Sarah's life were all equally good"?

The answer, Rabbi Sussya of Anipol used to say, is that Sarah, the most righteous of women, accepted suffering with love and grace. About everything she would say: "this, too, is for good". This righteous woman did not question, Heaven forbid, the qualities of the Holy One, and did not complain about the troubles that came her way. She met each wave of distress, each big upsurge of misery that passed over her with a nod of acceptance and blessed the bad just as she blessed the good. Hence, "The years of Sarah's life were all equally good".

Greater are the righteous in their death than in their lifetime.

This portion is called "Hayyei Sarah" or "The Life of Sarah" even though it depicts her death. Similarly, the final portion of the Book of genesis is called "VaYehi" or "And he lived" even though it tells of the death of Yaakov. Why? A hint is found in the saying of our sages: "the righteous, in their death, are called living" (Berakhot 18b).

Family man

In this portion we see Avraham as a sensitive and humane person. He weeps over the death of his wife to whom he was married for many years. He is very careful, and diligently works to find a proper burial site for her. Immediately after this, he begins the search to find a wife for his son Yitzhak.

Some might say Avraham was a cruel man. After all, he almost sacrificed his only son! Others might claim that he was stubborn – a man who lived only with, and only for, his God and did not understand the meaning of warm family relations. This portion, which depicts Sarah's death and the search for a wife for Yitzhak, complements the previous parasha. The binding incident takes on a deeper and more sublime dimension when we discover just how emotional and fearful Avraham was regarding his wife and son. The portion on the binding of Yitzhak does not tells us of the pounding heart, the awesome fear, and the emotional torment that Avraham experienced while guiding his only son "to one of the mountains". Only now, when Avraham the husband and father is revealed to us, can we understand the lengths to which this loving husband and compassionate father was able to go in order to fulfill the will and command of God.

Avraham came to mourn for Sarah, and to weep for her. (Gen. 23:2)

God raises up the poor from the dust (Ps. 113:7)

When the wife of Rabbi Shalom of Belz died, the rabbi burst into tears and sobbed in sorrow.

Rabbi, his followers asked him, how long will you mourn? Rabbi Shalom answered them: I am weeping before the Holy One, asking for mercy for the people of Israel and this is what I am saying: "Master of the worlds, it is revealed and known before You that were I able to raise my spouse from the dust, from her grave, nothing in the world would be able to stop me from doing so, but what can I do when such is not up to me? You, however, have sent down from Heaven a land that is the glory of Israel, which serves as your countenance to the world and Your particular virtue, yet her soul has been bowed to the dust in the degradation of exile. You have the power and the might to raise it again, but you do not...

The model mother

When Avraham mourned for Sarah and wanted to eulogize her, he noted the incident of the binding of Yitzhak that took place on Mount Moriah. Sarah raised and educated a child who was willing to give his life joyfully. So, one must appreciate how great a person she was. Thus the midrash states: "From where did he [Avraham] come? From Mount Moriah". From which point in her lifetime did Avraham come to mourn her? On which activity did he specifically dwell in his mourning? The answer is "from Mount Moriah" – from the event that occurred there. That served as the substance for his mourning.

I am a stranger and a sojourner with you; give me a burial site with you, that I may bury my dead from before me. (Gen. 23:4)

A living memorial

A Zionist activist, in a conversation with Rabbi Avraham Yitzhak Kook, spoke disparagingly of those Jews who came to the Land of

Israel to die there. Rabbi Kook answered him and said: The very first Jewish presence in the Land of Israel, the first four cubits owned by Jews, was a grave. It began with "give me a burial site". And subsequently, at the time of the exodus from Egypt, the Children of Israel came into the Land of Israel with the bones of Yosef for reburial. It is because of these burials that the living Land of Israel arose and came about.

The field I give to you, and the cave that is in it, I give it to you; in the presence of the sons of my people I give it to you. (Gen. 23:11)

A gift accompanied by its rewards

A person who gives a gift wholeheartedly tends to minimize the value of the gift, while one who gives less than wholeheartedly tends to exaggerate its value, as though saying: "Look what I am giving to you". That was what Ephron did. He didn't just say, "I give the field to you"-which clearly would have included the cave. Instead, he emphasized the word "give" three times: "the field I give... the cave I give... In the presence of the sons of my people I give...". When Avraham heard this threefold "giving", he understood that he had to buy the field for its full price and said: "I will give you money for the field" (Gen. 23:13).

The field, and the cave that was in it, were made over to Avraham for a possession of a burying place by the sons of Chet. (Gen. 23:20)

The redemption of the Land of Israel

Why does the Torah need to relate in such great detail the negotiations between Avraham, Efron, and the sons of Het when, in the end, Avraham purchased the land for full price? Rabbi Shumel Mohaliver responds: The Torah teaches us that when the time comes for us to redeem our holy land from the hands of strangers, we will also know not to bargain and, we too, will have to pay the full price for every inch of land.

The servant ran to meet her, and said, "Let me, I beg you, drink a little from your water jar" (Gen. 24:17)

The power of character

Rashi comments: Because he saw that the water rose [in the well] to meet her.

It is surprising that, after Eliezer had seen such an overt sign as this, he still had to test her to see if she was kindhearted. Was the sign not sufficient to demonstrate Rivkah's importance to the Divine One? Rabbi Ezekiel of Kozmir replied: From this we can conclude that one good character trait exceeds a hundred signs.

I blessed Adonai, God of my master Avraham, who had led me in the way of truth. (Gen. 24:48)

His lack is his merit

As a rule, a marriage broker will use a little falsehood and exaggeration, without which it is not possible to make a match that will work out. And so, Eliezer gave thanks to "the one who led me in the way of truth", that in brokering this marriage he was able to walk in the way of truth, without having to resort to any falsehood.

When the marriage was arranged for the Rabbi of Biala with his second wife, he met with her and said to her: In order to avoid any purchase in error, I consider it my duty to tell you in advance: If anyone has convinced you that I am a Torah scholar —do not believe it; that I am righteous – do not believe it; that I am wise – such is definitely not the case; that I am rich— it is a complete fabrication. The woman turned to him and said: so these are your faults. What are your good qualities? He replied: My only good quality is that I am hiding nothing from you and am telling only the whole truth.

Things of truth are recognized

Rabbi Hanina stated: "God's seal is truth" (Shabbat 55a). Rabbi Avra-ham Yitzhak Kook explained this as a wax stamp imprinted on the sealed envelope of a letter. When the stamp is broken, it no longer has any value. The letter is open to all. Such is the measure of truth. There is no such thing as a half truth, or a quarter truth. The truth must be whole, like the seal itself. He added: just as our sages said "god's seal is truth", so is the seal of every person who was created in the image of God. People's inner truth is the basis of their character and it is the seal of their lives.

Yitzhak went out to meditate in the field at the evening time. (Gen. 24:63)

His conversations are his prayers

Rashi explains "To meditate in the field" to mean prayer. Rabbi Nah-man of Bratzlav used to pray: Master of the World, make me worthy to go out to the field each day, among the trees, the weeds, and all the plants of the field and to converse with my Creator – this is prayer, to meditate there on everything in my heart.

Yitzhak brought her to his mother Sarah's tent, and took Rivkah, and she became his wife, and he loved her. (Gen. 24:67)

True love

Look at the difference between former generations and latter genera-tions. Nowadays, everyone thinks that the couple should be in love with each other before they get married. The result is that sometimes the love cools off and, after the wedding, it happens more than once that "love at first sight" ends with "divorce at second sight".

That, however, was not the way things were done in previous genera-tions. Scripture testifies about our patriarch, Yitzhak, that first he mar-ried Rivkah and only afterwards are we told that "he loved her".

Parashat Toldot

These are the generations of Yitzhak, son of Avraham.... (Gen. 25:19)

A tragic error

Parashat Toldot begins with these words. This is the only portion in the Book of Genesis which centers around Yitzhak. Even so, Yitzhak remains a passive person who does not look for struggles or challenges – in contradistinction to his father and son.

Avraham, for example, chased after the four mighty kings to rescue Lot, his kinsman, from their hands (Gen. 14:14-16). Yitzhak, on the other hand, distances himself from all quarrels and disputes as he dwells in the land of the Philistines. He does not insist on his rights to the water wells dug by his servants (Gen. 24). In his own home, too, Yitzhak is not a dominant or controlling figure. This is particularly evident in the great drama described in chapter 28 – the drama of the blessing. Yitzhak had lived his life mistakenly believing that his first-born son, Esau, would follow his ancestors' footsteps. Yitzhak expected Esau to be fit to receive from him the blessing of the first-born. At this point, Rivkah became involved. She was able to correctly assess the qualities of the two boys. She then succeeded in transferring the father's blessing to the son who was most fit to receive it.

Yitzhak remained passive even at the time of the great confrontation between his two sons – when Esau vowed to kill Yaakov his brother. It is not Yitzhak who takes measures to frustrate this scheme, but Rivkah. She is the one who suggests to Yaakov that he flee from his father's house to find shelter far from the land of Canaan; and it is she who finds the reasonable grounds to convince Yitzhak that his son Yaakov must urgently leave his home and his country – marriage to a suitable wife from the daughters of the extended family.

Adonai said to her: Two nations are in your womb, and two peoples shall be separated from your bowels. (Gen. 25:23)

A proper education

"Two nations are in your womb, and two peoples shall be separated from your bowels" – this means that the two are very distinct – different in character and separated in their ways, and they are destined to live and act, not side by side, but rather one before the other, one against the other.

Their physical differences were already apparent at birth. When they grew up, the difference in their character and spirit also became apparent: "And the boys grew: and Esau was a cunning hunter, a man of the field; but Yitzhak was a plain man, dwelling in tents".

Two sons, two worlds apart. Both need to be raised and educated as the sons of the family, in the spirit of the Torah. The younger, Yaakov, does not pose a problem. His body is soft, his soul is honest, and his way is correct. "A plain man" – literally – he is all innocence, internally and externally unified. "A dweller of tents" – the tents of Avraham and Sarah, Yitzhak and Rivkah, the tents of Shem and Ever, the tents of wisdom, ethics and knowledge of God and God's ways. He acts with consistency (in Hebrew: ikvi –like his name, Yaakov) and trustworthiness as he travels along the path of his ancestry.

The firstborn, Esau, however, poses a severe problem. He is different in every way. Even his physique is surprising. His skin is a different color and texture. This body is filled with fervor and excitement and his soul stirs up a storm. His home seems too confined for him, he is drawn to the field and the forest –not to work the land, but to roam afar, free from yoke and framework, to go after anything that his heart desires. Fear and danger do not deter him, and with the bow in his hand he would feed himself.

How was it possible to raise and educate such different children in one home? The wisest man who ever lived, King Solomon, answers this question: "Educate the youth according to his way", according to each child's natural tendencies. "According to the opinion of the son should the father teach him" (Jerusalem Talmud Pesahim 116:8).

How should one raise and educate a child who has undesirable tendencies? Here the task is harder. One must understand the inner workings of this child's hear, and take advantage of every hour of ability and bypass every instance of failure; one has to dismiss the destruction in the heart of the child and rebuild the child's outlook, measures, and deeds. All of this can be done only by getting close to the child. This is the only way to raise and elevate such a child. There is no other way. Would that it will succeed.

Beware of the hypocrites

What comfort did the Matriarch Rivkah draw from God's answer — "two nations are in your womb"?

Rivkah feared that she was carrying one child, a hypocrite showing two sides and that this child was causing spasms in order to exit her womb both in the ways of the Torah of Shem and Ever, and in the ways of idolatry. Therefore she protested and cried out "why am I thus?!"

However, when she was told "two nations are in your womb", one of them righteous and one evil, she was comforted. It is better to have an evil child than a hypocrite.

Rabbi Barukh of Mezbush once said to a man who pretended to be pious and who he (the rabbi) suspected of hypocrisy: Who are you trying to deceive when you pretend to pray with such devotion and intention? It is impossible to deceive God because Adonai tries hearts and reads people's thoughts. Neither can you deceive people because the public is not so foolish. You must be trying to deceive yourself, but what is the point in deceiving a fool?

The boys grew. Easu was a cunning hunter, a man of the field; While Yaakov was a plain man, dwelling in tents. (Gen. 25:27)

The strength of innocence

"Yaakov" and "Esau" are not simply the names of two brothers. They are symbols of two different points of view, of two different ideologies, of two different worlds.

It is said about our patriarch Yaakov "And Yaakov was a plain man" – Yaakov was plain, innocent, complete, and sincere. Yaakov's world was a world of good measure, of faith. There was no gap between his words and his actions.

Rabbi Yishayahu Horowitz (author of the Kabbalistic text "The Two Tablets") notes: Come and see how much we need to distance ourselves from the way of deceit and falsehood. Yaakov, of course, had incalculable good measures yet with all of his virtues and good measures, the Scriptures relate only that he was "a plain man". From this we learn that there is no greater measure in life than simplicity and honesty.

Yitzhak loved Esau, because he had taste for game; but Rivkah loves Yaakov. (Gen. 25:28)

True love

The Holy Shelah (Rabbi Yishayahu Halevy Horowitz), one of the great sages of Israel, writes: Yitzhak's love for Esau was based on a transient reason, as it is written "because he had a taste for game". The Sages, of blessed memory, said about such love: "All love that depends on something transient, when that thing ceases, the love ceases" (Pirke Avot 5:16). This is why Scripture states "And Yitzhak loved Esau" in the past tense. Because this love depended on something transient, on a taste for game, the love itself was transient and passing.

On the other hand, Rivkah's love for Yaakov was not transient and so it never ceased. This is why Scripture is careful to say: "Rivkah loves Yaakov".

Dwell in the land which I shall tell you of. (Gen. 26:2)

And we will plant on its borders

We find in Midrash: "Make a settlement in the Land of Israel, be a planter, be a sower". It also states: "Dwell (in Hebrew: Shekhon) in Israel" – Let the Shekhinah (the Divine Presence) reside in Israel with you. Indeed, these two acts – working the Land of Israel and bringing the Divine presence into it – are truly one and the same. (Gen. Rabbah 64)

I will multiply your seed as the stars of Heaven. (Gen. 26:4)

Stages of Redemption

Rabbi Avraham Yitzhak Kook once taught at a conference of the heads of the Yishuv (Pre-1948 Jewish settlement in the Land of Israel): The Torah outlines for us the main stages in the fulfillment of our budding national aspirations. Genesis 26 states there was a famine in the Land. Our patriarch Yitzhak asked to go down to Egypt – as did his father, Avraham, before him. Yet Adonai appeared before Yitzhak and instructed him not to leave the Land. Afterwards, God told him: "And I will multiply your seed as the stars in the Heavens, and I will give your seed all these countries; and in your seed shall all the nations of the world be blessed" (Gen. 26:4).

Here, before you, is a clear plan how we, with God's help, will fulfill our national aspirations in these our own time. First, "And I will multiply your seed" – we must strive to increase the number of Jews in the Holy Land via a great influx (Aliya). Then "and will give to your seed all these countries" – when masses of Jews assemble in Israel, we will, with God's help, achieve the state of independence we have yearned for. Finally, Rabbi Kook remarked excitedly – we will also reach the long awaited stage concerning our surrounding neighbors, as it is written: "and in your seed shall the nations of the world be blessed". The gentile neighbors, those hostile to us and who conspire against us all the time, even they will make peace with us and be blessed by us.

Then Yitzhak sowed in that land, and received in the same year one hundred fold - for Adonai blessed him. (Gen. 26:12)

Blessing of the giving

Where did Yitzhak's success come from? The Midrash suggests: "From that land. Rabbi Helbo said: The land was hard, and the year was difficult, nevertheless he was successful". (Gen. Rabbah 64)

In other words, this was an unnatural success, seen as a blessing from God. Our Sages (Yalqut Shimoni 26) saw this not only as the fruits of Yitzhak's labor, but mainly as a reward for a life filled with much accomplishment: "And he sowed" – he took all of the tithing from his money and sowed charity to the poor just as you say "sow for yourself by righteousness" (Hos. 10:12). For each and every thing he did, God gave him one hundred fold of blessings… So, as he knew the strength of righteousness, thus he devoted himself to it".

Yitzhak knew the secret – that assets are given to a person as a test. Therefore, he devoted himself to righteousness and his compensation was that he received "a hundred fold, for Adonai blessed him".

He moved from there, and dug another well; and they did not quarrel over it. (Gen. 26:22)

Do not despair

The Torah teaches us a great lesson. Although, from time to time, the Philistines came and quarreled and took the well which Yitzhak had dug, he nevertheless dug another well and did not despair. Because of this, in the end he succeeded. "And he moved from there, and dug another well; and they did not quarrel over it; and he called the name of it Rehovot; and he said, For now Adonai has made room for us, and we shall be fruitful in the land" (Gen. 26:22).

A story is told of Rabbi Levi Yitzhak of Berdichev who traveled to the provincial cities to collect money for redeeming prisoners. He spent much time on the road, going from town to town, but did not manage to collect as much as was needed. The righteous rabbi considered: perhaps I have not acted well, have not engaged in the study of Torah or in prayer and have thus come up only with broken pottery. It would have been better had I just stayed at home and engaged in Torah and worship. It happened, that in one of the towns where Rabbi Levi Yitzhak was staying, a Jew was caught stealing. He was punished and sent to prison. "See my son what you have done to yourself?" Rabbi Levi Yitzhak said to him, "Remember this and do not return to your bad ways". "So what?" replied the thief. If I was not successful stealing today, I will be successful tomorrow! At that point, Rabbi Levi Yitzhak realized a kal vahomer (an inference drawn from a minor matter to one of greater importance). If the thief did not despair because of a failed crime, how much more so should I not despair of performing a mitzvah! After all, if I am not successful today, I will be successful tomorrow or the day after.

So that my soul may bless you before I die. (Gen. 27:4)

What are you working for?

The Holy Yid of Pasishcha used say: A person is asked "what are you working for?" and the answer is always "were I to have to see only to myself, I would be happy with what I have, but the children... one has to see to the children...". When the children grow up, they, too, labor hard and for the very same reason – "everything is for the children".

Would that I may merit this perfect child, the Holy Yid concluded – for whom all the generations are concerned and labor so much!

Now, therefore, my son, obey my voice according to that which I command you. (Gen. 27:8)

Rivkah sees and knows

Rabbi Soloveitchik said: Rivkah commanded Yaakov to go out to the field to the flock. Why this harsh command? Because Rivkah saw that Esau is a man of the field, a hunter, a man who goes out into the world, acts, and takes control, while Yaakov sits in tents. She feared that Esau will remain the only man who goes out to the field, the only politician, the only diplomat, the only speaker, and ruler – and that he will take over the economy, the street, the outside world. If he remained the only man who goes out to the fields, he would eventually banish Yaakov even from his tents of Torah.

So she told Yaakov to go to the flock, the field, the street. She commanded: Take your Torah out of your tents and out to the whole wide world! This is a command to hold the plough in one hand, and the Gemara in the other.

If Yaakov goes out into the fields, the fields will also be sanctified, as, indeed, we read in Yitzhak's statement, "see, the smell of my son is like the smell of the field which God has blessed" (Gen. 27:27). Yaakov is an equal partner in the field, in society, in modern life. When Yaakov goes out to the field, this is the sanctification of the field. He, himself, brings holiness into the field.

Parashat Vayetze

Yaakov departed from Beersheba and set out for Haran. (Gen. 28:10)

Starting point and destination

Rashi asks why does it state "And Yaakov departed from Beersheba"? Does it matter where he was coming from? When a person goes from one place to another, sometimes it is motivated by the desire to leave, and other times by the desire to reacha new destination. In this instance, however, Yaakov was motivated by both of these. Rivkah ordered Yaakov to flee to Haran because of Esau's plan to kill him. Her intention, therefore, was that he should depart from Beersheba. On the other hand, Yitzhak sent Yaakov to Haran so that he would take a wife from the daughters of Lavan and not a Canaanite girl. It was his intention, therefore, that Yaakov should reach Haran. Yaakov wanted to keep the precept of honoring both his father and mother. Therefore, both purposes held sway over him. This is why the verse mentions both departing from Beersheba and setting out for Haran.

He took of the stones of that place, and put them under his head, and lay down in that place to sleep. (Gen. 28:11)

I will not move from here

Rabbi Menahem Mendel of Kotzk said: To what may this be compared? To a toddler who behaves very badly. When this child wants something, he lies on the floor and doesn't want to get up until his parents promise to hive him what he wants. Yaakov yearned to inherit the Land. What did he do? "and he lay down in that place to sleep" – and immediately – "and behold, God stood above it and said… the land on which you lie, to you I will give it, and to your seed".

Holy stones

The tosafists remark: This must be interpreted according to its simplest meaning – he took one stones from the stones of the place. Yaakov said: "I find the hard stones of the Land of Israel pleasant, pillows and soft cushions are of the Diaspora". (Hullin 91:75)

There are those who follow in Yaakov's footsteps, taking a small piece of stone from one of the holy places in Israel with them when traveling in the Diaspora. This, they believe, is a definite assurance that they would merit a peaceful return to the Holy Land.

The story is told of the righteous Jerusalemite, Rabbi Aryeh Levin, who sent his son Hayyim Yaakov to Rabbi Barukh Be'er Leibowitz so the won would learn Torah from him in his yeshiva in Kaminetz. Prior to boarding the train, the son took several Jerusalemite stones and put them in his pocket "in order to at least feel the sanctity of Israel every time every time I put my hand in my pocket..." But just before the train departed, the son burst into tears and said, "never mind me, I am going into the Diaspora to fulfill the commandment of my father who wanted me to personally fulfill what we studied in Tractate Avot: "exile yourself to a place of Torah, but you stones, the stones of Israel, why should you leave the Holy Land?" He removed the stones from his pocket and tossed them out of the window.

He dreamed, and behold! A ladder set up on the earth, with its head reaching to heaven; and behold! The angels of God are ascending and descending on it. (Gen. 28:12)

People are greater than angels

Rabbi Moshe of Kobrin used to say: "And he dreamed, and behold! A ladder set up on the earth" – this refers to each and every person. Every person should know: I am material substance, a piece of clay from the earth. There are countless like me, but "with its head reaching to heaven", my soul reaches Heaven. "... and behold! The angels of God are ascending and descending on it" – even the ascent and descent of the angels depends on my actions!

A dream and its interpretations

Yaakov did not leave his home and his land go to Haran just to have a fun trip or to look for adventure. He fled for his life from the threats of his brother, Esau, who hated him "because of the blessing with which his father blessed him" (Gen. 27:41). Young Yaakov was confused and bewildered having to leave his tranquil existence. According to Midrash, he also had to discontinue his study of Torah at the tents of Shem and Ever – study he greatly loved. His mother, who had warned him that Esau was planning to kill him and had advised him to flee, was now very far away from him. He was home-sick, he made sure to continue his studies and personal development, but he was also full of suspicion regarding the character of his uncle Lavan to whose home he was now fleeing and whose reputation as a crafty and devious man had reached the land of Canaan. How would this man receive him?

In the middle of this anxious and stressful situation, Yaakov had a wonderful dream in which the heavens touched the earth. In his dream he saw angels ascending and descending. He received a message from the heavens – the promise of a great future. When he woke up, he hurriedly declared: "This is no other than the house of God, and this is the gate of Heaven".

Despite the somber circumstances, Yaakov is sure that God will be with him, and that he will eventually return to his home. This man has a dream, a Divine dream, an angelic dream.

Yaakov left Canaan broken hearted. He reluctantly leaves the house of his parents and teachers, fleeing empty-handed to his uncle Lavan's house. All of this because of his brother's Esau's hatred, animosity, and his vow: "when the days of mourning for my father are at hand, then will I slay my brother Yaakov". Usually, a young man in such a situation would dream that he is stronger than his enemy Esau, and would repay animosity with animosity. At the very least, he would fantasize that his father's blessings, which he received through much sadness and torment, are being fulfilled and that he is rising to greatness and becoming his brother's hero. How astounding it is that Yaakov does not dream of revenge or of power. Instead, he dreams of exalted things, of Earth and Heaven touching one another. There is no jealousy here, no greed or competition, no passion for victory or murder.

The circle of life

God's angels – angels of mercy, angels of peace – are "ascending and descending on it". The ladder of life is a cycle that constantly turns and returns. Even one who rises to the peak then slides down and reaches its bottom.

Behold! Adonai stood above it and said, I am Adonai the God of Avraham your father, and the God of Yitzhak; the land on which you lie, to you I will give it, and to your seed. (Gen. 28:13)

Self-exertion

The text states: "I am Adonai, the God of Avraham your father, and the God of Yitzhak", and not "the God of Avraham and Yitzhak your father" as we would expect. So, too, in the Shmoneh Esreh prayer, we do not say "The God of Avraham, Yitzhak, and Yaakov", but "God of Avraham, God of Yitzhak, and God of Yaakov".

The Baal Shem Tov used to say: the reason we say "the God of Avraham, the God of Yitzhak, and the God of Yaakov" is to teach us that our ancestors did not rely on their parents' theological investigations but each of them exerted himself, did his own thinking, and each concluded the unity and existence of the Creator based on their own philosophical work.

A nation and its land

Rabbi Hayyim Vital stated: The fulfillment of the Divine promise begins with Yaakov. It is because of Yaakov that we are called the House of Israel, the nation of Israel. "The land on which you lie, to you I will give it, and to your seed" - it is from that moment that we are considered a nation, and there is no nation without its own land.

Your seed shall be as the dust of the earth, and you will spread abroad to the west, to the east, to the north, and to the south. (Gen. 28:14)

The strength of unity

It is well known that Israel has been compared to stars, to sand, and to dust. However, there are significant differences between these three substances. The stars are distant from one another and they will never have any contact whatsoever between them. Granules of sand, although gathered and piled one on top of the other, never cling to one another. Dust, however, is given the quality of sticking together and being unified.

For this reason God blessed Yaakov "and your seed shall be like the dust of the earth". In this way, God insinuates, if Yaakov's children will live in unity and friendship and will be close to one another like the dust of the earth, in them will be fulfilled the statement "and you shall spread abroad to the west, to the east, to the north, and to the south", because there will then be no greater strength in Israel than the unity of the people.

Yaakov awoke out of his sleep, and he said, surely God is in this place, yet I knew it not. (Gen. 28:16)

An undeserved gift

"And I knew it not" – Rashi explains: because if I knew, I would not have slept in this holy place.

But the sleep brought him this wonderful dream! What is then the reason for this sorrow? Rabbi Avraham Yitzhak Kook said: Yaakov did not want to receive an undeserving gift – a gift that was not the result of hard work or labor. If he had known, he would have attempted to merit this gift while awake through hard personal work.

Yaakov vowed a vow, saying: If God will be with me... and will give me bread to eat, and garment to put on... then Adonai shall be my God. (Gen. 28:20-21)

A broad mind and a tranquil spirit

The Kotzker Rebbe used to say: Yaakov prayed for his needs to be taken care of by God and not by people.

Rabbi Shlomo Leib of Lentzner added: Master of the Universe! Give bread to Israel so that they may eat with heartfelt you, for when a person is sick or is in a state of sorrow, that person is not capable of eating.

Rabbi Levi Yitzhak of Berdichev used to say: when Jews have bread to eat and a garment to put on, then they are able to recall at all times and at every hour that "Adonai shall be my God". But when they lack these basic necessities, it could happen, that out of deep bitterness, concern, and anguish, that – heaven forbid! – this fact could be forgotten by them.

Yaakov served seven years for Rahel; and they seemed to him but a few days, for the love he had for her. (Gen. 29:20)

True love

Rabbi Avraham Heschel of Apt was asked: How is it possible that "they seemed ... [as] days"? If anything, because of his love, each day should have seemed to him like a year! The Rabbi explained: There are two types of love. There is love that adheres to the loved object, and then returns to the one loving. In such cases, every hour seems long and heavy because the person longs to reach the loved object. And then there is the love of true friends, which does not return to the one loving – in which case it is all the same to whether the loved object is distant a thousand miles or just one mile.

And so it is said: "And Yaakov served seven years for Rahel; and they seemed to him but a few days, for the love he had for her". He loved her, truly her. So his love adhered to her and did not return to him. His intention was not for himself or for his longing, but his was true love.

Yaakov's anger was kindled against Rahel, and he said: Am I in the place of God, who has withheld from you the fruit of the womb? (Gen. 30:2)

Salvation belongs to God

Why was Yaakov angry with Rahel? Because she put her trust in him ("Give me children!") when she should have asked God to give her children; and because she said: "or else I die" – for she had despaired of mercy and sought to die. She forgot that a person is not the master of her own soul, that it belongs to the Master of all souls, in whose hands is the soul of every living creature.

The story is told of a peasant couple who came to visit the Seer of Lublin to seek his blessing for them to have a child. It was ten years since they had been married, and God had given them no children. The seer said to them: I am prepared to give you my blessing but, in return, I want from you sixty silver dinars. The peasants began to haggle: They began with ten dinars, and went up to thirty. More than that they were unable to pay. But the Seer insisted: Not one penny less than sixty dinars. Finally, the wife said to her husband: Come, let us put our trust in God. The Divine One, too, can help... When they left, the Seer said to those around him: I had no intention, heaven forbid, to take money, for how is it possible to benefit through the sufferings of others? My intention was only to extract those very words from their mouths, lest the Jews forget that the Master of the Universe also has the ability to save...

God hearkened to Leah, and she conceived and bore Yaakov a fifth son. (Gen. 30:17)

Yearning of the heart

Where is it written that Leah called out to God? This verse teaches us that the expression "and God hearkened" can relate not only to a specific prayer but also to the yearning of a suffering soul. The sound of the tears of the oppressed, the sorrow of the dejected, all of which come from the depths of the heart –all of these are prayers.

Parashat Vayishlah

The messengers returned to Yaakov, saying: We came to your brother Esau, and he is also coming to meet you, and with him are four hundred men. (Gen. 32:7)

Not via a messenger

Rabbi Barukh of Mezhbush (the grandson of the Baal Shem Tov) said: When Yaakov wanted to abate his brother Esau's anger, he sent him messengers to appease him. What were the results of this? Nothing. It is written: "And the messengers returned to Yaakov, saying, We came to your brother Esau, and he is also coming to meet you, and with him are four hundred men". We should learn from this that Yaakov's messengers failed in their task to appease Esau and to bring about peace between the brothers. However, immediately following this, when the feuding brothers met face-to-face, they were appeased and made peace like two loving brothers.

This teaches us that when attempting to make peace between enemies, we mustn't rely on messengers. It doesn't matter who the messengers are: even real angels would not be sufficient. Rather, the people involved must appease and be appeased and attempt to reach an understanding. This way, enemies of the past will come around to live in love and peace with one another.

Then Yaakov was greatly afraid and distressed and he divided the people. (Gen. 32:8)

Fear and distress

Rabbi Yehudah the son of Illai commented: Are not fear and distress identical? This is the meaning of it: he was afraid —lest he will be slain; and he was distressed — lest he should slay. For Yaakov thought: if he prevails over me, will he not kill me? And if I am stronger than he, will I not kill him?

Another interpretation: "he divided the people"… Yaakov greatly feared the chaos and division of the people that was prevalent in the camp. He said: "If there is separation between my sons, if there is a separation of hearts among them, this I fear greatly – because if there is no peace there is nothing". If everyone were one camp, united like one protective wall, Yaakov would never fear, not Esau and not Ishmael.

Yaakov's fear

Having just been saved by God from the grip of the evil Lavan, already the anger of his brother Esau is upon him. Now the messengers come and tell him that Esau is coming toward them with four hundred men. This news causes Yaakov to fear, since nobody knows his brother Esau's great strength and abounding evil better than he.

Nonetheless, the sages severely chastised Yaakov for this fear. After all, how could he get caught up in fear when God had explicitly promised him "I am with you, and will keep you in all the places to which you go, and will bring you back to this land" (Gen. 28:15)?

Our sages of blessed memory tried in various manners to find an explanation and justification for Yaakov's fear so they could acquit him: "Then Yaakov was greatly afraid" –Yaakov said, All of these years Esau dwells in the Land of Israel, therefore, perhaps. he comes at me through the merit of having dwelled in the Land of Israel? All of these years he has dwelled and has respected his parents, therefore, perhaps. he comes at me through the merit of honoring his mother and father? (Mekhilta)

In other words, Yaakov suspects that Esau could come at him through the merit of the two commandments that Yaakov was prevented from fulfilling during the 20 years he dwelled abroad.

A war between brothers

It was said of Avraham "and when Avram heard that his brother was taken captive, he led forth his trained servants, and pursued them and he smote them" (Gen. 14:14-15). Because this old man heard that his brother Lot, a resident of Sodom had been captured, he immediately ran like a deer with the strength of a lion and pursued the four great kings who were drunk with victory. However, regarding Yaakov it says "then Yaakov was greatly afraid and distressed". How can it be that the grandson, who had armies of angels at his disposal, is filled with fear and terror?

Indeed, children inherit the strength of their parents, and young Yaakov too had a brave heart and the courage to fight the enemy at She'arim. What does this mean? With foreign armies, just as his grandfather Avraham fought. But here, Yaakov had to stand against his brother, his own flesh and blood. There is no war more bitter and destructive than a war between brothers. That is why he felt fear. Therefore he prayed: "deliver me from the hand of my brother, from the hand of Esau".

A man wrestled with him until the breaking of the day. (Gen. 32:25)

The evil inclination

The Talmud comments: One [sage] said: the man appeared to [Yaakov] as a heathen. Another [sage] said: the man appeared to him as one of the wise. This debate is about the two modes of the evil inclination. One is to openly and directly push a person into committing an offence. The other is to act with cunning and obscure the sin, explaining that there is actually no real offence. Sometimes the evil inclination, pretending innocence, says to the person: not only is this not an offence, but acting this way even involves keeping a commandment...

Transferring self-confidence

This entire Torah portion is shrouded in mystery. Yaakov is busy with his final preparations for the fateful meeting with Esau. He lodges in the camp, awake and ready for a fight that might begin at any moment. The atmosphere is saturated with anxiety. He prays to God and begs: Deliver me from the hand of my brother, from the hand of Esau, for I fear him.

Then, suddenly, in the dark of the night, a man shrouded in mystery enters the arena and forces Yaakov to come out, to engage in a combat that continues until daybreak. Who was this man? Where did he come from? And for what reason? This surprising episode served our sages as a topic of study. They did not want to accept Yaakov's cowardice and they severely denounced his fear. The struggle with the angel, as they saw it, had one great purpose which was to teach Yaakov about the wondrous strength that was hidden within him, to release him from his feelings of inferiority, and to imbue him with self confidence and with a belief in his own strength. "I am one of the first angels, you did this to me – and you fear Esau?!" the angel Michael asks Yaakov (Midrash Abkir)

A purifying struggle

What did Yaakov achieve in this struggle? Nothing! He did not conquer new territory. He did not find large spoils. He did not finish the struggle as a world conqueror.

Why, then, did he have to go through such a struggle? Rabbi Soloveitchik said: The struggle itself was holy. The life of Jews is a life of strength. We must thank the Creator of the world for the great compassion he has bestowed upon us by granting us the possibility, like Yaakov in his time, to experience the "and there wrestled a man with him until the breaking of the day". It is a privilege to be a minority among our Jews, girded in strength, to fight for the crown of beauty.

Your name shall be called no more Yaakov, but Israel. (Gen. 32:29)

The blame belongs to all of us

This blessing bestowed on Yaakov, renaming him "no more Yaakov, but Israel", has been disastrous for us to this day. In any other nation, when an individual sins, the whole public is not made responsible for his sin. In fact, it is inconceivable that the public should be punished for the deeds of the individual. But where the matter concerns a Jew, when one Yaakov commits some sin, then immediately "your name shall be called no more Yaakov but Israel"; you do not hear people saying that Yaakov so-and-so has sinned but that Israel, the whole People of Israel, is guilty...

As he passed over Penu-el the sun rose upon him, and he limped upon his thigh. (32:32)

The meaning of the limp

This is one of the most mysterious portions of the Bible. There was some metaphysical occurrence, the meaning of which we do not understand, with only its result being clear to us – the limp.

Prof. Israel Eldad says: This nighttime event stands in juxtaposition to the nighttime dream of the ladder. As he leaves the country, Yaakov has a dream – a powerful, clear, divine, logical and to the point dream. Returning to Canaan 20 years later, Yaakov is embroiled in a strange struggle in the middle of the night. It is the God of Avraham who appears to him in the dream of the ladder, but the God of Yitzhak who sends his angel against him in the struggle over the Yavok. The God of Avraham wants to raise him, to give him a mission. The God of Yitzhak seeks to subdue him and bind him. At this fateful hour, as he returns to the Land with a great vision in his heart, much property, and many children, these two fathers – the one with his head in the heavens and the other firmly placed on the earth – struggle within him. He struggles with people in the name of Heaven, and he struggles with God in the name of people. He survives both by virtue of the strength of that 20 year old dream. He internalizes both fathers, and, because of this internalization and blending, he is awarded the name 'Israel'. Although this name incorporates the struggles of his past life and the fate of his children in the future, he himself completes the active port of his life with this struggle. He blends together the qualities of both fathers and then bequeaths them to his offspring. He also bequeaths the limp with which he was left at the end of the struggle. To this day, we have not been healed of this limp.

Even if Yaakov himself arrived in the Land "Bodily whole and whole in his learning" (Shabbat 33b), and was apparently healed of his limp, it was not a permanent healing. Nothing from the heritage of our ancestors disappears forever. Everything lives on in the depths of our souls and in our veins. So, too, is the case with this limp. Sometimes we stride ahead confidently and securely, with truth and faith. At other times, we are hesitant and fearful; afraid of Yitzhak, Lavan, Esau, the people of Shekhem. Our name is exalted and lofty, our name is Israel, and we have a great heritage and a great designation – but this limp sometimes causes us to lag behind others.

Yaakov lifted up his eyes and saw, and behold! Esau was coming, and with him four hundred men. So he divided the children to Leah and to Rahel... and he passed over before them, and bowed to the ground seven times, until he came near his brother. (Gen. 33:1-3)

The sin of obsequiousness

The sages, of blessed memory, noted Yaakov's self effacement and syco-phancy before Esau. They lingered on this: Yaakov, the righteous one, calling himself "servant" and bowing down before the wicked Esau over and over again. The aggadah sees Yaakov's fear as pitiful, humili-ating, and depressing. Yaakov puts himself to shame, and diminishes his own status before a wicked person, while calling this wicked person "lord": When Yaakov called Esau 'my lord', the Holy One said to him: "you have abased yourself and called Esau 'my lord' eight times. I will raise up eight kings of his descendants before your descendants". As it is said: These are the kings that reigned in the land of Edom before there reigned any king over the children of Israel. (Gen. Rabbah 75:11)

The Holy Blessed One was angry with Yaakov for referring to himself as a servant: The Holy blessed One said to him: Yaakov! I said [before you were born] 'The elder shall serve the younger' and now you say 'Thus shall you speak to my lord Esau'?! On your life, so shall it be! He will rule over you in this world (Pirke deRabbi Eliezer, 37).

Esau said: I have enough, my brother. Keep what you have to yourself.
(Gen. 33:9)

He who is happy with his portion

Esau said: I have enough... Yaakov said: I have everything

The Hafetz Hayyim explained: Although Esau has enough, he does not
have everything. Precisely because he has enough, he wants more and
more. Yaakov, however, says "I have enough" —meaning, what I have is
enough, I am satisfied with it, and I am happy with my portion.

I will build an alter to God, who answered me in the day of my distress.
(Gen. 35:3)

Answer us

It once happened that the Baal Shem Tov saw a great denunciation of
Israel in Heaven. He consulted with his students and they fasted many
times. Still, they were unable to do anything. The Baal Shem Tov persuaded the rabbi of an adjacent town to decree a fast for everyone in
the town so that they could pray on the fast day, and implore that the
edict be revoked. Men and women gathered in the synagogue, where
they wept, prayed, and recited psalms. But not even this public weeping could remove the evil decree in Heaven.

A certain woman who had been sitting in the women's section spoke
before the Master of the Universe and said: Master of the Universe! Are
you not our Father? Are we not your children? I have five children and
when they open their mouths screaming and crying, my insides turn
upside down. Yet You, our Father in Heaven, care for so many children
and they are all crying and wailing. Is it a heart of stone that You have
that You do not hear their cry for help and for mercy? Is it not right and
proper that you should answer us? Answer us, Master of the Universe,
answer us! At that moment, a divine voice was heard proclaiming that
the decree had been revoked.

Parashat Vayeshev

Now Israel loved Yosef more than all his children, because he was the son of his old age, and he made him a coat of many colors. When his brothers saw that their father loved him more than all his brothers, they hated him and could not speak peaceably to him. (Gen. 37:3-4)

The moral of the story

Had Yosef and his brothers spoken with each other, matters would not have deteriorated and reached such acts of jealousy and hatred as they did. The sages sadly included Yosef's brothers in the list of brothers who hated each other. As they put it: You find all the brothers hating each other. Cain hated Abel, Ishmael hated Yitzhak, Esau hated Yaakov, and the tribes hated Yosef.

One of the reasons for this dangerous situation was Yaakov's behavior: "Now Israel loved Yosef more than all his children, because he was the son of his old age, and he made him a coat of many colors". Our sages commented about this love: "Love is as strong as death; Jealousy is cruel as Sheol" (Song of Songs 8:6). His brothers were jealous of him, but what place does love have alongside jealousy? What caused Yosef to fall foul of their jealousy? The excessive love with which his father loved him. (Tanhuma Yashan Vayeshev 19).

A parent has to know how to maintain a balance of love between his children and not to show preference for one over the other. An imbalance in this sphere can have far reaching consequences within the family circle. The sages taught: A man should never single out one child among his other children for on account of the two sela's weight of silk [of which the coat of many colors was made], which Yaakov gave Yosef in excess of his other sons, his brothers became jealous of him and the matter resulted in our ancestors' descent into Egypt (Shabbat 10b).

His mouth and his heart are equal

Rashi comments: From what is stated to their discredit, we can learn something to their credit: they did not say one thing with their mouths while thinking something quite different in their hearts.

The Talmud teaches regarding those who say one thing while thinking another: A tanna taught – on the day when Rabbi Eliezer ben Azaria was appointed as the head of the academy, the doorkeeper was removed and permission was given to all the students to enter. This was contrary to the former situation, for Rabban Gamliel had previously issued a proclamation that no disciple whose inside is not as his outside (i.e. whose character does not correspond to his appearance) may enter the school house. On that particular day a number of benches were added. (Berakhot 28a)

why did the students need so many extra benches? Could they not have crowded together as they sat on their benches? Rabbi Aryeh Levin replied: Jerusalem was blessed in Rabban Gamliel's day. People could stand pressed together yet were able to prostrate themselves with wide spaces between them... No-one said: the place is too narrow for me to stay overnight in Jerusalem. (Pirke Avot 5:5) There was a mental preparedness to crowd together and, even if they were pressed against each other, they did not feel it because of the love that reigned among them – just as a mother who hosts her children does not feel any over-crowding in her home. Rabbi Eliezer ben Azaria, on the other hand, had instructed that all the students be allowed into the school house, including those "whose inside was not as their outside". Each of these students needed greater space, for each of them would complain and grumble that the others were taking all the room, and they would elbow their fellow students so that they could sit with more space between them, separately from their fellows.

They hated him and could not speak a friendly word to him. (Gen. 37:4)

Communication

Rabbi Yehonatan Eibschutz explained: The main problem in this situation was that "they could not speak a friendly word to him". If the brothers had been able to speak to Yosef, they would discover a way to reduce their hatred.

This, explained the Rabbi, is the essence of all conflicts between people. One does not speak with the other, and neither side is prepared to listen and understand the view of the other side. If people would only speak to one another...

Yosef dreamed a dream, and he told it to his brothers, and they hated him even more. (Gen. 37:5)

Peace and its meaning

We have a series of dreams and their interpretation. The dreamers are many. Lavan dreams, Yaakov dream, Yosef dreams, the chief butler and the chief baker dream, even Pharaoh dreams!

In the period when Yosef lived, dreams and their interpretation played a central role. Describing his dreams to his brothers is what caused Yosef's sale into slavery and his exile from his homeland. The interpretation of dreams is what elevated him from prison into the royal house.

To begin with, Yosef is preoccupied only with himself, with his beauty, his aspirations, and his dreams. He is the focal point. It is as though the world had only been created to serve him and to bow down before him: the sheaves, the sun, the moon, the stars, his brothers, his father, his mother. The whole of creation was only for his sake. Without him, there would have been no meaning to anything created.

In prison, he begins to sense the grief and pain of others and expresses an interest in their problems and their fate. He sees ministers and that they are upset. He goes over to them and encourages them to share their problems with him. It is as though he had been cured of an illness

– the illness of "nothing but me". But it was not so. He was not yet totally cured but continued to suffer. He had not yet learned that "I was created to serve my Creator and all that is created in the Divine image". He ties his fate to that of others and has a personal request: "Remember me when all is well with you" (Gen. 40:14) he says to the chief butler.

He had to suffer for another two years in prison. It is only when he stand before Pharaoh that he forgets himself altogether. He interprets the dreams and prevents tens of thousands from suffering the disgrace of hunger. It is only when he understands the interpretation of others' dreams that he is finally worthy, and ascends to greatness.

His father rebuked him, and said to him: What is this dream that you have dreamed? (Gen. 37:10)

Brotherly hatred

The brothers hated Yosef for three very good reasons: The first is the coat of many colors. The second is the rumors that Yosef spread about his brothers. In the first instance, Yaakov was the cause of the jealousy but in this case the blame lies totally with Yosef.

Finally, the third reason was Yosef's dreams. Here, the father and son play equal roles. It is true that Yaakov reprimands Yosef for the arrogance of the dreams, but does he not know that it is the coat of many colors that made Yosef arrogant, that made him think he was superior to his brothers?

How great is the distance between the dream of the father and the dream of the son! The former is the dream of a person who had to extract a blessing from his father by deceitful means, who had to flee from his brother, who was himself a miserable pauper, who slept with a stone for a pillow, an exile. His dream came to him from above. He had a Divine dream that elevated him. Here, though, we have the dream of a spoiled child, who enjoys excessive paternal love, who has everything, who lives in the home of a rich man. What can this son do and not sin? What could he manage to do without arrogance? His dream does not com to him from on high, but from below. From the depths of his own personal cravings.

Yaakov's dream is philosophical. Yosef's dream is psychological. Yaakov's dream requires a life of struggle and battle in order to realize that great vision. Yosef's dream requires nothing. It is a matter of success, of letting things take their course. It commences with "And his father made him a coat of many colors" and ends with "And Pharaoh had him dressed in robes off linen". Success just came his way. Indeed, he is the only person about whom it is said "and he was a successful man (Gen. 39:2).

A certain man found him, and behold! He was wandering in the field; and the man asked him, saying: What do you seek? (Gen. 37:15)

Self examination

Rabbi Menahem Mendel of Kotzk said: The angel taught Yosef that when he is wandering bewildered, lost in the ways of life, sunken in a confusion of the spirit, he must clarify and interpret his desires, first of all for himself. He must determine "What do you seek".

Reuben heard it, and he saved him from their hands, and said: Let us not kill him. (Gen. 37:21)

Individual Savior

Why does scripture say: "and he saved him from their hands"? Reuven did not really manage to save Yosef from them!

Who was it who actually saved Yosef? Was it Reuben, who told his brothers to cast Yosef into a pit in the desert and "lay no hand upon him" – from which the brothers might have deduced that Reuben wanted Yosef to die in the pit without their having to shed his blood with their own hands? Or maybe it was Judah who saved him, by saying "what profit is it if we slay our brother" and counseled that Yosef be sold?

Rabbi Yaakov Dushinsky (president of the Rabbinic Court of Capetown, South Africa) used to say: The person who thinks independently, who opposes the murder plans of the mob, who formulates the slogan of opposition to evil deeds, who implants doubts in the minds of those who shout out loud and tells them that bloodshed and reliance on force are bad —he is the one who saves the intended victim. Where the mob demands "let us lay", the person who expresses opposition is the person who saves the victim. This is why scripture credits Reuben with saving Yosef's life.

Then Judah said to his brothers: What benefit do we gain if we kill our brother and cover up his blood? (Gen. 37:26)

No Benefit

There are two possible reasons for killing a person. One such reason is to satisfy the need for revenge. A second reason is to spread fear among others, "that they hear and are frightened". But in this instance, argues Judah, neither goal applies. We won't satisfy our need for revenge – in fact the opposite. We will always feel blameworthy and have a guilty conscience that we killed our brother. Neither will we spread fear among others, since we are covering up his blood and hiding the whole matter. Thus, "What benefit" – what possible gain can we have from this whole nasty need?!

Parashat Miketz

Pharaoh told them his dream, but there was none who could interpret them to Pharaoh. (Gen. 41:8)

In wisdom he alters time

The magicians and wisemen of Egypt had difficulty interpreting Pharaoh's dream because they had been educated in the erroneous opinion that the world is run only according to the laws of nature. Yet Pharaoh's dream went against all natural law. According to nature, the strong man is victorious over the weak and cows that were ill favored and lean of flesh fall before the well favored, healthy cows. Since Pharaoh's dream showed the contrary: the weak ate the strong, the magicians could not comprehend this.

Yosef, however, was educated differently in the house of Yaakov and immediately noted: God has declared to Pharaoh what He was about to do. There is a Creator and a Leader who lowers even the exalted, He gives the strong over to the weak and the multitude into the hands the minorities, because the Creator of the world is the One who determines the laws of nature and can alter them according to the Divine will.

Then Pharaoh sent and called Yosef, and they brought him hastily out of the dungeon. (Gen. 41:14)

And He will redeem us again

Yosef was imprisoned in a dungeon for twelve years. Every day lasted an eternity and nobody ever bothered to release him from there. However, the very moment that God ordered him to be released, as quick as lightning, they brought him from prison because, when the pre-destined time finally arrives, God does not delay even for a moment. Thus, on the eve of the Age of Redemption, our righteous Messiah will arrive

65

at the exact moment he is supposed to, and he will not tarry for even one moment. Rather, he will come and he will bring us, with the speed of lightning, from the Diaspora to the Land of our redemption.

Yosef called the name of the firstborn Menasheh - for God has made me forget all my toil and all my father's house. And the name of the second he called Ephraim – for God has caused me to be fruitful in the land of my affliction. (Gen. 41:51-52)

Longing for the land of Israel

In Egypt, Yosef attained greatness and status, as Pharaoh said to him, You shall be over my house, and according to your word shall all my people be directed (Gen. 41:40). Why then does Yosef nevertheless refer to Egypt as "the land of my affliction"?

Abravanel explains: Despite all the honor and wealth which Yosef had in Egypt, he was far from his father's house and from the Land of Israel. The great wealth, praise, and honor that Yosef earned in the alien land of Egypt did not make him lose his perspective, and did not alleviate his sense of alienation. He saw as his homeland the place where his family lived. This is why he called Egypt "the land of my affliction". Emotionally, this country remained foreign and alien and, to the end of his days, his soul pined for the Land of Israel.

Yosef saw his brothers, and he knew them, but he made himself strange to them, and spoke roughly to them... but they did not know him. (Gen. 42:7-8)

The will to forget

Why did Yosef decide to keep his identity a secret from this brothers whom he had identified with such certainty? Also, through the years, Yaakov and his children did not know where Yosef was. All that Yaakov could do was mourn the loss of his beloved son. The brothers also knew that they could not change what had been done. But Yosef knew where his father was the whole time. In the first years after his brothers sold him he was still in shock because of what they had done to him. He lived the difficult life of a slave and then he spent time in prison. Perhaps. it was the difficult circumstances that prevented him from contacting his father. But why did he not do so after he was raised to greatness and became an independent and respected person? Certainly he could have had no difficulty imagining the suffering his father underwent. Could he not have found an opportunity to make contact with his father?

Prof. Pinhas Peli explains that Yosef underwent several traumas when his brothers sold him to the Midianites and, perhaps. even more than that, during his slavery and prison experiences. These traumas imprinted a deep mark on his soul. Together with the changes in his luck and circumstances, there was also a change in his personality. From a dreamer of dreams about himself and his family, he became the interpreter of other people's dreams – specifically Pharaoh's dreams. The naïve dreamer of days past turned into a practical man who acquired for himself, in a sophisticated way, one of the highest positions in the kingdom.

Yosef seems to have enjoyed his new status and functions, the silk garments that went with the position, and the gold chain Pharaoh placed around his neck. Within a short period of time, the former prisoner became used to the luxury that came with his new position as second only to the king. He did all he could to become one of the Egyptians. He did not object to having his Hebrew name changed into an Egyptian name, and he intermarried into high society. The handsome thirty year old traveled throughout the land of Egypt. He felt truly at home in this country. He had good contacts in all the right circles. He was not thinking about the past.

This process could have continued uninterrupted but suddenly his brothers appeared before him and made him go back to a world that he would have preferred to forget. "And Yosef knew his brothers... And Yosef remembered the dreams which he had dreamed of them" (Gen. 42:8-9). In this unexpected turn of events, the interpreter of the dreams of others remembers that he had himself once been a dreamer of dreams. This is the turning point. From this point on, the story takes on new energy, and returns Yosef to his own people and to his dreams.

Yosef said to them: This is what I spoke to you, saying "you are spies". (Gen. 42:14)

We are culpable

Rabbi David of Levov said: Redemption does not come to the public until they have recognized their shortcomings and made an effort to rectify them. This also applies to individuals. So long as the public or the individual cannot see their own flaws, they will not try to remove them, and so are not fit for redemption. This is something that we learn from our Holy Torah. So long as the sons of Yaakov said to Yosef: "we are honest men", as long as they considered themselves to be honest and loyal and without wrong and fault, they were not fit for redemption. On the contrary, Yosef was angry with them and said: This is what I spoke to you, saying "you are spies". It was only after they recognized their shortcomings, admitted them and said: "we are truly guilty concerning our brother, in that we saw the anguish of his soul, when he pleaded with us, and we would not hear; therefore is this distress come upon us" (Gen. 42:21). Only then did their redemption begin. The Holy One then filled Yosef's heart with love and mercy toward his brothers: "and he turned himself away from them, and wept" (Gen. 42:24).

I fear God. (Gen. 42:18)

For this I toiled

Rabbi Pinhas Horowitz once said in a heart to heart talk to his brother, Rabbi Shmalki, that, thank God, he had finally reached the level of fearing God. "What are you saying, my brother" – Rabbi Shmalki asked in fear – "how can a Jew boast so much and affirm to himself that he has fear of God? Where is the humility in this?"

I learned this from the Torah, answered Rabbi Pinhas. We see that with regard to fear of God, one is permitted to praise himself. Did not Yosef boast such and call out "I fear God"? The reason for this is that with any other commandment, each of us needs Divine assistance to fulfill it- indeed, "one who desires refinement is (divinely) assisted".

Therefore one cannot boast about the performed commandment, since the deed does not totally belong to the individual. However, with regard to fear of the Divine, it is said: "everything is in the hands of God, except for the fear of God". This each person must achieve without any divine help. Therefore, it is permitted to praise oneself for it.

Take of the best fruits (zimrat) in the land in your vessels. (Gen. 43:11)

The strength of song and melody

The righteous Rabbi Nahman from Bratzlav explains: The text uses the Hebrew word "zimrat" which means song. The best fruits are the song of the land, the tune of the land. Just prior to their going down to Egypt for the second time, Yaakov told his sons: take with you at least some of the tunes from the Land of Israel so that your thoughts are not diverted from the Land of your family during those days that you will be away from her.

He lifted up his eyes, and saw his brother Benjamin, his mother's son, and said, Is this your younger brother of whom you spoke to me? (Gen. 43:29)

The meeting of the two brothers

How picturesque and moving is the dramatic meeting between Yosef and his brother Benjamin – whose souls were so connected. Every year when we read this Torah portion, our excitement is renewed and the story makes a great impression on our souls.

The first time Yosef sees his ten brothers, after twenty two years of separation, he holds back his emotions and refrains from bursting into tears. However, when he raises his eyes and sees Benjamin, he cannot control himself: "and Yosef made haste, for his affection was kindled towards his brother and he sought where to weep and he entered his chamber, and wept there" (Gen. 43:30).

According to Midrash, Benjamin told Yosef: From the day that my brother Yosef went into exile, my father went down from his bed and sat on the ground. Moreover, when I see my brothers, each of them sitting by his (maternal) brother and I am sitting alone, tears falls from my eyes. At that moment, Yosef's compassion for him erupted. (Mekhilta Vayigash 4)

Put my cup, the silver cup, in the sack's mouth of the youngest. (Gen. 44:2)

The Brothers give their lives for Benjamin

Yosef, the ruler, specifically commanded that the challis be hidden in Benjamin's sack; Benjamin, who gave all of his tens sons symbolic names in memory of the calamities that befell his older brother whom he so loved. Yosef did this because "he wanted to test the brothers to see if they would display love for their brothers to see if they would display love for their brother Benjamin and if they would give their lives for him or not.

When the challis was found in Benjamin's sack, the brothers suspected that he had stolen it – since they knew how connected Benjamin was to his brother Yosef and how much he loved him. They believed that their brother Benjamin risked stealing the challis since he believed that the person holding it had the power to see secrets and hidden things, and he wanted to use the challis for this purpose – to discover the location of their brother Yosef. Indeed, the brothers were angry with Benjamin and they even called him shameful names and beat him. Nevertheless, they were ready to give their lives for him. When Yosef had Benjamin arrested, Judah placed himself in front of Benjamin and said: You have cast your eye on Benjamin. If for greatness, here before you is Reuven. If for strength, here I am before you. You say he is a thief, why do you take him? One should not want a thief in his home! (Midrash HaHafetz)

Therefore the sages said: Come and see the greatness of the tribes. When Yosef put them all in prison, they were silent and did not recoil. However, with regard to their brother Benjamin, in order not to cause their father further sorrow, they all prepared themselves forward –to kill or be killed.

Yosef said to his steward: Arise, follow after the men; and when you catch up with them, say to them, Why have you repaid evil for good? (Gen. 44:4).

Ingratitude

The Italian commentator, Rabbi Avraham Menahem Rafa, remarked: Yosef does not command his steward to ask his brothers "why did you steal my goblet?", but tells his messenger to ask the brothers "why did you repay evil for good?" From this we learn that the sin of ingratitude is worse than the sin of theft.

Parashat Vayigash

Then Judah came near to him and said: Oh my lord, let your servant, I beg you, speak a word in my lord's ears. (Gen. 44:18)

The main spokesperson

Judah was prepared to be a slave so long as Benjamin was released and returned to his father. Judah felt that a great moral responsibility hung over him. He saw that his brothers were pointing their finger at him, blaming him for Yosef's sale: Since his sons saw that Yaakov was angry and would not accept condolences, they went to Judah and said to him: "You did this great evil to us". He answered them: "I said to you: 'What profit is it if we slay our brother', and you accuse me?" They said to him: "And did we not listen to you? You said 'come let us sell him' and we did. Had you said to us, 'come, let us return him to our father' would we not have listened to you? (Tanhuma Yashan 8)

A reason

What argument could Judah have now? After all, he himself sealed his own judgment when he said: "Behold! We are my lord's bondsmen, both we, and he also with whom the cup is found". Now, when Yosef has judged and said "the man in whose hand the cup is found, he shall be my bondsman" Judah suddenly reconsiders what he had said and decides to oppose it. Why?

The Holy Alsheich responds: at first Judah believed that the time had come for the brothers to be punished for the sale of Yosef. They had sold Yosef into slavery – now they were all being taken as slaves. Therefore he said: "What shall we say to my lord? What shall we speak? God had found out the iniquity of your servants" –the iniquity being the sale of Yosef.

However, when he saw that Yosef was releasing them all yet detaining Benjamin, Judah realized this could not be punishment for Yosef's sale, since Benjamin had no part whatsoever in the sale. Immediately Judah erupted with harsh, strong words.

It shall come to pass, when he sees that the lad is not with us, that he will die; and your servants shall bring down the gray hairs of your servant our father with sorrow to Sheol. (Gen. 44:31)

As a father is merciful to his sons

A certain hassid, one of the followers of Rabbi Menahem Mendel of Kotzk, once complained to the Rabbi about his difficult economic straits in his old age. What was particularly painful to him was that the sons and daughters whom he had brought up with devotion, and who were now earning a good living, were not showing him a proper degree of gratitude. They seldom supported him in his old age, when he was no longer able to earn his own living.

The Rabbi of Kotzk listened attentively to the words of the old hassid. When he had finished, the Rabbi said to him: Please do not be surprised by the behavior of your children, despite your devotion to them when they were growing up. We have already noted something similar in Yaakov's family. When Yosef, the omnipotent ruler of Egypt, decides to hold his brother Benjamin with him, Judah begs him to reconsider and suggests that holding Benjamin might cause Yaakov's death.

The question has to be asked here – Benjamin left at home ten children. Why does Judah not ask Yosef to have pity on Benjamin's sons who might die of sorrow at losing their father? We can conclude from this that parents feel more sorrow and pain over their children than the children feel over their parents.

Rabbi Halevy from Obtrovska used to say: All the generations continue in one line from Adam and Eve and the qualities of the parents are passed on by inheritance from one generation to the next. So, too, pity for one's children came from Adam and Eve. This, however, was not the case when it came to the quality of children's devotion to parents – for this is a quality neither Adam nor Eve could have had since they had no parents, and could not then transfer such a quality to their progeny.

Then Yosef could not restrain himself before all them that stood by him, and he cried: Cause every man to go out from before me. And no man stood with him, while Yosef made himself known to his brothers. (Gen. 45:1)

Reconciliation

Judah saw that the situation was getting out of hand, that the brothers would have to return to their father without Benjamin. Judah knew that this would totally devastate his elderly father and decided to speak with Yosef harshly, but at the same time in a reconcilable manner. He was prepared to appease Yosef with words and to surrender himself to him, yet at the same time he was ready to go to battle and to release Benjamin forcibly if necessary.

Judah spoke from the heart and described to Yosef the sorrow of his father, who has already lost one son, and is now on the verge of losing a second son. Yosef could not counter Judah's open admonishment. When Judah reminded him of Yaakov's sorrow, his heart yearned for his father and he decided to remove the mask and let his brothers know who he is.

Yosef knew that his brothers would be embarrassed because of their deeds, so he commanded: "cause every man to go out from before me". Rabbi Shmuel Bar Nahman said: Yosef faced great danger, since his brothers could have killed him to keep their secret from being discovered. So why did he send all the people out of the room? Because he said to himself: It is better that I be killed than to shame my brothers in front of the Egyptians. (Tanhuma Vayigash, 5)

He fell on his brother Benjamin's neck and wept, and Benjamin wept on his neck. (Gen. 45:14)

Unconditional love

And he wept – for the two Temples that were destined to be among Benjamin's portion and whose end was destruction. Benjamin cried for the sanctuary of Shiloh that was destined to be among Yosef's portion and whose end was destruction.

Why were these two crying now, at a moment of joy, over the future destruction? Why did each weep over the destruction of his brother's portion and not over his own portion?

It is well known that the Temples were destroyed as a result of baseless hatred. They wept because this baseless hatred – which was already responsible for so much pain and sorrow in their own lives – will end up causing such complete destruction.

The remedy is to increase mutual love so much that the sorrow of one's friend should trouble one more than one's own sorrow. So Yosef and Benjamin wept each for the destruction of his brother. Although Benjamin's sanctuary could not be built until after the destruction of Yosef's, nevertheless, Benjamin wept over it – preferring that his sanctuary not be built and if his brother's sanctuary be spared. A love such as this might be just the remedy for baseless hatred...

They told him, saying: Yosef is yet alive, and he is the ruler over all the land of Egypt. And Yaakov's heart fainted, for he believed them not. (Gen. 45:26)

Crying wolf

It is stated in Midrash: How are liars punished? Even when they speak the truth, they are not believed. So it was with Yaakov's sons. Initially, when they lied about Yosef's death, he believed them. Now, however, even though they told the truth, he did not believe them.

I will go down with you to Egypt, and I will surely also bring you up again, and Yosef shall put his hand upon your eyes. (Gen. 46:4)

The future sill waits

When the Holy Blessed One said: "I will go down with you to Egypt, and I will surely also bring you up again", Yaakov was full of despair. He thought, who knows if after such a descent and ascent is at all possible? Once one begins to sink, one cannot rise up again either easily or quickly. So the Holy One consoled him, saying "and Yosef shall put his hand upon your eyes" – let Yosef be a sign for you that one should not give way to despair. Yosef, too, went down and reached the lowest rung. Nevertheless, he too rose in one swoop and reached the grand level of governor of Egypt. So shall it be with your seed.

We will be redeemed

This is God's greatest promise to Israel, because the glory of God will always be declared throughout the world and the Divine Name will be sanctified by the redemption of Israel. As long as Israel is at the bottom of the scale – so will Divine glory be hidden, and when Israel is raised in their redemption – so too will the Divine glory be raised.

Parashat Vayehi

Yaakov lived in the land of Egypt seventeen years. (Gen. 47:28)

A permanent dwelling

This portion completes the story of the founding family to which the book of genesis dedicates ten of its twelve portions. Even though the family is destined to remain away from the Land of Israel for generations, still their strong bond with the land is expressed in Yaakov and Yosef's last wills made at the time they requested having their final resting place in the Land destined for the children of Israel by the Creator.

The sages explain: when Yaakov returned to Israel from Haran, it is stated "and Yaakov dwelled in the land in which his father had sojourned (Gen. 37:1). But regarding his time in Egypt it says: "Yaakov lived in the land". The concept of 'dwelling' signifies permanence and relates only to the Land of Israel. On the other hand, the life of Jews in the Diaspora is not a permanent reality and its purpose is only to awaken the soul temporarily.

Dancing to welcome the messiah

It once happened that Rabbi Dov Baer of Radishitz came to a rural inn to stay the night but his sleep was disturbed by the ticking of a clock in the adjoining room. For a long time, he tossed and turned on his bed. He tried to go over Mishnahyot in his head, but the sound of the clock upset his thoughts. Suddenly, he was overtaken by a strong desire to dance in honor of God, in movements matching the tick-tock of the clock. He was so caught up in this ecstatic dance that he danced all night.

In the morning, the innkeeper asked him why he had danced all night. The rabbi answered: If you can tell me the origin of the clock in the adjacent room then I might be able to know why I danced. The innkeeper told him that a certain person had once stayed at the inn and was unable to pay for his board and lodging. He left this clock as a pledge and promised to redeem it soon. Two months had passed since then and the pledge had not yet been redeemed.

Rabbi Dov Baer asked for the name of the person but the peasant said that he did not recall it, although he did know that he was related to some great tzaddik in Lublin. At that, Rabbi Baer told the innkeeper: I promised I would tell you the reason for my dancing. Through the ticking of any clock, one can hear the voice of the Angel of Death approaching. That is why they cause such sadness. But this particular clock belonged to my teacher, the Seer of Lublin, may his memory be a blessing. This clock proclaims and announces with every tick and with every tock that the Messiah is approaching, and that is good news. Therefore, I danced all night long welcoming the Messiah.

If now I have found grace in your sight… bury me not, I beg you, in Egypt. But I will lie with my fathers, and you shall carry me out of Egypt and bury me in their burying place. (Gen. 47:29-30)

The last wish

Great was the merit of Yaakov for" his death was perfect". Not only did his sons who lived together with him remain loyal and devoted to the deeds of the father, but even Yosef who was in Egypt, alone and abandoned, in a place of impurity and filth, remained steadfast.

Yaakov was allowed to say "I will lie with my ancestors". The expression "and he lay" is to be found neither with Avraham nor with Yitzhak, for they left Ishmael and Esau after them. It was only with Yaakov, who left after him twelve tribes, all righteous and decent, that it is said: I will lie with my ancestors (Midrash Shohar Tov).

Love of the land

The love felt by all the patriarchs to the Land of Israel is truly awesome. Avraham did not leave the land except during the famine. Even when he sent his servant bring a wife for his son, he warned him by oath "beware lest you bring my son back there" (Gen. 24:6). Not once during his lifetime did Yitzhak exit the boundaries of the land promised to his sons. Yaakov, who was compelled to leave the land twice for long periods of time, nevertheless did not forget to command Yosef "do not bury me in Egypt".

The way of the world is for people to revere their estate and property and possessions. The virtue of our ancestors was such that even when they had still not merited the Land promised to their descendents, they still felt, with all their being, that this was their inherited land and they remained attached to it with all their might.

Deal kindly and truly with me; bury me not, I pray, in Egypt. (Gen. 47:29)

Without compensation

Rashi explained: The kindness that is done for the dead is 'true kindness', since one does not expect anything in exchange. On this matter, Rabbi Israel from Modzitch said: The Torah is described as 'truth' (Mal 2:6) and 'kindness' (Prov. 31:26). Thus, anyone who engages in the study of Torah must do so as one who engages in sincere, truthful kindness-meaning one should not expect anything in exchange for the mitzvah of study.

That one told Yosef: Behold! your father is sick. (Gen. 48:1)

Illness

Since Yosef is told "Behold! your father is sick", it can be understood that previously Yaakov had never been ill.

The following is taught in midrash: Yaakov requested illness (that is, he asked God to cause a person to become ill before dying). Yaakov said to God: Master of the World, a person who dies without illness cannot settle outstanding family affairs. By being ill for a day or two before dying, a person can settle these matters with the children (by writing a will or orally imparting things to them). God said to him: On your life, you have requested a good thing and it will start with you.

Comfort

Rabbi Levy Yitzhak of Berdichev once visited a sick person and found him exceedingly despondent. Rabbi Levy Yitzhak asked him why he was worried? The sick man replied: Rabbi, I feel that my hours are numbered and my heart is filled with fear. I am about to come to the world of truth and what will be my portion and destiny in the next world? Rabbi Levy Yitzhak stood up and said to him: I wholeheartedly give you my entire portion in the next world.

The sick man was comforted and joyful, yet several hours later he died nonetheless. One of those close to the rabbi remarked: Obviously your intention was good, you wanted to keep a sick man alive a little longer. However, indeed you saw that his hours were numbered and your encouragement was of no avail. Why did you have the need to do what you did?

Listen, my son —Rabbi Levy Yitzhak responded- it is better for me to forgo all of the next world in order to save a dying Jew just one hour of sorrow and suffering.

As for me, when I came from Padan, Rahel died by me. (Gen. 48:7)

The strength of devotion

Rashi expounds: And even though I inconvenience you to bring me to burial in the land of Canaan, and act which I did not even perform for your mother Rahel since, after all, she died near Bethlehem and I did not even bring her to burial in Bethlehem itself but rather buried her on the side of the road, and I knew that you held this against me. Still you must know that I buried her there according to God's will so that she will be of assistance to her children. When Nebuzaradan discovers them and they will pass by that way, Rahel will go out onto her tomb and cry and ask for compassion for them. It is said: "A voice was heard in Ramah, lamentations and bitter weeping; It is Rahel, weeping for her children. She refuses to be comforted for he children". God replied to her: Your work shall be rewarded, and they shall come back again from the land of the enemy.

Dr. Max Nordau told the following story: One day in Paris, during the reception hours for the sick at my home, a poor woman from the Jewish quarter came to me with a nine year old boy to receive treatment. I saw that the boy was clever, but felt that his French was impaired. I asked him at what school he studied and he answered me with impaired French that he studied at Heder (religious Jewish school). As if to confirm this response, his mother added that her husband, the boy's father, was old fashioned and did not want the boy to go to a gentile school before completing his course of study at the Heder.

I pondered angrily over this man who had prevented his son from receiving a European education and, almost mockingly, I asked the boy what he learned in Heder. Immediately the boy became filled with astounding emotion and, in Yiddish, began to expound on Rashi's explanation of Rahel's burial as he had learned in Heder on the day before he fell ill.

At that moment, all of my organs trembled and my heart muscles began to vibrate with a new song. I stood up and hugged the boy and kissed him on his forehead. In my heart I said: a nation like this who preserves such memories for thousands of years and roots them in the hearts of their children, such a nation cannot die. It is promised a life of eternity. This occurred during the Dreyfus trial, when I had began to doubt the "justice" of the gentile nations toward Israel. I can say that this boy was one of the factors that returned me to Judaism, to a belief in the eternity of Israel, and that brought me closer to Zionism.

He blessed Yosef...the God who has succored me all my lifelong to this day. (Gen. 48:15)

The blessing of the soil

Rabbi Simhah Zissel of Kelm used to say: "I have never heard anyone, either of middle standing or even more so, one of the rich, say: Blessed be Adonai that I have had food to eat this past year. And here was Yaakov, the grandson of lord of the land, who said: "the God who has succored me...". Onkelos (the Aramaic translation) renders this: "God who has fed me and provided for me". I marveled on hearing from Yaakov something that I have heard from no one else.

I was still wondering about it when it was time for Birkat HaMazon. I was surprised at myself- how could I have not known what it was that I was blessing? Is not the whole of the "grace after meals" about the free gift of food? I thought to myself: We are impressed by the manna which came down from heaven. Why then are we not similarly amazed by the manna that comes up from the land each year?"

Yaakov called his sons and said: Gather yourselves together, that I may tell you that which will befall you in the last days. (Gen. 49:1)

The end of days

Yaakov gathered his sons around him. He began to disclose to them when the end of days would be. He thought that, by so doing, he would make the exile and the sufferings easier to bear. But, as he began to speak, it was hidden from him. He realized that he was prevented from disclosing to his children anything about the end of days. So he lifted up his eyes and, seeing the Divine Presence stationed above him, bade them "be heedful of the honor of the Holy One. He also warned them to show honor to the tribes of Judah and Benjamin.

Exodus

Parashat Shemot

These are the names of the Children of Israel, who came to Egypt with Yaakov. (Ex. 1:1)

A light to the nations

Rashi comments: "This is to show us how dear they were [to God] that they are compared to the stars". Each star has its own name and, just as they are needed for the existence of the world, so are the righteous needed. Each and every star has a function and a job to perform. One is responsible for cold, another for warmth. One brings humidity and another dryness. One merges the winds, another ripens the fruit. They are all part of the existence of the world and are for the good of humanity, even if we do not know their nature and are not aware of their function. One thing we do know, however, is that without them the world cannot exist. So it is with the righteous. Although they differ from each other in their actions and in their behavior, each has one name and title. One is called a hassid and another a tzadika. One is called rosh yeshivah, and another rabbi. One is a preacher and another is a judge - but all are needed for the existence of the Jewish People. Without them, there is no existence for our world.

Another interpretation: The Sefat Emet taught: The children of Israel must know that God loves them and just as He created the stars in order to light the darkness of night, so did He create Israel and scatter them throughout the world in order for them to distribute the Divine light and penetrate it into the darkest and most distant places, to fill their role in the world to be "a light unto the nations".

But the more they afflicted them, the more they multiplied and grew. (Ex. 1:12)

"pen" (lest) or "ken" (surely)

Rashi taught: Pharaoh, in speaking to his people about the Children of Israel, says: "pen yirbeh" - lest they multiply (Ex. 1:6). But the Holy Spirit said: "ken yirbeh" - they will surely multiply (Ex. 1:12).

You say "lest they multiply". You, Jew-haters, think that with your enactments, which embitter the lives of the Jews, the 'pen', the doubt, will increase for us, the desperation and disappointment will begin to penetrate. You hope that we might begin to question whether all this suffering for the sake of the survival of Judaism is worthwhile, that we might begin to question whether hope is still possible. You hope we might wonder if perhaps. our enemies were right in telling us that the curse of God is hanging over us, that God has abandoned and forgotten us, and similar such sad thoughts which you think might bring us to surrender. If so, it is a bitter mistake you are making! For God says: "ken yirbeh"! God is telling you all: I promise that all this will have the opposite effect. The more you afflict them, the more their "ken" - their daring and courage, pride and faith of the Jewish People – will multiply.

Hardship breeds strength

Rabbi Meir Shapira from Lublin was one of the leaders of Orthodox Jewry in Poland after WWI and, among his other positions, he served as a delegate in the Polish "Sim" (Parliament). One of the delegates in the Polish "Sim" once asked him what the Jewish custom of eating hard-boiled eggs at the Seder was all about.

Rabbi Meir responded: this custom symbolizes the typical character of the nation of Israel from its inception until this very. The egg is different from all other foods in that the longer it is cooked in boiling water the harder it becomes. This is just what Israel is like - the more their enemies persecute them, the more hardships. they suffer, the stronger they become. This national character trait was already referred to in the Bible: "But the more they (the Egyptians) afflicted them the more they multiplied and grew".

The daughter of Pharaoh came down to wash herself at the River... and when she saw the box among the rushes, she sent her maid to fetch it. (Ex. 2:5)

Father and daughter – worlds apart

Pharaoh spent much time and effort on plans to abuse the children of Israel. However "The One who sits in the Heavens will laugh". There, in the very house of Pharaoh, the redeemer of Israel was raised, saved from the river by none other than Pharaoh's daughter herself!

This chain of events demands consideration: The father plans mass destruction. The father commands that every Jewish male child be hurled into the river. However, the daughter saves a Jewish child from the river and finds him a wet-nurse. Pharaoh's daughter must have known that the child she had found in the small box that floated silently on the river was from among those same children that her father, the King, had commanded to have thrown into the river. Despite her father's command, she cared for the crying child and sent for a wet nurse.

She named him Moshe, "because I drew (Hebrew: Mashiti) him out of the water". The child bears that name throughout his life, as if to emphasize the good deed of this Egyptian woman - Pharaoh's daughter - who drew him out of the river that her father had converted into a river of death for the Hebrew children. Does this story not teach us that even in the house of the most evil person, a decent, loving, and compassionate child can be found?

Furthermore, is it possible that Pharaoh's daughter did not acting innocently, or simply out of compassion for the Hebrew child that she has drawn out of the river? Perhaps. this was a clear expression of youthful rebellion, of the anger of the next generation, which does not want, and is not willing to accept, their fathers' insane hatred. Amid the darkness of Pharaoh's actions, it would be a serious mistake to ignore this speck of light.

It came to pass in those days, when Moshe was grown, that he went out to his people and looked upon their burdens. (Ex. 2:11)

Unlike the Way of the World

The Midrash teaches: "(he) was grown in an 'unnatural' manner (Ex. Rabbah 1:32). The 'natural' way is that when someone gains prestige and rises to the top, he forgets - or pretends to forget - his people, relatives, and friends. He avoids them, their problems and their hardships. However with regard to Moshe, it is written: "and Moshe was grown"; had risen to greatness, had become a family member in Pharaoh's court. He had grown "not in the way of the world". With all of his prominence and prestige he did not forget his brothers and acquaintances, but rather "he went out to his brothers"; specifically at that time (when he had attained prestige) he was interested in their destiny and their condition, and searched for ways to free them from their distress.

... and the people of Israel sighed because of the slavery.... (Ex. 2:23)

The Power of a Sigh

The story is told of a scholar and a poor craftsman who lived as neighbors. The scholar would rise early in the morning and go off to the school-house where he would study Torah, then pray with purpose, return home for a short time to eat a quick breakfast and then go back to his studies in the school-house until lunchtime. He would engage for a short while in negotiations for his limited income and return to the school-house to study Torah until the afternoon prayers. After the evening prayers, he would continue studying, and so it was each day.

The poor craftsman would also rise at the morning watch, pray hastily at home and go to engage in his craft. He was dejected and poor, time was always pressing on him and throughout the week he was not able even to look through a book. Come Shabbat, he would pick up a book but he was so very tired that he would fall asleep.

Every now and again, these two neighbors would bump into each other as they left their homes or returned to them. The scholar would look reproachfully at the craftsman, who was always worried by the concerns of making a living and who had no time in his heart for Torah and prayer. And when the craftsman saw the scholar, he would sigh deep down and wonder: He rushes and I rush. He rushes to the Torah and to prayer, while I rush for inconsequential things.

In due course, the two neighbors were summoned to the "yeshivah on high". They both appeared before the great court, the scholar with his Torah and his prayers while the poor craftsman stood empty-handed. The defense counsel took all the bundles of the Torah and the commandments of the scholar and placed them before the court on high. The prosecuting counsel stood up and argued: The Garden of Eden is not the place for this man who was proud of himself in the face of the poor craftsman and even looked at him reproachfully from time to time. The craftsman was also summoned before the court on high and was asked: "What do you have?" He sighed from the depths of his heart and said: "I have no Torah and no prayer to my credit. I was a poor man, troubled with earning a living. My time was short and I was unable to spare any for proper study of the Torah and for prayer".

The court on high immediately ordered that scales be brought and that the bundles of Torah and prayer of the scholar be placed on one side and the reproachful look on the other side. The reproachful look tipped the scales. Then they placed on the first side all the days of the poor craftsman, which were devoid of Torah and prayer, and, on the other side, the sigh that came out of his heart when he saw his neighbor engaging in Torah and commandments. The sigh tipped the scales.

Moshe answered and said: But they will not believe me, nor hearken to my voice. (Ex. 4:1)

Redemption

So what if the people would not believe him? Was Moshe's mission to Pharaoh related to their belief? The main point of his mission was to go to Pharaoh and convince him to let the children of Israel out of Egypt. Would they not be happy if he succeeded in his mission? Still, a prophet does not act in a vacuum. Without the nation's belief in him, it would be impossible for Moshe to be their redeeming messenger. Without the nation's power of belief, it would be impossible for the redeemer to hasten the redemption.

I am not eloquent ... I am slow of speech, and of a slow tongue. (Ex. 4:10)

The Divine Presence speaks through Moshe

The question is asked: Why did the Almighty chose Moshe who was "slow of speech, and of a slow tongue" to be the leader of Israel at the time of their exodus from slavery to redemption? A national leader has to be able to address the leaders of other peoples and countries; how could it be right that a person who speaks slowly and stammers should take upon himself such a high and responsible position, and appear before kings and rulers?

If, however, we look at the history of Moshe our Teacher, we will come to realize that it was the very fact that he was "slow of speech and of a slow tongue" that made him fit to serve in his most important role: the Giving of the Torah to his people Israel. Had Moshe been a talented and enthusiastic preacher, who influenced his listeners through his eloquence, it would have been a possible to argue that the Torah was not given by God but that Moshe our Teacher, through the power of his speech and the magic of his tongue, influenced the Children of Israel into calling out unanimously: "We will do and we will obey" (Ex. 24:7). But since it was common knowledge that Moshe was "slow of speech and of a slow tongue" and the Children of Israel nevertheless agreed wholeheartedly to accept the Torah from him - this is clear proof that the Divine Presence had spoken out of his mouth, and that Moshe our Teacher was the devoted and loyal messenger of the Holy Blessed One.

You shall no more give the people straw to make brick. (Ex. 5:7)

Peace of Mind

Would it not have been better to give them straw so that they could double the number of bricks they made? Rabbi Yitzhak from Vorka stated: from this you learn that a troubled mind and a worrisome heart are harder on a person than long, hard and tiring work.

The officers of the children of Israel, who Pharaoh's taskmasters had set, were beaten. (Ex. 5:14)

Devotion

A despotic ruler, who oppresses a foreign nation, appoints taskmasters from among the oppressed nation who cooperate with him, and thus facilitate the task. These taskmasters alienate themselves from the people in order to find favor in their master's eyes.

What were the nation's taskmasters in Egypt like? The Torah tells us: "the officers of the children of Israel were beaten". Midrash Tanhuma explains: "He appointed the Egyptian oppressors over the taskmasters of Israel, and the taskmasters were appointed over the rest of the nation. When he told them "You shall no more give the people straw to make brick", the oppressors would come and count the bricks. If they were found to be lacking in number, the oppressors would beat the taskmasters. The taskmasters would be beaten for the rest of the people, but they would not turn them over to the oppressors. They said: "It is better for us to be beaten than for the rest of the people to fail. Thus, "And the officers of the children of Israel were beaten". From this you learn that they were like the emissaries that devoted themselves to the people of Israel and suffered beatings in order to ease their burden.

Therefore, when God told Moshe: "Gather me seventy men", and Moshe said: Master of the World! I do not know who is worthy and who is not worthy, God told him: 'Those who are known to me as the elders of the people and their taskmasters' - those same taskmasters who consigned themselves to be beaten in Egypt for the number of bricks - they shall come and partake of this greatness".

Parashat Va'era

Since I came to Pharaoh to speak in Your name, he has done evil to this people: neither have You delivered Your people at all. (Ex. 5:23)

Chastising God

Would the Prophet of prophets, Moshe, the servant of God speak rebelliously against God? Rather, taught Rabbi Levi Yitzhak of Berdichev, Moshe is advocating for Israel. He said: All the hatred against them originates from the fact that "I came to Pharaoh to speak in Thy name", that we sanctify Your Name and we speak in the name of Your holy Torah. Because of you, Creator of the world, we are suffering. Because of you, we are hated. It is for you that we have been killed each day. Therefore the obligation rests with you to save us from those who hate us.

I will bring you out from under the burdens of Egypt. I will deliver you out of bondage. (Ex. 6:6)

The Feeling of Bondage and Redemption

This narrative should have, perhaps, began with "and I will deliver you out of bondage" prior to "and I will bring you out from under the burdens of Egypt" since, in actual fact the bondage ended before the departure from Egypt.

Rabbi Ben-Zion Meir Hai Uziel said that this textual reversal comes to teach us that until they tasted freedom, they did not feel or understand the feeling of redemption.

Only after the yoke of Egypt was broken and the yoke of exile was removed from them were they able to comprehend the bitterness and sorrow of exile, and only then could they conceive and understand the great miracle in "and I will deliver you out of their bondage" in its entirety.

I will take you to me for a people ... and I will bring you into the Land. (Ex. 6:7-8)

Two Gifts

The Sages taught: "The Torah and the Land of Israel were given to Israel only through suffering" (Berakhot 2a). This statement refers to the promise that God gave to Moshe at the beginning of the portion. "and I will take you to me for a people" – this refers to the giving of Torah, "and I will bring you into the Land" – this refers to the entry into the Land of Israel.

In these verses, Israel was given a clear and explicit promise that the difficult bondage in Egypt was destined to make them worthy of receiving the two most precious gifts: the Torah and the Land.

Everlasting Promise

Rabbi Naphtali Berlin remarked: The promise of the Land was given not only to the generation departing Egypt, but also to all of the future generations of Israel. For this reason it is said: "and I will give it to you for a heritage" - it is a heritage to you from God and you will bequeath it to your children after you.

Just as the Torah was given not only to the generation who merited being present at Mt. Sinai, but to each and every generation of Israel, so was the Land of Israel given as a worldly inheritance to all the future generations of Israel that are destined to arise.

Moshe spoke so to the children of Israel, but they did not listen to him for anguish of spirit and for cruel bondage. (Ex. 6:9)

Spiritual Preparation for the Redemption

The children of Israel "did not listen to Moshe for anguish of spirit and for cruel bondage"- people do not always refrain from listening only because of cruel bondage. Often their inability to listen is because of anguish of spirit.

One may address people, ask them to participate in community life, to take part in study groups, to read a book, however they often turn such invitations down with the excuse that they are too busy, they work too hard, they do not have the time. Often, however, the excuse is totally different. It does not stem from "hard work" but rather mainly from "anguish of spirit" (*kotzer ruah*). The spiritual part of such a person is very deficient (*katzar*), very small, very narrow and very insignificant. If this is so, why should we complain? Why should such a thing matter to us?

It should matter because redemption, the departure from our current exile, is delayed not because of hard work but mainly because of anguish of spirit. The objective conditions are not what prevent the redemption of our nation. Rather, it is the lack of belief in the nation's basic redeemability and, even more so, the absence of a heartfelt need or wish to be redeemed that keeps. delaying the redemption and prolonging the exile.

Moshe spoke before Adonai, saying, Behold! the people of Israel have not listened to me; how then shall Pharaoh hear me? (Ex. 6:12)

The road to freedom is long

The enslavement of the Israel in Egypt under the rule of Pharaoh reaches its lowest point with this verse. The bitterness mounts, but even as it does, the Children of Israel do not express any anger against Pharaoh. It is much easier for them to accuse Moshe and Aharon. The policemen of the Children of Israel do not want to hear even one word about freedom. They are willing to live with the situation as it is, so long as their own skin is saved.

Moshe is hurt and is at a loss as to what to do next. He sees no chance that the task imposed on him will be successfully completed. This is the lowest point in the entire story of the exodus. Even Moshe, the leader, is ready to give up and to surrender as he views the sorry results of his actions to that point and as he hears the complaints of the people. But then Adonai is revealed to Moshe again, and says to him: The road to freedom is long; there are many obstacles and no short cuts.

Freedom is not easily obtained by a one-day uprising of the oppressed masses. In fact, the suffering masses rarely recognize the fact that they are enslaved. The redemption, Adonai tells Moshe, will come about because it is anchored in a deep commitment, in the covenant God made with Israel's ancestral family. The Children of Israel will win freedom because somewhere, beyond the horizon, is a land waiting for them and expecting them.

Adonai ... gave them a charge to the people of Israel ... to bring the people of Israel out of the land of Egypt. (Ex. 6:13)

Adonai is our Redeemer

It was the religious custom of the Admor Rabbi Henoch of Alexander, that, when he reached the end of the recital of the Haggadah on the eve of Passover, and came to the declaration: "Next Year in Jerusalem", he would tell the following story: A certain Jew leased a bar in a certain village. When this Jew came to the paragraph: "Next Year in Jerusalem", he reflected on his respectable position in the village, so distant from his Jewish brethren, and that he was unable to bring up his sons in Torah and public worship. He became depressed and with great enthusiasm cried out at the top of his lungs: "Next Year in Jerusalem", "Next Year in Jerusalem".

The village land owner happened to pass by just at that time and he heard the shouts in astonishment. He went in and asked his barman: "What's with you, Jew, that you shouted like someone scared and woke up all the inhabitants of the village? The barman told him the whole long story of the exile and of the waiting for the Messiah, and how he waited for his coming daily. He explained to him, from what he recalled of his childhood studies, the meaning of the words "Next Year in Jerusalem". The land owner nodded his head and said: And so, listen, Jew: If, by this time next year, you have not kept your festive promise to move to Jerusalem, know that you are going to be ignominiously expelled from the village.

A year went by and the Messiah had still not come. Since it was Passover time, the land owner summoned the barman and asked: So, Jew, where is your promise "Next Year in Jerusalem"? Did I not warn you? And now, either you uproot yourself from the village and take yourself off immediately to this Jerusalem of yours, or you abandon your belief in the coming of the Messiah and stop proclaiming: "Next Year in Jerusalem". The barman started to weep in front of the land owner, saying conciliatory things to him and pleading with him to allow him another year. He sweet-talked him until he had softened the heart of the land owner. The latter then said to him: Good, I am giving you an extra year this time, provided that you pay double the rent for the bar. And you should know - added the land owner angrily - that this is the last extension and warning, one year only and no more, not even one day more. If, by the end of this year, you are still standing here in my village, no more ifs and buts, no more tears and pleadings.

For the whole of the year, the barman tried to move from there because of the threats of the land owner, but did not manage to do so. When the fourteenth of Nissan dawned, the eve of the searching out the leaven, the miserable man stood there in prayer and said: Master of the Universe! It is revealed and open before You that I am ready and willing to give my life for Your sake and to be degraded at the hands of this cruel land owner, but my conscience afflicts me. What will be with Your great Name, with the profanation of the Name!? Why should the gentiles say that the Children of Israel are liars for every year, twice a year, at the greatest moments, on Passover Eve and on the Day of Atonement, upon conclusion of the closing prayer of the day, they say: "Next Year in Jerusalem", but they do not go there, and the Messiah does not come. We are ashamed and embarrassed to raise our heads in the presence of gentiles, who tell us: "You are liars". Master of the Universe! Send us Your Righteous Messiah and "Next Year in Jerusalem" ...

Adonai said to Moshe: See, I have set you in the role of God to Pharaoh, and Aharon your brother shall be your prophet (Ex. 7:1)

True Love Between Brothers

In the beginning, Moshe refused to fulfill his mission because he feared that his brother, Aharon, would be insulted by his Moshe's foray into what was, essentially, Aharon's territory. Our rabbis ask: "Do you imagine that Moshe would have really refused to go? This is not so! Rather, because Moshe respected Aharon. he said: Before I stood to redeem Israel, Aharon my brother prophesized to them for eighty years. Now I will enter my brother's arena and he will feel sorrow. For this reason he asked not to go". (Ex. Rabbah 3:16)

Moshe had such a remarkable soul that he did not want to take the mantle of greatness on himself for fear that this would insult Aharon: "God said to Moshe: Your brother Aharon does not feel sorrow over this, but is happy for you. Know that he comes to meet you as it is written (Ex.odus 4:14): 'Behold, he comes to meet you, and when he sees you, he will be glad in his heart', not only in his words is he happy, but also in his heart" (Tanhuma Exodus 24).

Moshe nearly did not recognize Aharon because they were separated from one another while still children. "Rabbi Hama said: At the age of twelve Moshe was plucked from his father's house" (Ex. Rabbah 5:2). For many years the brothers did not see one another and this was why Moshe feared that Aharon, his older brother, would be insulted that Moshe took the staff of rule upon himself.

But the opposite happened: When Moshe took the kingship and Aharon the high priesthood, they were not jealous of one another but rather each was happy at the greatness of the other.

Moshe was eighty years old, and Aharon eighty three years old (Ex. 7:7)

Young at Heart

Why does the Torah disclose Moshe's and Aharon's ages?

Most people think that only youngsters are able to bring about change and, in their struggle, bring redemption and freedom to the entire people. The Torah comes and notes that this is not necessarily the case and that, in times of need, when God commands, and the time is ripe, a Jew of eighty years and a Jew of eighty three years are able to cause great changes.

Parashat Bo

Pharaoh's servants said to him, How long shall this man be a snare to us?
Let the men go that they may serve Adonai their God: know you not yet
that Egypt is destroyed? (Ex. 10:7)

"Who are They that Shall Go?"

"How long shall this man be a snare to us"? Pharaoh's advisors argue
before him without stating Moshe's name. It is understood that they
are not suggesting that "this man" be awarded any political or military
status. He is but a "snare". However they admit that Moshe is causing
serious harm to the land of Egypt and its people: "know you not that
Egypt is destroyed"?

Pharaoh then invites Moshe and Aharon to come before him and he
proposes a deal. In principle he is now ready to consider granting of
permission for the Hebrews to leave, as per their request. "Go, serve
Adonai your God", he says: but "who are they that shall go?"

Pharaoh is willing to permit the "trouble makers" to leave - says Prof.
Pinhas Peli - yet he denies the existence of a "Jewish problem" in Egypt.
He hints that in actuality only a minority, all of whom are rowdy "activists", will take the historic opportunity, pack their belongings and
leave his country.

We will go with our young and with our old, with our sons and with our
daughters ... for we must hold a feast to Adonai. (Ex. 10:9)

Each generation

Rabbi Moshe Teitelbaum commented: Moshe our teacher tells Pharaoh: "We will go with our young and with our old...". If we continue
to uphold "we will go with our young and with our old" - if the young

101

will go hand in hand with the old, and continue the magnificent chain of generations that began with our ancestors, then our entire future as Jews and as a nation is secure.

Rabbi Yosef Kahanman, founder of the Ponevitz Yeshiva in Bnei Brak, once said: Moshe specifically emphasizes here "our sons and our daughters" since the future of the nation of Israel depends upon the younger generation in its entirety. If a child without parents is called an "orphan" - a nation is called an "orphan" when it does not have children to continue the tradition of the parents....

Then Adonai said to Moshe: Stretch out your arm toward the heavens that there may be darkness upon the land of Egypt, a darkness that can be touched. (Ex. 10:21)

The meaning of Darkness

"A darkness that can be touched": The darkness of Egypt was so heavy and so thick that it was possible to feel it and to touch it with the tips. of the fingers. Our sages asked: "What was the thickness of the darkness of Egypt?" Their answer: "As thick as a gold dinar".

Rabbi Israel Salanter used to say: "With two eyes, a person can see the world and all that is in it but, if two small coins are placed over the pupils - one over the left eye and the other over the right eye, nothing at all will be seen!"

They saw not one another, neither rose any from his place for three days... But all the Children of Israel enjoyed light in their dwellings. (Ex. 10:23)

Hidden Light

Rabbi Yisrael of Rizin taught: There is no such thing as a Jewish soul in which a spark of the Divine hidden light does not shine, as it says - "all the Children of Israel enjoyed light in their dwellings", all of them according to the place where they live and their standing. They are like precious stones, the value of which a person does not recognize so long as they are buried in the sand. Only when they are set in jewelry of silver and gold is their value noticed. So if you see a Jew whose light is darkened, whose Jewish sparkle is eclipsed, do not judge. Rather, observe the situation instead.

Concern for other people

Rabbi Henich from Alexander would say: Because "they saw not one another" but rather each cared only for himself, each tried only to save her own body. Therefore, "neither rose any from his place": not one person among them could rise up from the basest, lowliest condition.

The Magid from Kuzhnitch, used to say: When true peace will exist among the children of Israel, when they will give a hand to one another, rely on and help one another, then all of the hands will become one strong hand that will reached out and seemingly touch the Divine Throne bringing down all kinds of goodness, redemption and prayers for the entire nation of Israel.

Speak now in the ears of the people, and let every man ask of his neighbor, and every woman of her neighbor, jewels of silver and jewels of gold. (Ex. 11:2)

There is no compensation for children's blood

In the heated discussion held in Israel during the first years of statehood for and against receiving compensation from Germany, various arguments were presented.

This dilemma was not new since, indeed, it already came up in national discussion thousands of years ago. In a certain way, that epoch was similar to our present era: After suffering endless torture and hardship, our ancestors left the slave camps. in Egypt and headed for the Promised Land. God addresses Moshe: "Speak now in the ears of the people, and let every man ask of his neighbor, and every woman of her neighbor, jewels of silver and jewels of gold".

Echoes of the claim for compensation are found in the following Aggadah: The children of Egypt once had a debate with Israel in the presence of Alexander the Great. The Egyptians told him: it says - "Adonai gave the people favor in the sight of the Egyptians and they asked them" - return to us the money and the gold that you took from us!

Givihah ben Pashisah asked the wise men for permission to argue before Alexander. They gave him permission and he went and debated. He asked the Egyptians: From where do you bring this evidence? They told him: From the Torah. He said to them: so I will not bring you evidence (from any other source) other than the Torah. It is written: "and the dwelling place of the children of Israel (who) inhabited Egypt (was) four hundred and thirty years" – so, give us the employment salary of the six hundred thousand men who you enslaved in Egypt for four hundred and thirty years [and we will return the gold we took]. Alexander the Great said to the Egyptians: Respond to him. They answered him: Give us three days. He gave them time. They examined the matter and found no answer. Immediately they left their sown fields and their planted vineyards and fled" (Sanhedrin 91a).

For those children of Israel who were hurled into the river, there is no compensation. The human being does not have the power to exact blood revenge for innocent babies. This role is given to Adonai, "And God heard their groaning". The children of Israel demanded remuneration only for the hard work they performed in the slave camps. This is an accounting that people can make, and therefore - they are required to make it.

This day shall be to you one of remembrance: you shall celebrate it as a festival to Adonai throughout the ages; you shall celebrate it as an institution for all time. (Ex. 12:14)

So long as he directs his heart to heaven

Rabbi Levi Yitzhak of Berdichev once kept the Seder on the first night of Passover in all its minutiae and with full intent, so much so that every saying and custom shone at the table of this righteous rabbi with its hidden meaning. At the end of the seder, as the dawn broke, he sat in his room, happy that the seder had gone so well.

Then he heard a voice saying: "Why are you so proud of yourself? The seder of Hayim the water drawer is more pleasing to Me than yours". The rabbi summoned the members of his household and students and asked them about Haim the water drawer, but no one knew of him. He immediately gave sent several of his disciples to search for him.

For a long time, they wandered through the streets until, finally, they reached a slum neighborhood at the edge of the town. People there pointed out to them the house of Hayim the drawer of water. The disciples knocked on the door and a woman came out and told them: "Hayim the water drawer is indeed my husband. But he cannot go with you because last night he drank a lot and he is now sleeping deeply. Even if you wake him up, his legs will not carry him".

The visitors replied: "The Rebbe has ordered us to bring him!" They entered his room and shook him. He gave them a strange look and did not understand what they wanted from him. He wanted to go back to sleep. So they lifted him off his bed and carried him in their arms until they brought him to the Rebbe. The Rebbe ordered that a seat be prepared for him close to him. As Haim sat there, silent and confused, the Rebbe bent down to him and said: "Dear Rabbi Hayim, what were your hidden intentions at the time when you made the seder?"

A spark appeared to have been kindled in his eyes as he replied: Rebbe, I will not hide the truth from you. I had heard that it was forbidden to drink certain spirits for all eight days of Pesah as there was a suspicion that they might be hametz. So yesterday morning, I drank enough to last me for all the days of the festival, then felt tired and fell asleep. My wife woke me up later and asked me why I was not conducting the seder like all the other Jews. I told her: "What are you asking of me? I am a simple person and my father, too, was a simple person. I don't know what I have to do, nor do I know what is forbidden, and I certainly don't know how to conduct a proper seder. But this I do know: Our forefathers were captives in the hands of the Egyptians, and we have a God in heaven who brought us out from slavery to freedom. And look, now we are enslaved again, and one thing I know with certainty and can tell you: the Holy One will bring us too to freedom". And then I saw the table, all laid, with a shining white cloth on it and, on the table, were bowls with matzoth and eggs and other things to eat and a bottle full of red wine. So I ate from the matzoth and from the eggs and I took some wine and I also gave to my wife to eat and drink. I was then overcome with joy and I lifted up my glass to heaven and said: "See, my God, this glass I drink to Your health! And you will pay heed to us and will redeem us". So we ate and drank and were merry before the Creator and later I became tired and lay down and fell asleep.

It came to pass, that at midnight, Adonai smote all the firstborn in the land of Egypt. (Ex. 12:29)

Celebrating Redemption

The children of Israel were on the verge of redemption, the eve of their departure from slavery to freedom - and already they were commanded to celebrate their redemption even before it happened! They were informed that the plague of the firstborn will take place only at midnight, on the night of the fifteenth day of the month of spring (Nissan). The Pascal sacrifice, however – whose sole purpose was giving thanks for their redemption – this they were commanded to perform at nightfall, prior to the redemption that will only happen several hours later.

It is here that the greatness of Israel was revealed. They were celebrating the great miracle that was about to occur wholeheartedly, as if the miracle had already happened. This is because they are "believers, children of believers" (Ex. Rabbah 3:15). Belief is our inheritance from our ancestors and is rooted in us so deeply that no power in the world can extract it from our hearts.

Pharaoh rose up in the night, with his servants ... and called for Moshe and Aharon by night. (Ex. 12:30)

At Midnight

At midnight, when the final plague hit and the firstborns died, Pharaoh's rigidity and stubbornness finally crumbled. In the middle of the night he went out to look for Moshe, and when he found him, he begged: "Rise up and get out". The children of Israel, however, only left Egypt in the morning - in daylight and not in darkness: "even on that very day it came to pass, that all the hosts of Adonai went out from the land of Egypt" (Ex.odus 12:41).

"Why 'even on that very day' (midday)? Because the Egyptians were saying "If we sense that they are still here, we do not let them leave". So God said: I am taking them out at midday and anyone who has the power to protest – let them come and protest" (Sifri, Ha'azinu 32:48).

One Torah shall be to him that is home born, and to the stranger that sojourns among you. (Ex. 12:49)

Free Will

The nation of Israel was the first to throw the shackles of slavery off itself and to raise high the torch of freedom and equality that enlightened the entire world. It sounded the claim for equal rights, for one law and one Torah for the citizen and the foreigner alike. This claim became an integral part of the Torah of Israel from the moment when it announced the liberation of the nation from slavery.

Some of our Sages went even farther. They said: "The convert is more beloved by Adonai than those people who stood at Mount Sinai. Why? Because all of those who stood at Mount Sinai, had they not seen the voices and heard the shofars, they would not have take upon themselves the yoke of the kingdom of heaven. The convert, however, saw nothing of this yet came, surrendered to God, and took on the yoke of the kingdom of heaven. Is there anyone more beloved than this"?!

Parashat Beshalah

Now when Pharaoh let the people go, God did not lead them by way of the land of the Philistines, although it was nearer, for God said: 'The people may have a change of heart when they see war, and return to Egypt'. (Ex. 13:17)

There is room for suspicion

Had all the Children of Israel despised the life of exile and servitude, and had their souls been yearning to be a people, to accept the Torah, and to enter their land - then there would have been no room for any suspicion that they might want to return to the slavery and the lowly status that had been their lot in Egypt. But since they had been expelled from Egypt - rather than leaving of their own free will - there was certainly room to suspect that they might have a change of heart and wish to return to Egypt. The sole desire of Israel in Egypt was to be liberated from the burden of hard labor. They did not have a vision of the complete redemption from the house of servitude, as it is said: "The Children of Israel groaned under the bondage ... and their cry for help from the bondage rose up to God" (Ex. 2:23). That was their entire vision – this, and nothing more. This is the source of the suspicion that, at the first opportunity, they would return to Egypt - because "For lack of vision a people loses restraint" (Prov. 29:18).

Acclimation

Rabbi Judah Leib from Gur (author "Sefat Emet") comments: The Scripture here informs us that God did not lead Israel "through the way of the land of the Philistines" because this path was too close and it would not be good for the Israelites to enter their destined land via a short route. Rather they needed to experience a long hard path in the desert in order for them to become accustomed to the hardships. that awaited them in their inherited land. The Israelites' years of wandering

109

in the desert would serve them as a period of preparation and acclimation during which they could learn how to settle and inhabit an arid and desolate land, and how to live a life of toil.

Rambam also sees the period of wandering in the desert as a vital necessity, as the only way to prepare the tribes of Israel for the life of a free nation in its own land. In his book "Guide to the Perplexed" (Moreh Nevukhim Part 3, chapter 24), Rambam writes: "It is not natural for a person to be educated in the subservience of slavery, in clay and bricks, and then immediately be able to fight the children of the giants and be a brave warrior. It was Adonai's desire to delay the children of Israel for forty years in the desert until they became strong- as it is known that the wilderness and savagery of the landscape commanded courage- and until a generation was born that was not used to submission and slavery".

Moshe took the bones of Yosef with him: for he had laid an oath on the children of Israel saying: God will surely visit you; and you shall carry up my bones away from here with you. (Ex. 13:19)

Yosef's Coffin

The Law of Moshe is the law of good deed. The point is not study - but rather deed. Furthermore, it is the small deed done for the individual that is of utmost importance, not a great deed done for society. Moshe himself served as an example and model of his law. While masses of people were removing the shackles of bondage and breaking forth to a life of freedom, the great liberator, Moshe, retired and dealt with the "smaller" matters – such as fulfilling the promise made to Yosef to bring his bones to the Land of Israel.

Adonai said to Moshe, Why do you cry to me? Speak to the children of Israel that they go forward. (Ex. 14:15)

Confidence and Insecurity

How can one understand Moshe's insecurity when the Egyptians were chasing the Israelites? After all, God had just promised him: "And I will harden Pharaoh's heart, that he shall follow after them; and I will gain honor by Pharaoh and by all his host" (Ex. 14:4). Is it possible that Moshe, God's servant and most righteous person of the generation, doubted the fulfillment of an explicit promise given to him by God? Is it possible that, in a moment of crisis, Israel's leader became feeble and had doubts regarding the Creator's ability to fulfill the promise made to the of Israel?

Rabbi Yisrael Lipkin of Salant replies – It is precisely in Moshe's demonstrated impatience and insecurity that the greatness of his leadership is exemplified. At a time when the fate and future of the entire nation is in possible jeopardy, this loyal shepherd cannot behave calmly and tranquilly. A true leader may not exhibit confidence in matters affecting the entire nation.

The waters returned, and covered the chariots, and the horsemen, and all the army of Pharaoh that came into the sea after them; there remained not so much as one of them. (Ex. 14:28)

Mercy and Justice

The Egyptians, of course, did not expect the sea to be a death trap for them, nor did they suspect that in the end they would come to drown in the abyss. "At that same hour, the ministering angels asked to sing for Adonai. He said to them: The creations of my hands are drowning and you want to sing for me?!" (Megillah 10b)

These words of God, determined the fate of the Israelite nation. They left their mark on the nation's consciousness for generations to come. From then on, there was no total happiness for Israel as long as God's creations were in trouble. Israel's fate is interconnected with the fate of all humanity. Only when final redemption will finally come to all of humanity, will the day of celebration also come to Israel.

But the Children of Israel walked upon dry land in the midst of the sea (Ex. 14:29)

An Overt Miracle

Rabbi Elimelekh of Lizensk used to say: People are impressed only when they see overt miracles. They do not understand that nature itself is nothing but one large miracle in which one can constantly see the greatness of the Creator and can wonder at it.

It is only on seeing an overt miracle that one begins to believe that there is also divine providence in the simple, natural life and that wonderful miracles take place even though everyone is used to them and pays no attention to them. This is what the Torah means: "But the Children of Israel", having seen such an overt miracle - that they walked on the sea as though on dry land - come to the recognition that they had "walked upon dry land in the midst of the sea" - that even when they were walking on terra firma, that in itself was a great miracle, as great as though they were actually walking on the sea.

Thus Adonai delivered Israel that day from the hand of the Egyptians ... and the people feared Adonai, and they believed in Adonai, and in his servant Moshe. Then Moshe and the people of Israel sang. (Ex. 14: 30 – 15:1)

About that they sang

Rabbi Yisrael of Rizin was asked: Were further great miracles not performed for Israel in the wilderness? Why did they not sing about them?

It was not about the miracle of the crossing of the Red Sea that the Children of Israel sang, replied Rabbi Yisrael replied. Rather, it was because of the crossing of the Red Sea that the Children of Israel came to a total belief, to a full recognition "and they believed in Adonai". That is why they burst out in song.

The Almighty has many messengers

A poor Jew who had to marry off his daughter came to Rabbi Menahem Mendel of Kotzk. The rabbi gave him a letter addressed to a rich man in the near-by town, asking him to help the poor Jew as Adonai had been good to him.

The poor man took off to the town and found the home of the rich man. The latter received him warmly enough. The poor man showed him the letter of request from the rabbi and thought to himself that the rich man would surely provide him with all the expenses of the wedding since he had brought him a personal letter from the well-known rabbi of Kotzk.

The rich man read the letter, then took a small amount of money from his pocket and gave it to him. The poor man was astounded, for the costs of getting there had come to more, apart from the troubles of the actual journey. The main thing, however, was that he could not cover the costs of the wedding with this meager contribution. No arguments were of any use. The rich man would not give him anything more. Having no other choice, the poor man left bitterly disappointed and returned home on foot.

No sooner had the poor man left the rich man's house than the latter quickly prepared everything necessary for a wedding: he bought expensive clothes and other necessary items, loaded everything onto carts and took the same road along which the poor man was walking, until he caught up with him and gave everything to him.

The poor man was surprised and asked the rich man: Since you have given to me so generously, why did you cause me such anguish for nothing? The rich man replied: When you had in your hand the letter from the Rabbi of Kotzk addressed to me, you forgot that Israel has a God who will assist you. I wanted, therefore, to guide you so that you would trust in Adonai. And so now, make your way home in peace.

Trust

Rabbi Menahem Mendel of Kotzk used to say: When a person is facing calamity and misfortune and can see no natural way out, then such a person casts the burden upon Adonai and trusts in God - but this is not yet the quality of trusting in Adonai a the true level, for does such a person have any other choice?

However, if a person is well-off and lacks for nothing and, nevertheless, trusts in Adonai - that is true trust.

The Strengthening of Belief

Moshe's mission was not only to save the children of Israel from the yoke of slavery but also to bring them to the land of their ancestors. The departure of the children of Israel from Egypt freed them not only from their physical slavery but also from their emotional bondage.

When they saw with their own eyes the miracle of the splitting of the Red Sea, they began to sing thanks to the Creator of the world who behaved toward them with kindness and mercy. The strong belief "in Adonai and in God's servant, Moshe" was apparently born not in Egypt but on the shores of the Red Sea.

Adonai is my God and I will praise him; my father's God and I will exalt Him. (Ex. 15:2)

Knowing the Creator

Rabbi Menahem Mendel of Kotzk used to say: A Jew must first say: "Adonai is my God" – must first personally know the blessed Creator. Only afterwards will this Jew be able to walk in the path of his ancestors and exalt their God.

Then the chiefs of Edom shall be dismayed; the mighty men of Moab shall be gripped by trembling; all the inhabitants of Canaan shall be aghast. (Ex. 15:15)

Fear and dread shall fall upon them

It would seem difficult to understand why Moshe was so happy that fear shall fall upon Edom and Moab. After all, the Children of Israel had no intention of attacking these two peoples. The Holy Blessed One had warned Moshe regarding these nations: "You will be passing through the territory of your kinsmen, the descendants of Esau ... do not provoke them, for I will not give you of their land so much as a foot can tread on" (Deut. 2:4). And "Do not harass Moab or provoke them into war, for I will not give you any of their land as an inheritance" (Deut. 2:9).

The answer, Rabbi Yosef Soloveichik used to say, is that sometimes one has to sing a song over fear that falls upon our enemies, even if it is baseless fear. This is because fear is a sign of respect. It signifies, in the clearest possible manner, that those who hate us nonetheless recognize the people of Israel as a living, dynamic kingdom.

I will put none of these diseases upon you, which I have brought upon the Egyptians; for I am Adonai that heals you. (Ex. 15:26)

The Power of Weeping

It once happened that a certain woman came to Rabbi Moshe Leib of Sassov and burst into tears: "Rabbi, holy one of Israel, please pray for my daughter who is dangerously ill". So the Rabbi prayed: "May He who dwells on High send her perfect healing". "No, rabbi", said the woman out of the bitterness of her soul, "I am not moving from here until you swear on your portion in the world to come that my daughter will be healed". "I swear", said Rabbi Leib, "on my portion in the world to come, that your daughter will be healed, if God so wills it. Now, go in peace and trust the Healer of all flesh".

After the woman had left, one of his students asked the rabbi: "Rabbi, why did you see fit to swear on your portion in the world to come that the woman's daughter would recover her health seeing that she is dangerously ill?" Rabbi Leib replied: "One hour of consoling a Jewish mother is worth the whole world to come of a Moshe Leib who lives in Sassov".

But Moshe's hands were heavy. So they took a stone, and put it under him and he sat on it. (Ex.17:12)

Do not take leave of the community

Our Sages of blessed memory praised Moshe's exemplary behavior during the war with Amalek. In their opinion, this behavior of a leader of Israel in the desert must serve as instruction to every person to avoid forsaking the community, and to actively participate in the sorrow of the people.

At a time when the community is shrouded in sorrow, one should not say: I will go to my hose and eat and drink and peace be upon my soul. Rather, one should feel the sorrow of the public. We find this characteristic in our teacher Moshe, who felt sorrow with the community - as it is stated: "but Moshe's hands were heavy, and they took a stone and put it under him and he sat on it". Did Moshe not have even one pillow or cushion on which to sit? Rather, Moshe said: "Seeing that Israel is shrouded in sorrow, I too will be with them in sorrow". One who is saddened with the public, earns and sees the comfort of the public. (Ta'anit 14a)

Parashat Yitro

Now Yitro, the priest of Midian, Moshe's father-in-law, heard all that God had done for Moshe and for Israel His people. (Ex. 18:1)

Will he who listens not hear?

The students of Rabbi Shmuel Yitzhak Schor once asked him: Our sages of blessed memory taught: "Every day a bat kol [the echo of the Divine Voice] goes forth from Mount Horev, and says: Woe unto men on account of [their] contempt towards the Torah [through neglect of its study and practice]". Why don't we hear this voice?

He replied: Scripture says: "Now Yitro heard". Did only he hear, or did others also hear? Does Scripture not also say: "The people shall hear, and be afraid" (Ex.15:14)? There are different levels of hearing: The Prophet Isaiah says "They hear, but do not understand" (Is 6:9). In other words, one can hear something but not understand the meaning of what one hears. Thus, everything depends on the listener. Everyone hears, and many things are heard. But all ears are not the same and all hearts are not equal. For one person, the sound may penetrate the ear and play on the chords of the heart as on a violin while, for another person, the sound may reverberate on the ear drum but never reach the heart. In the case of Yitro, the Torah testifies "Now Yitro heard". Since he wanted to hear, he knew and understood what he heard. Therefore he merited entering under the wings of the Shekhinah (the Divine Presence) and finding shelter there. Furthermore, he merited having an important portion named after him, the portion in which the Ten Commandments were given: Parashat Yitro.

Now I know that Adonai is greater than all the gods. (Ex. 18:11)

Searching for the Truth

Rashi comments: This teaches us that Yitro knew every idol in the world, and that there was no idol which he had not worshipped.

The implication of this is that Yitro never stopped searching for the truth. That is why he went and worshipped all the gods and all the religions that existed in the world in those days. When he came to the realization that the way and means of a particular idol were not right, he left and sought a different faith, until, finally, he came to the faith of Israel and to the Torah of Adonai and its precepts. Then, when he had attained some satisfaction and his tempestuous spirit, which had unceasingly sought the truth, was quiet, he stood up and proclaimed the joy of truth: "Now I know that Adonai is greater than all the gods".

The people stood by Moshe from the morning to the evening. (Ex. 18:13)

I Give You Servitude

Rabbi Shmuel Salant, was once asked why he did not schedule a special time to receive people, to decide on halakhic questions and other such matters.

He responded: A Jew, especially a leader in Israel, must act according to the ways of God and be devoted to God's character. The way of the blessed Adonai, is to respond to every person any time God is addressed, just as we say in the Grace After Meals: "You feed and sustain us continually every day, at all times and at all hours". God does not have scheduled reception hours....

You shall provide out of all the people able men, such as fear God, people of truth, hating unjust gain. (Ex. 18:21)

Money Commands All

Rabbi Sushi of Anipol used to say: Of all the character traits that demand guiltlessness from the leaders of the nation, the only ones that are stated are that they be: "God fearing, and people of truth". Yet the Torah points specifically to only one specific trait: "hatred of unjust gain", as this is the worst of all desires. No desire runs as deep and is as insatiable and there is no desire that is as hard to uproot - as greed.

Monetary Greed

Regarding people's greed, Rabbi Nahman of Bratzlav said: We instinctively see that even those who have enough money to support themselves, and even the very rich, greatly toil all their life to earn more money. They risk accidents, endure much running around, and cause themselves great anxieties in their quest for money. It is as if some great debt is tied around their necks. Yet the debt is only something they must have for themselves, in order to fulfill their desire.

It has been found that they do, in fact, have a debt. Throughout their life, they do not stop paying what they owe their desire. Desire knows no limits and no boundaries because "a person leaves the world with half his cravings unfulfilled".

The difficult matters they would bring to Moshe, but all the minor matters they would decide themselves. (Ex. 18:26)

The Law of Truth

It once happened that a poor widow, sobbing uncontrollably, knocked on the door of Rabbi Tzvi Hirsch of Rimanov. The Tzaddik of Rimanov asked her: What are you crying about? The woman replied in a voice choked by tears: I have just been in the court before Judge so-and-so. To my total chagrin, the judge ruled against me and I was made to look like a charlatan.

Rabbi Tzvi Hirsch immediately sent someone to summon the judge and asked him to show him the halakhic sources on which he had relied in the ruling he had given that morning. The judge opened the Shulhan Arukh and pointed to the section according to which he had made his ruling. But, as he was looking at it again, the judge realized that he had erred in his interpretation of the section in the Shulhan Arukh, and that he should have, in fact, found in favor of the woman and against the other litigant.

The judge started to make excuses to Rabbi Tzvi Hirsch about the distorted ruling he had issued that morning, and explained to the Tzaddik that even a veteran judge who is well versed in the laws can make a mistake and find against an innocent party.

Rabbi Tzvi Hirsch mollified his guest and expressed his joy that the Divine Providence had assisted in preventing a misruling and deprivation of a poor widow. Wine and cookies were immediately brought to the table and everyone drank a toast and blessed each other, as is the way of the Hassidim.

After partaking of the spread, the judge got up to go and Rabbi Tzvi Hirsch accompanied him to the door. As they were shaking hands before parting, the judge asked his host: How did the suspicion enter your mind that the ruling I gave this morning was an error? After all, you had not heard the particulars of the case which were brought before me for a ruling.

It was the bitter weeping of the woman, replied Rabbi Tzvi Hirsch. This was what gave me the incentive to do what I have just done. It is said about our Holy Torah: "The teaching of Adonai is perfect, renewing life" (Ps. 19:8). Had you made a correct ruling, according to the law of the Torah, the woman would not have broken out in bitter weeping, as she did here.

Simple and easy or complicated and difficult

Rabbi Hayyim Berlin taught: Yitro said: "every great matter they shall bring to you (Moshe)", yet the Torah states: "the hard cases". Among the nations of the world, judicial authority is determined according to the amount of money around which the conflict revolves. Legal suits regarding large sums of money are brought before the district courts, and small sums of money are brought before the regular courts.

However, according to the law of Torah, there is no difference whatsoever between a large sum of money or a small one. Rather, the difference is mainly in the nature of the case – whether it is simple and easy, or complicated and difficult. A complicated case was brought before the more brilliant students – "the hard cases they brought to Moshe" – even when the case did not concern a "great matter".

...and you shall be My treasured possession among all people. (Ex. 19:5)

Torah and Israel – Which comes first?

Even before the Children of Israel received the Torah on Mount Sinai, and even before they were commanded about its laws, they had already heard clear statements to the effect that the Torah was designed for them, and for what it would, in the future prepare, them: "you shall be My treasured possession among all the peoples ... And you shall be to Me a kingdom of priests and a holy nation" (Ex. 19:5-6). In other words, the purpose of the Jewish People was to be an example to all the peoples and this obligation preceded the Ten Commandments.

Perhaps. This is why Eliyahu used to say: "I was once going from one place to another, when a certain person came to me and asked about matters in the Torah. He said to me: Rabbi, I have two things in my heart, and I love them both dearly: the Torah and Israel. But I don't know which comes first. I said to him: People say that the Torah precedes everything but I would say that the holy of Israel come first". (Tanna devei Eliyahu 15)

Rabbi Shimon Bar Yohai said: "Now what was created for the sake of what? Was Torah created for the sake of Israel or vice versa? Surely Torah was created for the sake of Israel! Since the Torah, which was created for the sake of Israel, endures for all time, how much more must Israel, for whose sake it was created, [endure for all time]!" (Eccl. Rabbah 1:9)

I remember the affection of your youth

A woman approached the Magid of Kuznitz and bitterly told him that her husband had began to hate her, and to claim that she was ugly.

"Maybe you really are ugly to him?", asked the Magid. This made the woman sob even more: "When we went under the huppah I found favor in his eyes, and he showered me with compliments, and said that I was pretty. Now, in one second, I became so ugly to him?!"

When he heard these words, the Magid of Kuznitz raised his hand to the heavens and said: "Master of the Universe! This woman is right and we make this very same claim about You with our mouths: as we stood before You on Mount Sinai and said "we will do and we will hear", You showered us with praise and chose us from among all the nations. Now, alas, suddenly we have become despicable to You, and You do not want to look at us at all?!

Adonai said to Moshe, "Behold! I come to you in a thick cloud". (Ex. 19:9)

...and your faithfulness every night... (Ps. 92:3)

Rabbi Meir Shapira, the head of the Yeshivah of the Seers of Lublin, used to say: One finds believers, the offspring of believers, who sometimes disclose a weakness of faith at difficult times when such befall them. Scripture here calls to those of a weak faith: "Behold! I come to you in a thick cloud". One should never despair - even when visited by difficult times – for on many occasions when darkness covers the land and a person feels that no hope remains in life and that there is no way out, suddenly rays of hope shine, and the full glory of salvation is seen once again.

Rabbi Avraham Yitzhak Kook said: Why did the Holy Blessed One advise Moshe "I come in a thick cloud"? Many times, a person may only see a heavy cloud, darkness, and blackness. Such a person will wonder: From where shall my help come? (Ps. 121:1) There are two possible reasons for this fear: It is possible that observer is short-sighted, and cannot discern the Divine Presence. It is also possible that, because of the shining bright light of the Divine Presence, the human eye is temporarily blinded and can no longer sense it. Only in such times of confusion, does the Holy One promise us: "Behold! I come to you in a thick cloud". It is precisely in times of distress that I will be there to save you, for salvation belongs to Adonai.

Honor your father and your mother. (Ex. 20:12)

A Double Commandment

One Shabbat evening, Rabbi Kook's mother, who was then an elderly lady of 84 years, fell ill. The Rabbi asked his servant to call her grandson, the doctor. When the doctor arrived, the Rabbi told him that his mother's throat hurt, and that her temperature had gone up.

In the room where the old lady lay, there was only a very weak light from an electric night light. The doctor wanted to examine her throat, for which he needed a stronger light. The doctor wanted to bring in the portable paraffin lamp, which was on the table, and to move it close to her face so that he would be able to examine her properly. He therefore asked the servant to hold the burning paraffin lamp. Even though it was Shabbat evening, the servant agreed willingly.

Rabbi Kook immediately rushed towards him, and insisted that he, himself, hold the paraffin lamp in his own hand. He said to the servant: You are fulfilling just one mitzvah - that of saving life. For me, this is a double precept – saving a life and honoring a parent!

You are not exempt from this commandment

A man once came to Rabbi Moshe Sopher and complained about his son, who did not honor him sufficiently. Rabbi Moshe Sopher sent for the son to him and asked him: "Why do you not keep the precept of honoring your father?" "Rabbi", the son apologized, "my father has money but does not support me. Accordingly, I do not feel obliged to show him honor". "You are mistaken", replied Rabbi Moshe. The commandment of honoring parents was given to the Children of Israel when they were in the Wilderness, at a time when they were not dependent on each other in any way - neither parents on children, nor children on parents. At that time, in the Wilderness, the Holy Blessed One provided all their needs with the manna, which descended from Heaven. From this, it can be deduced that children are required to honor their parents, even when the parents do not provide for their needs.

Parental Respect

An elderly Jerusalemite received financial support from his son who lived in America. The father was apprehensive about taking pleasure from this money because he knew that the son managed his business affairs on the Sabbath and his heart would not allow him to take money that perhaps. came from business done on the Sabbath.

The elderly man went to the home of Chief Rabbi Avraham Yitzhak Kook to ask for advice in this matter. The Rabbi responded: According to what you have said, you regret that your son does not fulfill the commandments. Yet, there is one commandment that your son wants to fill wholeheartedly: honor thy father. Yet you desire to deprive your son of this commandment too?

Parashat Mishpatim

He shall bring him to the door...and his master shall bore his ear. (Ex. 21:1)

Unable to Understand

How was the door used for boring the servant's ear different from any other location? It can actually be said that this door is the place most worthy of this action. The doors were opened before this Hebrew servant who was offered the possibility of throwing off the fetters of servitude and acquiring freedom, liberty and independence. Yet this slave, whose life and soul is bound to servitude in the Diaspora, is comfortable in this position, accepts this life, and has no desire to take pleasure in the sunshine of freedom and liberty. Therefore it is written: "He shall bring him to the door".

When a man steals an ox or a sheep, and slaughters it or sells it, he shall pay five oxen for the ox, and four sheep for the sheep. (Ex. 21:37)

Extenuating Circumstances

When Rabbi Yisrael Salanter would engage in his studies, it was clear to the world how he dove into the depths of halakhic literature, and how he would bring up from there pearls and treasures filled with empathy for all those in pain, and for all the lowly among the Jewish People.

He was once teaching his students the section of Talmud, which explains the Torah's requirement that a person who steals an ox or a sheep and slaughters or sells it should pay fivefold for the ox and fourfold for the sheep. "Rabbi Yohanan ben Zakkai said: Observe how great is the importance attached to the dignity of people, for in the case of an ox, which walks away on its own feet, the payment is five-fold, while in the case of a sheep, which was usually carried on the thief's shoulder, only four-fold has to be paid" (Bava Kama 79b).

Rabbi Yisrael turned to his students and excitedly said to them: Listen and pay heed to the extent to which the Torah participates in a Jew's sorrow, even when that Jew commits an offence. Are we not talking here about a Jew who steals a sheep from a fellow Jew? The animal could have been the last important thing from which the owner and his household were eking out a living but, nevertheless, when the thief is caught and placed on trial, the Torah feels for him and sees fit to punish him leniently in that he has to pay only fourfold, while one who steals an ox pays fivefold. This is because the Torah makes allowance for the tribulations of the thief in that he had to carry the sheep on his shoulders.

Keep far from a false matter. (Ex. 22: 7)

I am not a rebbe nor yet am I a liar

Rabbi Azriel of Lublin, once asked the Seer of Lublin: Why have you set yourself up as the rebbe of the Hassidic community? Are there not greater and better men than you who are fit for that? The Seer of Lublin asked: What should I do when Jews come to me and say that I am a rabbi?

Rabbi Azriel suggested that he should proclaim and announce before all the Hassidim who came to his house that he is not a rebbe but a simple Jew, and then the Hassidim will leave him alone. The Seer did just that. At the Shabbat meal, he declared before the community of Hassidim who were eating at his table: I want you to know that I am not a rebbe, nor am I the son of a rabbi, but just a simple Jew. I have no Torah, no fear of Heaven and no good deeds. Leave me alone and do not come to my house. The Hassidim wondered greatly at the words of their rabbi and felt in their hearts a great love for that righteous man. Instead of talking about his own greatness, he spoke of his humility and of his deep pain. Not only did they not abandon him, they even increased his good name in public and the Hassidic community continued to grow.

Some time later, Rabbi Azriel asked the Seer: Did you do as I suggested? Did it work out? The Seer replied: Yes, rabbi, I followed your advice but, to my regret, nothing changed. The Hassidim, seeing that I was humble, bonded with me more than ever. Rabbi Azriel immediately gave the Seer different advice, suggesting that he should tell his Hassidim: "You should know that I really am a great rebbe, great in Torah and in good qualities". Rabbi Azriel reasoned that, when the Hassidim will see their rebbe speaking his own praises so arrogantly, they will leave him and go their own way.

The Seer replied to Rabbi Azriel: With all due respect to the rabbi of Lublin, I admit that I am not a rabbi nor am I a rebbe, but neither am I a liar. Heaven forbid that I should praise myself before my Hassidim for what I am not!

Truth and Falsehood

Rabbi Menahem Mendel of Kotzk used to say: The evil inclination has found a new way, which is working successfully for it. It no longer fights day and night. It labors only to take from you the thin thread of truth which is in your heart. After that, it leaves you to do whatever you want: work, study, pray. Without that thread of truth, it is no longer of importance to the evil inclination what you do.

You shall not afflict any widow, or orphaned child. If you afflict them in any way, and they cry to me, I will surely hear their cry. (Ex. 22:21-22)

Courtesy

When the position of Chief Rabbi of Jerusalem fell vacant, many of the religious leaders turned to Rabbi Hayim Yaakov Levin (the son of the Jerusalem Zaddik, Rabbi Aryeh Levin) who had immigrated to Israel from the United States, and who served as rabbi in Pardes Hannah. They offered him this respected position, for which many other good rabbis were competing.

When Rabbi Levin refused to submit his candidacy, Menahem Begin, then a minister in the Government, went to his home and personally asked him to submit his candidacy. He told him that there was a consensus with respect to him and that he was assured of a majority in the electoral committee. But Rabbi Levin was adamant in his refusal.

A delegation then went to see him, consisting of representatives of most of the members of the appointments committee. They had the signatures of the leading rabbis and rabbinical judges of Jerusalem, asking him to submit his candidacy - but he continued with his refusal. The members of the delegation were greatly astonished. The position was being offered to him on a silver platter and his election was assured. Why, then, was he stubbornly refusing them?

Rabbi Levin told them: One of the rival candidates is Rabbi Bezalel Zholti. In my youth, we used to study together and I well remember Rabbi Zholti's mother. She was a poor widow who worked so hard cleaning the houses of others that her son, the prodigy, could study diligently and grow in Torah. And so now that that elderly mother can see her learned son ascending the throne of the rabbinate in Jerusalem and can have some pleasure in her world - I cannot permit myself to prevent this righteous widow from enjoying this pleasure.

If you lend money to My people, to the poor among you…. (Ex. 22:24)

So that you may feel their distress

The Hatam Sopher once called on a rich miser to solicit funds for a good cause. It was freezing cold at the time. The rich man came out to greet the rabbi in the outer room, without wearing an overcoat. The rabbi remained standing in the outer room and there he explained to the man about his request. The rabbi talked at great length, until his host began to shiver from the cold. The man asked the rabbi to come inside into the heated room.

The rabbi replied: I wanted to speak with you specifically in the outer room, so that you would understand the situation of the poor in town who cannot afford to buy wood to heat their rooms. This, too, was the Rashi's intention: "To the poor among you - look at yourself as though you were that poor man".

Charity

The first and foremost concern of every Jewish community in the world was establishing public institutions. These were the glory of the community. The oldest and most established among these was the charity fund that offered aid and assistance to the poor and needy. This precept was deeply rooted in the Jewish soul thanks to tireless exhortation of the Sages who trained the people and infused them with love and a devotion to aiding others. Our Sages warned the affluent who clenched their hand and did not loan money to the poor. They stated this warning as if it came directly from God: "God said: Be it known that I made him poor and you rich. I can bring you back and make you poor" (Yalqut Shimoni, Mishpatim 22). Midrash Rabbah adds: "God has judged, this will be lowly and this will be honorable". What is this world likened to? Like the clay buckets of a (well) wheel in a garden; the bottom ones come up full and the upper ones go down empty. Thus, not everyone who is rich today will be rich tomorrow and someone who is poor today may not be poor tomorrow. Why? Because the world is a wheel (cycle)". This wheel obligates mutual aid between people. Moreover, our Sages saw this phenomenon as a vital arrangement, one that rules all of nature, and they advised people to learn a lesson from it. They said: "Come and see. Each of God's creations borrows from one another. The day borrows from the night and the night borrows from the day, and they do not converse like people... God's creations borrow from one another and make peace with one another without speaking. But a person of flesh and blood borrows from a friend, who then tries to devour the person through interest and robbery". (Ex. Rabbah 31)

For that is his only covering, it is his garment for his skin; in what shall he sleep. (Ex. 22:26)

And Your Brother Shall Live With You

During the years when Rabbi Soloveitchik headed the Rabbinical Board in Brisk, the community supplied him with all of his needs, including a candle for light and wood for heating. One day the heads of the community checked the account and saw that the heating expenses of their Rabbi's home cost several hundred Rubles per year. They were very surprised by the expense. They investigated and found that the wood-shed was not locked, and that the city's poor folk would come and take wood from there as if it belonged to them. The heads of the community had the wood-shed locked and gave the key to an attendant. When the Rabbi heard this, he demanded that the lock be removed immediately so that the woodshed was again open to all. The heads of the community complained that the community fund is not enough for all of the poor people in the city. "In that case", Rabbi Hayyim replied, "neither shall my house be heated. I cannot sit in my heated home where I am warm while the poor people of this community freeze from the cold"

Keep yourself far from a false matter. (Ex. 23:7)

Education

One must labor for many years in order to develop the characteristic of truthfulness. This character trait can only be procured by virtue of continuous spiritual training. This is why our Sages instructed us that an extra obligation falls on parents to educate their children to speak the truth. They must be strict in this regard while the child is still very young: "Rabbi Zira said: A person should not tell a baby, I will give you something - and then not give it, because this teaches the baby falsehood" (Succah 47a). Once people become accustomed to falsehood, it is difficult for them to return to telling the truth. Moreover, even if they do, other people will still not believe them: "This is the punishment of the liar, that even if he speaks the truth - nobody listens to him" (Sanhedrin 89b).

The Liar is Always at Work

In one of his sermons, the Magid of Kelm remarked: You may think that lies are not a very big deal, but the fact is that a liar is worse than a thief or a robber. The thief works when nobody is looking, mostly at night. The robber, although acting both in daytime and nighttime, usually acts directly against a particular individual. The liar, however, can strike any time, any place, at any hour of the day or night and against an individual as well as against a group.

Parashat Trumah

Adonai spoke to Moshe saying: Speak to the children of Israel that they bring me an offering: of every man whose heart prompts him to give you shall take My offering. (Ex. 25:1-2)

The Correlation Between the Torah Portions

With the Terumah portion, the Torah introduces a comprehensive topic: the work and vessels of the Temple. Five portions, beginning with Terumah and ending with Pekudei, are dedicated to this subject.

The question is raised: In what way is parashat Terumah connected to parashat Mishpatim? The Sages responded: The Torah teaches every member of the nation, that a Terumah (an offering) is acceptable to God only when it is given from money that has been righteously and justly collected or earned. However, an offering that comes from property purchased through extortion and fraud or through exploitation is not at all acceptable to God, since such an offering is considered "a good deed rooted in transgression".

Accustom Yourself to Giving

Why was Israel commanded: "you shall take My offering"? After all, is it not written that "God's is the earth and its fullness". Is all silver and gold not God's?

God provided totally for the Israelites during their wandering in the desert - giving to each one - with a full, wide, open hand - an equal portion and leaving not one among them in need of anything whatsoever. This means there was no need for people to give charity to one another nor do charitable deeds for each other during all of those years, and they were becoming accustomed to clenching their fists. Since habit soon becomes nature, they were commanded to give an offering to the Temple, so they could learn and become accustomed to giving. This way, when they arrive in Israel, their hand would be open to fulfill "indeed give", so that there would be no pauper in Israel who would be lacking.

The Hour of Trial

The book "Tanya Devei Eliyahu" states: "You shall take My offering",,, Since the nation of Israel said "We will do and we will hear", the Almighty immediately said to Moshe" "you shall take My offering". Rabbi Israel Baal Shem Tov said: If someone was spiritually awakened and driven to fulfill a mitzvah, this person must clothe this awakening in deed, otherwise the awakening will leave no impression whatsoever. This is the explanation of the verse: "Let us lift up our heart with our hands" (Lam 3:41). One must transfer the excitement of the heart to the action of the hands so that it does not simply dissipate. Therefore, with the great awakening and excitement at receiving the Torah, when the Israelites rose to the level of angels, God told Moshe, see to it that the excitement is clothed in action - in the building of the Temple.

An urgent need

One day, when Rabbi Shimon Netanel Rothschild from Frankfurt was taking a walk, a well-dressed Jew approached him and began unraveling his sorrowful tale before him. The words greatly touched Rothschild and since he did not have any money with him, he removed the gold chain from his pocket watch and gave it to the man. The latter stood confused and embarrassed and, at first, did not want to take it. "What is the meaning of this?" he asked, "It can only be that the Baron is mocking me. God save me, and how can I take the gold chain of his watch. Tomorrow I will come to his office. The situation is not so pressing and urgent, God forbid, to the point that...". Rabbi Rothschild replied: "Indeed, very pressing and urgent. At this moment a feeling of compassion overcomes me and I do not want to miss it. After all, who knows if I will ever have that feeling again or if it will weaken? Even King Solomon cautioned: "Do not tell your friend go and return, tomorrow I will give you, if you have (at that moment) in your possession".

Ignore Not Your Own Flesh and Blood

Rabbi Menahem Kalisch from Amshinov, arrived early one morning at the home of a nobleman in order to convince him to support one of his kinsman who lived in great poverty and who cared for a large family. But the nobleman was not a benevolent person and tried to evade Rabbi's request, claiming that the pauper was merely a distant relative that he hardly knew.

Rabbi Menahem asked the man: "Do you pray the morning, afternoon and evening prayers daily?" "What a question?" the nobleman answered resentfully, "Does the Rabbi suspect that I am not strict in my daily prayers?" The Rabbi then asked the man to recite the beginning of the Shmoneh Esre. The nobleman responded with obvious impatience: "Everyone knows that the Shmoneh Esrei prayer opens by recalling the Patriarchs, God of Avraham, God of Yitzhak and God of Yaakov".

"When did these Patriarchs live, that you and all the people of Israel recall them three times a day?" asked the Rabbi. "As is well known, the Patriarchs lived three thousand years ago", the nobleman answered, surprised at the Rabbi's questions. "You answered very nicely: three thousand years ago" Rabbi Menahem stated in a louder voice. "Yet still you recall these Patriarchs three times a day, and thanks to these 'distant relatives' of three thousand years ago, you want to be saved by the Creator of the universe. Yet when I come to you to ask for support and aid for your relative, who is alive today - you dare to claim that he is only a 'distant relative'?!"

Speak to the people of Israel, that they bring Me an offering; from every man that gives it willingly with his heart you shall take My offering. (Ex. 25:2)

Word and Deed

God, having brought the Children of Israel out of Egypt, having given them the laws and judgments, having divided the sea so that they could cross it safely, having brought manna down from Heaven and provided them with all their needs in the Wilderness, now asks them to bring offerings of gold, silver and copper. Was God really in need of their gold, silver and copper?

No! God could certainly have managed very well without their gifts. Rather, they were intended as a test, to see whether they really meant what they said when they unanimously declared: "We will do and we will hear" (Ex. 24:7).

Before they came bearing their gifts, it would have been difficult, if not impossible, to accurately assess the extent of their commitment. It was obviously very easy to be carried away in the storm of emotions that permeated the scene at the foot of Mount Sinai. Then they called out, in trepidation and excitement: "We will do and we will hear".

It is much easier to proclaim enthusiastic acceptance of the burden of the commandments than to put down money. So, in order to test the seriousness of this commitment, Adonai commanded: "Speak to the people of Israel, that they bring Me an offering". By their willingness to give and by the amount of their contribution, we will see whether their financial generosity is equal in size to their verbal pledge.

I am ready and willing

Rabbi Simhah Bunam of Pasischa was once on his way home from Danzig when he happened upon the township where Rabbi Zalman Hasid lived. Rabbi Zalman was great in Torah and in good deeds but desperately poor. When Rabbi Simhah Bunam arrived at the inn, he immediately sent someone to call Rabbi Zalman. He saw that he was dressed in rags and worn-out garments even though it was winter, the cold was severe and the snow was piled high.

Go - Rabbi Simhah Bunam said to him - and prepare me a whole meal, a meal for Hassidim. Here's some money. And he gave him a hand-full of coins, without counting them.

Rabbi Zalman went to the market and spent with largesse to buy everything necessary for a meal: meat, fish and all sorts of drinks, and he still had money left over.

While Rabbi Zalman was out, Rabbi Simhah Bunam sent for a furrier and bought an attractive fur coat from him. He sent out for some boots, cloth for suits and other items of apparel.

Before the meal, he instructed the janitor of the inn to take all the new clothes he had bought to the house of Rabbi Zalman Hasid. He also went round to Rabbi Zalman's house himself, sent everybody out of the house and dressed Rabbi Zalman from the top of his head to the soles of his feet. Then he noticed Rabbi Zalman's family, also dressed in rags and worn-out garments. He sent out for fabric and cloth for all members of the household. The house was filled with light and joy and they sat down and ate and enjoyed themselves.

As Rabbi Simhah Bunam was getting ready to leave on his way, he went to Rabbi Zalman to receive a blessing from him. Rabbi Simhah Bunam gave him a gold dinar, which Rabbi Zalman refused to accept.

"Rabbi", he said, "I still have the change left over from buying the products for the meal, in addition to the clothing you bought for me and for the members of my household".

"Let me tell you", Rabbi Simhah Bunam replied, "One who gives charity out of pity for the poor, who is unable to see them in this sorry state, has not kept the commandment of giving charity. Such a person has been charitable for personal reasons. This is not a case of "gives it willingly with his heart" but of giving out of a sense of pity. What I have given to you so far was only because my pity was aroused and I was unable to see you and your family in such a sorry state, wearing rags. But now that you are dressed in new, attractive clothes, I am ready and willing to keep the commandment of charitable giving".

Counsel of the inclination

A widow once came and tearfully told Rabbi Aharon of Karlin how the betrothal of her daughter to her fiance might be annulled if she could not come up with the promised dowry in a timely manner. Rabbi Aharon asked her how much she had promised. The widow stated the amount and Rabbi Aharon went over to the cupboard, took out a bundle of money and gave it to the woman so that she could pay the dowry she had promised.

A few weeks later, the woman came to Rabbi Aharon again, weeping bitterly. She could not set the date for her daughter's wedding because she had no money to make her a wedding gown. Rabbi Aharon asked her how much money she needed for the wedding gown. The woman told him. Rabbi Aharon pondered for a while and then gave her the necessary money.

When Rabbi Aharon's wife saw this, she said: "You gave her money for the dowry, to fulfill the commandment of "bringing a bride under the wedding canopy" since the betrothal might otherwise have been annulled. But why did you give her money for a wedding gown? Would the betrothal have been cancelled because of the wedding gown? Had you distributed this money of the wedding gown to the poor, you would surely have performed a greater mitzvah".

Her husband replied: What you say makes sense. I also gave the matter some thought, maybe it would have been better to give this money as charity to the poor. I paused for a while and wondered whether to give this money or some other money but I immediately changed my mind. I said: Had the argument to give the money to charity come from the good inclination, why did the good inclination not place this suggestion before me yesterday or the day before? Now that I was about to do a favor for a widow, and to make the heart of a poor bride happy rather than being embarrassed at having to wear an old dress on her wedding day, there is no choice but to say: it was not the good inclination which has come to give me good advice but the evil inclination which wants to divert me from fully keeping the precept of "bringing a bride under the wedding canopy".

Let them make Me a sanctuary; that I may dwell among them. (Ex. 25:8)

Doing out of habit rather than thought

Rabbi Simhah Bunam of Pasischa commented: The main thing about prayer is that the soul should pray. The body has to follow on after the soul, as a sheaf of straw is dragged behind the cart. And so it is with all matters to do with worship of the Creator. If the body is dragged after the inner self, it is also refined. Through "that I may dwell among them" - among the souls literally - the body becomes a home "Let them make Me a sanctuary". Without the content, without the inner feelings, it would not have been a sanctuary but just planks of wood connected to each other.

The Magid of Mezeritz added: You find people studying all day long and praying but without any vitality or enthusiasm. They behave that way out of habit rather than thought. They can sometimes be worse than criminals. A criminal can experience remorse, can begin to pray and beseech the Almighty with great enthusiasm, truly repent of wicked deeds and change for the better. But, people who keep all the commandments as a matter of routine are righteous in their own eyes. They feel that they are doing their job in the best possible manner, and they never scrutinize their own actions. Never will such people attain a higher level because they are of the opinion that what they are doing is complete and perfect. In reality, however, they are as remote from the Blessed Almighty as is east from west.

You shall make boards for the Tabernacle of acacia wood standing up. (Ex. 26:15)

Fruit Trees

The Torah protects fruit trees and thus prohibits destroying them or chopping them down. The Midrash expounds: Why in the building of the Temple does it say "acacia wood"? The Almighty taught proper conduct for all generations. Thus, a person wants to build a home from a fruit-bearing tree is told: And what of the King of Kings, to whom all belongs? When the Tabernacle was being built God said: Bring only from a tree that does not bear fruit. You, for your homes - all the more so should avoid using fruit trees!

Parashat Tetzaveh

You shall command the children of Israel, that they bring to you pure olive oil beaten for the light, to cause a lamp to burn continually. (Ex. 27:20)

A Light for the Entire World

The whole intention of this commandment to light the lamp in the Temple, is to kindle God's lamp in this world so that it lights the entire world and banishes the darkness that envelopes humanity. The purpose of the lamp of Israel that brightly burns "pure olive oil", is to infuse all of civilization with a pure, moral, and noble lifestyle in every area, and to saturate all of humanity with this concealed light. The worldly nations who sling mud at one another and war against each other will recognize the great light bursting forth from Israel. Each nation will succeed in preserving its own character, but will also design an amended social image, a proper social order, and a system of law and justice to restrain the human impulse. At that time the flame spreading from the candles of the lamp will light the entire world.

Rabbi Avin Halevi said: A person wants to make windows; he makes them wide from within and narrow from without. Why? So that they should draw in the light. Yet (the windows of) the Temple were wide from without and narrow within. Why? So that the light would leave the Temple and light the world. (Midrash Tanhuma)

The Eternal Light

Students and followers of Rabbi Yisrael Salanter often quote him as saying that at times it is possible to learn a lesson even from a simple conversation with a person who speaks out of total innocence. The story is told that Rabbi Israel Salanter left the Beit Midrash in the middle of the night and saw a small light flickering in the shoemaker's window. Rabbi Yisrael, who empathized with the sadness and stress of each member of Israel, entered the shoemaker's home and found him sitting and fixing a shoe in the candlelight. Rabbi Yisrael asked him: "Why do you sit so late and work?" "Rabbi", the shoemaker answered, "as long as the candle burns, I must work and mend". Rabbi Yisrael immediately returned to the Beit Midrash, called the men who were studying and said to them: "My brothers and friends. I just received a great Torah lesson from the shoemaker: As long as the candle burns, we must work and mend".

A similar story is told of the Baal Shem Tov. It happened one day that a craftsman approached his house and asked: "Perhaps. you have in your home tools such as barrels or buckets that have broken and need repair?" "No", the Baal Shem Tov answered, "in my home, thank God, everything is completely whole". "Check and look carefully" the craftsmen said again "you might find something that needs mending". The Baal Shem Tov addressed his students saying: "I just learned an entire Torah from the mouth of a simple craftsman: Even a person who thinks that everything in his home is completely whole, needs to examine and search; certainly he will see and find something that needs mending....

You shall bring forward your brother Aharon, with his sons, to you from among the Children of Israel, to minister to Me as priests. (Ex. 28:1)

Without Divisions

Rabbi Meir of Premislan remarked: It is known that Moshe and Aharon had different ways in their contacts with other people. Moshe our teacher had a great tendency for solitude, as it is written: "Now Moshe would take the Tent and pitch it outside the camp, at some distance from the camp" (Ex. 33:7). Aharon his brother, on the other hand, was very involved with people, loving peace and pursuing peace.

That is why Adonai here says to Moshe: "You shall bring forward your brother Aharon to you". Bring close to yourself the good attribute of your brother Aharon, who is involved with other people at all times. As a true leader, you have to live among the people every day, and must not set up any division between yourself and the people.

You shall speak to all that are wise hearted. (Ex. 28:3)

Friends

Rabbi Menahem Mendel of Kosov said: Before roads were paved, men would travel on them only during the daytime hours and, with dusk, they would enter an inn for the entire night, sit and read a book or befriend another for friendly conversation which brought about closeness. There were those who segregated themselves, to think about their deeds and perform moral self-evaluation. Since roads came into existence, everyone is running around, both day and night. There is no time to read books or speak to another person. People are in haste, always traveling; the roads exhaust their strength and they have no time to speak to themselves or with their friends....

Aharon shall bear the names of the Children of Israel on the breastplate of judgment upon his heart, when he goes in to the holy place, for a memorial before Adonai at all times. (Ex. 28:29)

Breastplate

The description of the making of the ephod and the breastplate takes thirty verses (Ex. 28:6-35). Despite this long description, it is difficult to get a clear and accurate picture of how they were made or what they looked like. But, from the text, we do know the main purpose of this special apparel. The names of the tribes of Israel were engraved on the two stones which were a part of the ephod: "Six of their names on one stone, and the names of the other six on the other stone, according to their birth" (Ex. 28:10). The names were engraved so that "Aharon shall bear their names before Adonai upon his two shoulders for a memorial" (Ex. 28:12).

The ephod and the breastplate were apparently designed to teach us a most important lesson about leadership and accountability. Many leaders, immediately after being elected to high office, forget those whom they are supposed to represent. The names of the twelve tribes of Israel had to be borne "on Aharon's shoulders" so that he would never forget

141

the weight of their needs and would always remember that it was not he who was being carried on their shoulders to enjoy a life of pleasures and opulence as part of the ruling elite. On the contrary, they were always resting on his shoulders so that he would concern himself with the needs of his people and would be their true spokesman.

Furthermore: It is true that bearing the task on one's shoulders was essential but it was not sufficient for a true leader such as Aharon, whose personality became an example to be emulated through all generations. He was unable to make do with bearing the burden, as required by his position, and he had to harness more than just his shoulders, he also filled his heart with love and compassion for every individual member of the people. And so we learn from Aharon, the Jewish People's first high priest, that a true leader bears the needs of the people on the leader's shoulders and engraved deeply in the leader's heart.

... and his sound shall be heard when he goes in to the holy place before Adonai ... (Ex. 28:35)

State what you have to say

Rabbi Moshe Sopher used to say: Modesty is a good quality in anyone, and even more so in a community's leader. This, however, is only true in secular matter and daily affairs. However, when the matter concerns the sacred issues of the people, when an important and fateful decision has to be made, the leader has to speak out, to be in control, to speak out with fortitude and courage.

You shall make a plate of pure gold, and engrave upon it, like the engravings of a signet, "Holy to Adonai". (Ex. 28:36)

God's actions

Rabbi Avraham Yitzhak Kook commented: The tzaddik always stands between God and the world, connecting the violent, dark, world to speech and to the Divine Light. All the senses of a true tzaddik are given over to the divine connection of all the worlds. The righteous person's passions, desires, inclinations, thoughts, actions, conversations, customs, movements, nerves, sorrow, and pleasure are all, without exception, chords of holy music. The life of the Godhead, inasmuch as it flows through all the worlds, give its voice, a powerful sound, to humanity. And souls innumerable, living treasures without end, fill all of existence. Only they, as they struggle to rise from the deep abyss of the boredom of their baseness to the majesty of the divine joy of freedom, the source of pleasure and delight, only they are the ones who urge on all the actions of the tzaddik, who is always engaging in divine worship and whose life in its entirety is sacred to Adonai.

This is the thing that you shall do to them, to sanctify them to minister to Me in the priest's office. (Ex. 29:1)

Sanctity of the Heart

One summer, many visitors, among them simple folk, farmers and craftsmen, came to spend a Shabbat with the Baal Shem Tov. At the Friday Evening meal, he invited these simple people to join in, and they began to recite psalms with feeling.

Many of the guests who were present there and who heard the psalms recited by these innocent people reflected to themselves: "Would that we would be able to pray just once with such innocence". The Baal Shem Tov noticed this, and said to those around him: "I am jealous of this sweet prayer which is being said with such devotion and spiritual outpouring by these simple Jews - would that my portion were with them".

Pure prayer

Rabbi Levi Yitzhak of Berdichev used to tell this story: In the days of Czar Nikolai, small Jewish children used to be kidnapped from their parents and sent to remote regions of Russia to be brought up and conscripted into Nikolai's army.

One Day of Atonement, the children gathered together secretly. One of them said: "Let us pray to God on this great and awful day". Unfortunately, they could not recall a single prayer. A second child said: On the Day of Atonement, one does not only pray. One also recites psalms. Maybe one of us can remember a chapter of psalms? But none among them did. A third child said: I don't remember the words of any psalms but I do remember the melody of the psalms. And he started singing the melody. The rest of them all responded, and the tune was accompanied by a great weeping.

As Rabbi Levi Yitzhak of Berdichev finished the story, he said: The force of that melody shook the very heavens. The tears of children are stronger than prayers, and had the strength to cleanse the sins of the House of Israel and to swing the fate of the Jewish People for acquittal in the Heavenly Court. One must always balance 'holy fire' against 'strange fire', but the tear of a young child is a pure tear and it always purifies.

A child's prayer

Rabbi Avraham Yehoshua Heschel was once in a beautiful synagogue during prayer. He saw the ushers sending away a small boy who had been sitting with his father and who had suddenly burst out in a loud cry. Rabbi Heschel asked them: "Why are you expelling this boy from the synagogue"? They answered: "Because his crying is interrupting the prayer". Rabbi Heschel told them "And I precisely feel that this boy's voice that sounds throughout the synagogue, is the only true voice that has been heard here throughout the entire time of prayer...".

Take of the blood, and put it upon the tip of Aharon's right ear, and upon the tip of the right ear of his sons, and upon the thumb of their right hand, upon the great toe of their right foot. (Ex. 29:20)

Three Limbs - Three Characters

Our Sages noted: these three things - the ear, the hand and the foot - must be excellent and exemplary in each priest of Israel. First, his ear should hear — he should listen carefully to the cry of the suffering masses, constantly examine the needs and requests of those who call for help, and to do the utmost to ease their lamenting and suffering.

Second, his hands should be open - not only to receive the "gifts of the priesthood", but also to give plenty of what is needed to the nation's wretched and oppressed. Finally, his feet should be light - to hurry and run in order to hasten assistance to all who need it, to all who extend their hand requesting help.

Parashat Ki Tisa

This is what every one who is entered in the records shall give: a half-shekel by the sanctuary weight ... as an offering to Adonai. (Ex. 30:13)

Two sides to a coin

"This is what [they] shall give". Rashi comments: God showed Moshe a kind of fiery coin and said to him: "Like this shall they give".

Why a "fiery" coin? Rabbi Elimelekh of Lizansk explained: This is a hint here. A coin has a fire-like quality. Just as fire can be beneficial, a motivating and warming force, it can also be a destructive force. So, too, can a coin be used for good and sublime purposes - for charity and good deeds - but it can also be used for bad and destructive purposes.

Rabbi Menahem Mendel of Kotzk used to say: Moshe Rabbeinu was surprised that a simple coin had the power to atone for a soul. The Holy Blessed One showed him a fiery coin. "Like this shall they give". -if the giving is not reluctant, but done with fire and enthusiasm of the spirit, then that coin can atone for a soul.

It is up to you

Why a half-shekel and not a whole shekel? The sages taught: "A person should always view himself as half guilty and half innocent. If he performs one precept - he is happy, as he has weighed the scales down on the side of his innocence. If he commits one offence - let him regret it for he will have weighed the scales down on the side of his guilt ... Rabbi Eliezer the son of Rabbi Shimon says: Because the world is judged after the majority, if he performs one precept, he is happy as he has weighed the scales down on the side of innocence for himself and for the whole world. If he commits one offence, let him regret it for he will have weighed the scales down on the side of guilt for himself and for the whole world". (Kiddushin 40b)

That is why the Torah says that he should bring "half a shekel", so that a person will always remember, every day and every hour, through every step taken, through every deed done, that the scales of righteousness and justice are in one's hands, and that these scales can be tipped with just one good deed, affecting the entire world.

Moreover: The Torah also says to all Jews that they will never reach wholeness alone, but only when they join with other Jews. Each one of the Children of Israel, in the census conducted by Moshe, gave only a half-shekel. Two acts of giving have to come together to make a complete shekel. Not only that, but no Jew has ever known who it was who completed the half-shekel into a complete shekel. This teaches us that the simplest Jew has the potential to complete even the greatest of Israel.

... and in the hearts of all who are wise-hearted I have put wisdom. (Ex. 31:6)

Keepers of a Confidence

Rabbi Nahman of Bratzlav told the story of a king who sent three of his men to a foreign country on a mission for him. Many people lay in wait and followed the king's confidants. One of the messengers acted wisely and seemed to totally disregard his mission. Thus no-one knew that he was carrying a confidential message with him and he traversed the country safely.

The second was not as cautious as the first and was caught by countrymen who wanted to coerce him into revealing the secrets to them. He managed, however, to escape from them with clever tricks and heroics.

The third messenger, who was not cautious and was also caught, was not clever enough to flee from them and he suffered at their hands great troubles and tortures. But he withstood the trials and did not reveal to them a hint of anything. When they saw that he went through so many tribulations but did not reveal anything to them, they concluded that he had nothing at all to tell them, that he carried no hidden message, and so they let him go on his way.

When the ministers of the country from which the messengers had been sent learned of what had happened, they were divided as to which of the three was the most worthy. Some said that the first had earned a great reward because, from the very beginning, he had been wise enough to conceal the mission from everybody. Others thought that the second messenger should be most congratulated because of the tricks he had devised to escape from captivity. But the king ruled that the reward of the third was to be greater than all the others. This was because he had withstood a great test and had suffered indescribable tortures, yet had managed to ensure that his captors were deceived into thinking that he had no secrets at all. Had he wished to betray the trust placed in him, not only would he have not had to undergo the torture but he would have been given a high position by his captors. Yet he chose to remain silent.

Sages are that way too. Some are naive to the extent that no one at all would suspect they were sages. Others are suspected of being sages but use various evasive tricks to avoid the trap of honors. And there are those on whom honors are forced but they, nonetheless, withstand the trial and save their souls. The eminence of the latter is greater than of the two former.

The Children of Israel shall keep the Sabbath, observing the Sabbath throughout the ages as a covenant for all time. (Ex. 31:16)

An extra soul

The Sabbath breathes, as it were, a new spirit into the soul itself. This is that "extra soul" that raises a person to a higher spiritual level. Rabbi Shimon Ben Lakish taught: "The Holy One gives each person an extra soul on the eve of the Sabbath and takes it back from at the end of the Sabbath" (Betzah 16a).

This extra soul leaves its imprint on a person's body even though it cannot be actually discerned: "And God blessed the seventh day and sanctified it" (Gen. 2:3). God blessed it with the light of humanity's countenance (panim); He sanctified it with humanity's inner (penim) light. "The light of a humanity's countenance is not the same on weekdays as it is on the Sabbath". (Gen. Rabbah 11)

When the people saw that Moshe took so long to come down from the mountain, the people gathered themselves together against Aharon, and said to him: Arise, make us gods, which shall go before us. (Ex. 32:1)

Psychology of the masses

According to the Midrash, Moshe arrived at the camp with a delay of six hours. The Children of Israel were not ready to suffer the uncertainty and they already hurried to find a replacement for him.

Something even more serious was to occur a short time after this. When they cast the molten calf, they arose and proclaimed: "These are your gods, O Israel, which brought you up out of the land of Egypt" (Ex. 32:4).

In this chapter, the entanglements and deviousness of human nature are exposed. Moshe is just six hours late and they are already rushing off to rewrite history and to proclaim unreservedly and without extraneous doubts, or even a hint of shame, "These are your gods, O Israel, which brought you up out of the land of Egypt".

They forgot all about Moshe, the prophet and architect of the exodus from Egypt, the spokesperson of the people who fought with great courage for the sake of their freedom, the teacher and lawgiver. Now it is: "These are your gods, O Israel" - a golden calf.

This, as Prof. Pinhas Peli has noted, is so very typical of mass psychology. The masses are not prepared to remain leaderless for even a short time. How deep is the gaping abyss between Moshe and a man-made calf! Nonetheless, "Arise, make us gods, which shall go before us", they call. They are prepared to follow any leader blindly, whether it be Moshe or a molten calf.

Rabbi Shmuel Mohilever added a further characteristic to the psychology of the masses which can be learned from this episode. When Moshe was late and the Children of Israel were in need of a leader, they turned to Aharon and asked him to appoint a new leader instead of Moshe. Rabbi Mohilever asks: Why did the people not ask Aharon himself to take on the leadership and to step into Moshe's shoes? All being said, Aharon was a person whom they knew and loved, he had always stood at Moshe's side, from the early stages of the exodus. Was he, therefore, not the most "natural" heir for the tardy Moshe?

The fact that the Children of Israel did not appoint Aharon as their leader but preferred a molten calf teaches us that people prefer something "external", even if it is a senseless calf, over someone well known to them, even if he is an outstanding and experienced person, such as Aharon the High Priest to whom all showed honor.

All the people took off the gold rings which were in their ears, and brought them to Aharon. (Ex.32:3)

A Positive Side

Come and see, Rabbi Yitzhak of Slonim used to say, how even the corrupt in the generation of the Wilderness stood at a high level, for they were ready and willing to give up their silver and their gold in order to make a god, while in more recent times, people give up God in order to make silver and gold.

The people sat down to eat and to drink, and rose up to play. (Ex. 32:6)

Spite or captivity?

When transgressors sin but do not break out into dancing, they are not "apostates out of spite" but rather are "babes in captivity", that is, they do not know any better. They erred, they made mistakes but that is no reason for breaking the tablets or for issuing the edict: "slay every man his brother, and every man his neighbor" (Ex. 32:27). On the contrary, it is an occasion for Eliyahu the Prophet to come and to "turn the heart of the fathers to the children, and the heart of the children to their fathers" (Mal 3:24), in the hope that fire will issue from Heaven and will light up the path for the return of the children to their Source and for the redemption of their souls, until they cry out aloud: "Adonai is God!"

Rabbi Sussya of Anipol commented: We read in Pirke Avot (4:11): "A person who commits one transgression acquires for himself one accuser". From every transgression, an angel is created who accuses the person in the world of truth. I, however, have never in my life seen a wicked Jew. I have, however, seen the wicked angels, the angels of destruction who are created from the offences committed by Jews, and I can testify that I have never seen a whole wicked angel, healthy in all his limbs. These wicked angels are all handicapped - one has an arm missing and another has a leg missing. This is because, when a Jew commits an offence, he does not do so wholly. His inclination prompts him and his heart pulls on his conscience. From such an offence, which a person does not commit wholeheartedly, an incomplete, handicapped angel has to be created ...

Then Adonai said to Moshe, Go down; for your people, whom you brought out of the land of Egypt, have corrupted themselves. (Ex. 32:7)

It is a Time of Descent

We read in the Midrash: "Then Adonai said to Moshe: 'Go down.'. Moshe replied to the Holy Blessed One: 'Master of the Universe! Yesterday, You said to me: Come up (Ex. 19:24), and now You are saying: Go down?' Replied the Holy Blessed One: 'You have not come up here for your own glory, but for the glory of My children. I once said to Yaakov: "And behold the angels of God ascending and descending on it" (Gen. 28:12). [In other words] if your offspring are righteous, they and their prophets will rise higher and higher; but when they suffer a decline, then they and their prophets will decline. And so now: Go down, for your people, whom you brought out of the land of Egypt, have corrupted themselves. Since they have sinned, you, too, must share their downfall". (Ex. Rabbah 42:2)

Adonai repented of the evil which he thought to do to his people. (Ex. 32:14)

A spiritual spark

Rabbi Menahem Mendel of Kotzk asked: Why were the Children of Israel forgiven for the sin of the Golden Calf even though they had not repented for it, but were not forgiven for the sin of the spies, even though they did repent? In the sin of the Golden Calf, there was a spark of spirituality, a craving and a thirst for a supreme power. "Make us a god", they said to Aharon. With the sin of the spies, the craving was only for worldliness, "to spy out the land" (Num. 13:16), and that made all the difference.

When Moshe saw the calf and the dancing, he became enraged. (Ex. 32:19)

Insult to injury

Rabbi Ovadia Sforno wrote: "When he saw them rejoicing in the ruination they had made, he despaired of ever being able to remedy the injustice in such a way that they would be restored to their purity".

Until then, he had judged them on the side of innocence, saying: They would not have committed such a great sin were it not for a mistake. They saw that I was a long time in coming down from the mountain, and, having no leader, without choice, they made themselves a molten calf. They are surely sorry that they had to recourse to that. They certainly only made the calf out of unsteadiness and broken heartedness. But when Moshe saw the calf and the dancing, then he became enraged. He did right to be enraged at the joyousness of the people, at the dancing extravaganza. People can err and fail, but how could they dance at such a time of falling and plunging into the depths?

So long as a sinner feels discomfort with the sin, there is hope. One who has sinned can return and again be healed. But for a person who rejoices in the sin there is no remedy.

No one will covet your land when you go up to appear before Adonai your God. (Ex. 34:24)

A precept for its own sake

It is said in the Talmud (Pesahim 8b): "Why are the fruits of Ginossar not available in Jerusalem? - So that the pilgrims will not say: "Had we only gone up to Jerusalem to eat the fruits of Ginossar, it would have been enough". That is to say, their going up to Jerusalem would not have been for its own sake".

"From this", said Rabbi Avraham Yitzhak Kook, "we can deduce that going up to the Land of Israel has to be for its own sake, not for any benefit, not for business and profit".

Parashat Vayakhel

Moshe assembled all the congregation of the Children of Israel together, and said to them: These are the words which Adonai has commanded you to do. (Ex. 35:1)

To assemble all the congregations of Israel

We read in the Midrash: 'And Moshe assembled' - from the beginning to the end of the Torah, there is no other portion where it is stated at the outset: 'And he [Moshe] assembled'. Said the Holy Blessed One: Make for yourselves large assemblies so that the generations to come may learn from you and assemble congregations every Shabbat, that they may gather in the academies to learn and to teach words of Torah, what is forbidden and what is permitted, so that My great Name may be praised among My people. (Yalqut Shimoni, Vayakhel)

Ongoing Unity

Rashi claims this assembly was gathered on the day after the Day of Atonement. In the normal course of events, on the Day of Atonement, all Jews are God-fearing and good. On the Day of Atonement, each Jew makes peace with all other Jews and everywhere there is peace, love and unity. This, however, does not continue. It remains so only to the end of that day.

And so: "And Moshe assembled all the congregation" on the day following the Day of Atonement, and demanded of them that they be together and united not only on the Day of Atonement but also on the next day, and thereafter.

Check Thoroughly

Our sages asked: Why is it stated at the time of the calf: that "all the people took off the golden ear rings which were in their ears" (Ex.

32:3), that all the people gave a donation, while at the time of the building of the Sanctuary only "those whose hearts moved them" (Ex. 35:22) gave, only the generous few gave? The Gemara replies: "It is impossible to understand the nature of this people! They are asked to give for the calf and do so; they are asked to give for the Sanctuary and do so" (Jerusalem Talmud Sheqalim 1:1).

How does this answer the question of the whole people giving for the calf while only those whose hearts moved them gave for the Sanctuary? Rabbi Meir Shapira of Lublin said: It frequently happens that donors are convinced that the money being collected is for something holy, for a sublime religious or national purpose. Later, they realize that they were deceived and that the money which was collected served for other purposes. So it was with the episode of the molten calf. The Children of Israel did not all know that the money was being collected to make a calf, for idolatrous purposes. Did they not say: "These are your gods, O Israel" (Ex. 32:4)? In other words, they thought it was "for the sake of Heaven" and so the whole people gave. Subsequently, they saw that they had been misled, that they had been deceived and they started to exercise caution. When they were approached and asked to give for the building of the Sanctuary, they were apprehensive about giving, lest they again be deceived and so we find that on this occasion only "those whose hearts moved them" gave.

Let all among you who are wise of heart come and make all that Adonai has commanded. (Ex. 35:10)

Wise-heartedness

We learn from this verse that, in order to do all that Adonai has commanded, one has to be not just wise-headed but also wise-hearted. "Wise of heart", Rabbi Meir Rubman used to say, "means wise in his inner feelings and his perceptions. Let us take Balaam, for example. On the one hand, he had wisdom. The Gemara says (Berakhot 34b) that he was a prophet like Moshe Rabbeinu. On the other hand, he is known to have been evil. Where, then, is his wisdom? He might have been wise of head but he was not wise of heart.

To what can this be likened? To a person who has a supply of medicines. This fact is, in no way, a guarantee that one will recover from various maladies. To be healthy, one has to swallow the medicines needed so they can work on fixing the problem. Such is the Torah. It is, saving one from the evil inclination, as it says in the Talmud (Kiddushin 30b): "I created the evil inclination and I created the Torah with which to season it". The Torah does not heal the soul until one fixes the words of the Torah in one's innermost feelings and heart.

The extent of one's fear of transgressions should be examined to determine whether one's heart is imbued with the wisdom of the Torah or whether it is just a matter of wisdom of the mind. A God-fearing person, for example, will be deterred from committing some offence. The same person will also balk at eating dangerous food, in which some poison has been mixed. Are the fear and apprehension in both cases the same? So long as they are not the same, this is evidence that the fear of poison is enrooted in the heart while the fear of committing some offence is only in the mind - but not in his heart.

This is why we say in the morning prayers "Put into our hearts [the desire] to understand and discern, to learn and teach, to observe, to do and to fulfill all the words of Your Torah". We ask the Holy One, , to "put into our hearts" and not only in our minds.

He has filled him with the spirit of God, in wisdom, in understanding, and in knowledge, and in every kind of workmanship; And to devise finely done works. (Ex. 35:31-32)

You favor man with knowledge

Rabbi Nahman of Bratzlav said: "The thoughts that are in the brain are a matter of great wonder and an expression of the greatness of the blessed Creator. For the thoughts are arranged within the brain, one on top of the other, like packages lying on each other. When a person needs one of them and remembers them, that thought is pulled out exactly as it is needed.

How puzzling it is! For where was that matter lying until now? There must be connections and markings in the thoughts as they lie one on the other in the brain. When a person recalls something which has some connection to a matter entailing a particular thought, the thought needed is immediately summoned from amongst all those packages in the brain.

So, when a thought is pulled out from its treasures, all the thoughts are turned over in sequence, but the person is not aware of this. This is not the same as with physical objects. If one pulls something out from the middle of pile of objects, the whole pile gets turned over, but a person's brain is not so turned over.

And Rabbi Nahman continued: More than a wicked government can arrest and imprison a person, an unfit thought, sent by the evil inclination, can bind a person in its jail. The wicked government can release you but the unfit thought will never allow you to feel a free person again. You say that you will release yourself? From where will you find the strength for that, if you willingly agreed to be imprisoned?

One should realize that the higher an organ is within a person, so can it reach further and attain more. For example, with one's foot one can kick something upwards but, with one's hand, one can throw it higher. Speech can achieve and reach even higher because speech can be heard from a distance. And hearing even more so, because one can hear something from an even greater distance, such as a gunshot. And sight can reach even further because with sight one can perceive the heavens.

Thus, the higher the organ is in the body, so can it achieve more and attain more. And thoughts, which are higher than anything else, can reach the furthest and the highest. That is why one should take good care of one's thoughts.

It is up to each person

Rabbi Simhah Bunem of Peshischa used to say: A person can be most righteous and, at the same time, a great fool. The Gemara tells us that, before a person is created, it is proclaimed in the Heavens whether that person is to be rich or poor, wise or foolish, but righteousness and wickedness are not proclaimed - because this is something each person has freedom of choice in the matter. Thus, a person can be righteous, for this depends on one's own desire, and, at the same time, such a person can be a fool, for this depends on Heaven alone.

Let, then, Bezalel and Ohaliav, and all the skilled persons whom Adonai has endowed with skill and ability to perform expertly all the tasks connected with the service of the sanctuary. (Ex. 36:1)

Democracy

Overseeing the tremendous venture of building God's sanctuary is the artist par excellence, Bezalel the son of Uri of the tribe of Judah. Bezalel was a man endowed with "a divine spirit of wisdom, ability and knowledge in every kind of craft". Nevertheless, the Holy One did not appoint him to the task of building the sanctuary until there was public agreement for this appointment.

We read in the Talmud: (Berakhot 55a): "R. Yitzhak said: We must not appoint a leader over the community without first consulting it. The Holy Blessed One, said to Moshe: Moshe, do you consider Bezalel suitable? Moshe replied: Sovereign of the Universe, if You think him suitable, surely I must also! Said the Holy One: All the same, go and consult the people. Moshe went and asked Israel: Do you consider Bezalel suitable? They replied: If both the Holy One and you consider him suitable, surely we must do so also!"

He made the laver of copper and its stand of copper, from the mirrors of the women who performed tasks at the entrance to the Tent of Meeting. (Ex. 38:8)

Lust can be a good thing

Women played a big role in the construction of the sanctuary. They handed over what was most dear to them and contributed with a willing heart for the building of the sanctuary. But the piece de resistance in this great epic was "the mirrors of the women", which were made of polished copper and played a decisive role in the Egyptian exile.

It is related in the Midrash: "When the Children of Israel were under hard labor in Egypt, Pharaoh decreed that they were not to be allowed to sleep in their homes and they were not to be allowed their women (so that the women would not become pregnant and give birth to boys). What did the women do? They went down to the Nile and drew water, and the Holy Blessed One would summon small fish into their pitchers. They would sell the fish and, from the proceeds, make food and wine and go out to the fields and feed their husbands there. As they ate and drank, the women would take out their mirrors and look into them with their husbands. The women would say: I am better-looking than you. And the men would reply: I am better-looking than you. In this way, their passions were aroused and they were fruitful and multiplied" (Tanhuma Pikuddei 9).

Now, with the building of the sanctuary, it was these "mirrors of the women" that angered Moshe. The Midrash continues: "After the Holy Blessed One told Moshe to make the sanctuary, all the men came and made contributions. Some brought silver, some gold and others brought copper. The women asked: "What do we have that we can give for the sanctuary? They arose, took their mirrors and came to Moshe. When Moshe saw those mirrors, he was furious at them and said to the men: Take sticks and break their legs. What do they need the mirrors for? The Holy Blessed One said to Moshe: These you regard with contempt?! These mirrors were the cause for all the babies being born in Egypt. Take the mirrors from them and make of them a laver of copper for the priests, that the priests may become sanctified out of it, as it is said: "And he made the laver of copper and its stand of copper from the mirrors of the women who performed tasks at the entrance to the Tent of Meeting".

Moshe Rabbeinu, who abstained from his wife and distanced himself from the passions of this world, despised mirrors that could arouse lust. He saw the women's gift as a disgraceful act that had to be denounced. But the Holy One thought otherwise. God fully appreciated the praiseworthy devotion of the women. Furthermore: The Holy One gave Moshe explicit instructions: "And you shall anoint the laver and its stand and you shall consecrate it" (Ex. 40:11).

Judaism recognizes the positive element in lust and desire. It recognizes that it is possible to raise it to the level of sanctity. Of all people, it was imposed upon the priests, those who served in the sanctuary, to sanctify themselves from the laver, made, as it was, from "the mirrors of the women" who gave birth to the numerous offspring of Israel who came up out of Egypt.

Parashat Pikkudei

In Parashat Pikkudei, the last of the Book of exodus, the epic story of the construction of the Tabernacle is completed. Five weekly portions were devoted to it (Terumah, Tetzaveh, Ki Tissa, Vayakhel and Pikkudei). According to rabbinic tradition, it was the day after Yom Kippur, after Moshe descended from Mount Sinai with the second set of tablets, that the Children of Israel were commanded to construct the Tabernacle. As to the date of completion, it is stated explicitly in this week's portion: "In the first month of the second year [following the exodus from Egypt], on the first day of the month, the Tabernacle was set up" (Ex. 40:17).

The work of construction of the Tabernacle, in all its parts and with all its accessories, took, therefore, less than six months. The swiftness of the work is explained by the people's recognition that establishing the Tabernacle could restore the balance, could return them to the time before the Shekhina (the Divine Presence) left the Children of Israel as a result of the sin of the calf.

These are the records of the Tabernacle, of the Tabernacle of Testimony, as they were kept, according to the commandment of Moshe ... and be guiltless before Adonai, and before Israel. (Ex. 38:21-22)

Here they ask?!

Rabbi Meir Shapira of Lublin remarked about this: For the molten calf, they gave all their silver and gold "And all the people took off the golden ear rings which were in their ears ..." (Ex. 32:3). Only one calf resulted but no-one demand an accounting. For the construction of the Tabernacle, each person gave only "half a shekel" and with this they built the whole Tabernacle and all its utensils. And here, of all places, they complained and were suspicious! When they give for the calf - everyone is happy, but when they give for the Tabernacle, for something sacred, they ask questions and demand accounts.

Moshe assured his people that he would give them an accounting of the money deposited with him by the public and the financial expenditures incurred in the construction of the Tabernacle. This was because he had heard the people gossiping behind his back, suggesting that he had embezzled the contributions which had been entrusted to him. It is not enough for a person to be confident and to know with certainty that his conduct with public funds is above reproach. Nor is it sufficient for even the Holy One to testify as to this person's integrity.

So long as the construction of the Tabernacle was at its height, Moshe took no time off to put a stop to the slander against him. He felt that the best way to refute it would be publication of all the records after the completion of the whole operation. There is great lesson here: Do not be deterred and do not halt the work, despite slanderous accusations. Gossip and suspicions may not be totally preventable yet the Halakhah lays down a number of rules to be followed when running a public fund.

We read in the Mishnah regarding a similar matter: "The charity fund is collected by two and distributed by three people" (Peah 8:7). The disbursement must be made in the presence of three adjudicators in order to ensure an equitable distribution according to just criteria. The Talmud expands on this ruling: "Our Rabbis taught: The collectors of charity are not permitted to separate from one another [while collecting funds], and must keep an eye on each other". Moreover "Our Rabbis taught: If the collectors [still have money but] no poor to whom to distribute it, they should change the small coins into larger ones [as the small coins might rust], but not from their own money, [lest anyone suggest that they did not give full value] (Bava Batra 8b). In the same vein, if they have to invest any cash surpluses remaining in the charity fund, they must do so with others so that they cannot be accused of having gained any personal benefit from the investment. (Mishneh Torah, Laws of Giving to the Poor, chapter 9).

A place to preach

The good men in charge of the community of the Great Beit Midrash of Vilna, deliberated and resolved to enact a ruling to forbid smooth-talking preachers from speaking in the Great Academy. The reason was that so many people would gather to hear them that they disturbed the regular classes.

The Gaon of Vilna sent for them and invited them to his house, where he said to them: The sanctuary which was built at Adonai's command by Moshe was only called a sanctuary [mishkan] because the Divine Presence [Shekhinah] dwelt [shakhnah] in it. And the Shekhinah only dwelt in it because of the Tablets of the Testimony which were housed in the Ark of the Testimony, as it is written: "These are the records of the Tabernacle, of the Tabernacle of Testimony" (Ex. 38:21). Similarly, the Academy is only called Beit Midrash because of the sermons which are preached in it, thus increasing Torah and morality. Those in charge then changed their minds and restored the former glory of the preachers to them.

Slavery without authority

This is the face of the leader of the nation. The jokers of the day permit themselves to pass judgment on him and to express their criticisms of him. In this respect, nothing has changed to our day. One who faithfully occupies himself with public affairs does not earn recognition. This "secret" was well known to Rabbi Akiva: "They wanted to appoint him as a leader of community but he said to them: I must consult my wife. They followed him and heard his voice saying: "To be denounced, to be reviled" (Jerusalem Talmud, Peah, chapter 5).

He had doubts as to whether he should accept this appointment because he knew that his only "remuneration" would be that he would be denounced and reviled. Rabbi Akiva did well to consult with his wife. Women have a discerning eye and know that public office is a bother and a burden. While the neighbors might be jealous that he had risen to a powerful position, she - the wife of the leader - knows that it is no more than a form of bondage, as we learn from the Midrash: Adonai said to Moshe "Gather for Me seventy of the elders of Israel" (Num. 11:16). Said Rabbi Abba, the son of Kahana: "When the elders were appointed, the whole of Israel lit candles for them and rejoiced for them. Miriam, Moshe's sister, saw the burning candles and asked Zipporah, Moshe's wife, "What is this business of the burning candles?" She told her the reason. Miriam said: May the wives of these men be happy. For what do they see? How their husbands have risen to a position of authority! Zipporah said to her: Woe to them! (Yalqut Shimoni, Behaalotekha 12).

Zipporah, who had herself seen how the people of Israel had rewarded Moshe, her husband, with bad for good, well knew that one should not be jealous of those who had risen to positions of authority.   Indeed, it is the nature of people to be unwilling to recognize the greatness of their leaders. Instead, they rise up against them and harm them. Even outstanding people are burnt by the nonsense spoken by their contemporaries and are not accorded due esteem and appreciation in their lifetime.

Half a shekel a head, half a shekel by the sanctuary weight. (Ex. 38:26)

Taking trouble is worthwhile

Rabbi Soloveitchik was very active in public affairs and would walk great distances to assist charity and Torah institutions in the country. On one occasion, Rabbi Soloveitchik went to the home of one of the affluent men of Brisk to raise a contribution for an important public institution. The man welcomed the Rabbi politely enough and, after he had heard the reason for the Rabbi's coming to him, he said with great respect: Our Rabbi has known me for years, and, whenever he has called me on some public matter or other, I have come to him without delay. What is the reason that, this time, the Rabbi has gone out of his way to come to my house? Is it not honor enough for me to be summoned to come to the Rabbi? Why, then, this additional honor of the Rabbi coming to me?

Rabbi Yosef Dov was moved by the endearing words of his host. After a short pause, he replied: The truth of the matter is that it would be fitting for the householders of Brisk, for the honor of Torah, to take the trouble to go to the Rabbi's house. In this instance, however, I made a simple calculation for myself. Had I asked you to come to me, that would have been tantamount to asking you for a favor. And that would have prejudiced the crucial cause for which I am working at the present time because it is unbecoming to ask somebody for one favor after another. But now that I have put myself out and come to you, I have only one favor to ask of you, namely: that you make a generous contribution to the cause which is on the agenda of our city! The words of the Rabbi touched the heart of the host and he gave a contribution which was more generous than he had ever given before.

Leviticus

Parashat Vayikra

Adonai called to Moshe, and spoke to him out of the Tent of Meeting, saying.... (Lev. 1:1)

Wholeheartedly

Traditionally, the last letter of the word Vayikra, the letter aleph, is written smaller than the other letters in the Torah scroll. We are taught that God originally dictated "Vayiqar Adonai to Moshe" – God appeared before Moshe, but Moshe had not wanted to write Vayiqar since it is used regarding Balaam: "And God met (Vayiqar) Balaam" (Num. 23:4). So the Holy Blessed One told Moshe to add the letter aleph to the word Vayiqar, changing its meaning to "And God called to Moshe". Moshe did so but wrote it in a smaller size.

Rabbi Simhah Bunam of Pasischa taught: This can be likened to a person standing on top of a mountain. It would not occur to him to brag about how high up he is, because his elevation is not due to his personality. Rather, it is due to the mountain upon which he is standing. Moshe also understood that his elevation derived from God and not from any innate personality traits.

We read in the Midrash: "Whoever pursues power, power flees from him; whoever flees from power, power pursues him" (Tanhuma Vayikra 50). Since Moshe was humble and fled from honor, honor pursued after him and the Almighty called to him alone to come to the Tent of Meeting. If one does not want honor, why should this honor be imposed as a burden?!

The author of "Sefat Emet" remarks that the one who truly flees from honor is the one who takes the honor and raises it up to Adonai, for Adonai is the true recipient of Honor. Accordingly, "honor pursues him" because if such a person has the strength to raise the honor up and return it to its root, it, the honor, yearns to return to such a worthy person.

It once happened that a certain man complained to Rabbi Simhah Bunam of Pasischa. "I am always fleeing from honor", he asked him, "so why is it that honor does not chase after me? Where is the truth in the saying of our sages of blessed memory? Rabbi Bunam answered: "It can be deduced from your question that at the very time you are fleeing from honor, you occasionally turn around and look back to see whether honor is indeed pursuing you...".

Elective Sacrifice

If his offering is a burnt sacrifice ... he shall offer it of his own voluntary will at the door of the Tent of Meeting before Adonai. (Lev. 1:3)

A person who offers a sacrifice in order to satisfy the conscience, for a theft or some act of wrongdoing, without admitting any wrongdoing and without making restitution for the sin, is not offering a voluntary sacrifice. Only one who worships. Adonai out of cognitive reflection, in fear based on the love of Adonai and keeping God's way, offers voluntary sacrifices.

Primitive peoples who offered up sacrifices did so as a sort of gift, to bribe the gods, to quiet their jealousy, and to satisfy their appetite in a magical way. They brought their sacrifice out of compulsion, out of an inner coercion, to assuage the feelings of sin in the soul and to silence their conscience.

The purpose of the sacrifices in the Torah is different. The burnt offering is an expression of the individual's surrender to God; the peace offering is an expression of spiritual peace between a person and the Creator. The guilt offering gives concrete expression to the feeling that the sinner should have been the sacrifice and gratitude to Adonai for accepting penitence.

This sublime form of offering sacrifices is one in which the person offering the sacrifice does so willingly and with a spiritual outpouring.

Such sacrifices are an expression of the spiritual desire, the yearning for the proximity of God. Such worship is elective and, therefore, acceptable to and accepted by the Creator.

The Inner Desire

Rashi asks: How is this possible? - They pressure him until he says: I wish to do it.

But how can such be thought of as willingness or desire, when it derives from coercion? Rambam explains (Hilkhot Gerushin 5:2): The concept of coercion only means that a person is pressured and required to do something that is not an obligatory mitzvah of the Torah - for example giving a present to someone, or buying an article from someone. But in a case where a person's evil thinking leads to annulling a mitzvah, or to committing a transgression, and they pressure the person to keep that mitzvah or to avoid that transgression - such is not called 'coercion'. The contrary is true. This course of action helps. the person to overcome the evil thinking which is the cause of the transgression. Every Jew has a true desire to observe the mitzvot and to keep away from offences; the evil inclination, however, does not leave people alone but pressures them into doing wrong. If people are forced not to give in to their evil inclination and are punished until their materialistic tendencies weaken, and their body also says: "I wish it". – then we say that they observe the mitzvah willingly, of their own free will.

Speak to the Children of Israel, saying: When a person (nefesh) unwittingly incurs guilt in regard to any of the mitzvot of Adonai about things not to be done, and does one of them.... (Lev. 4:2)

Body and Soul

The body steals, destroys and commits adultery, but around whose neck does the Torah hang it? The soul's (the nefesh)! Our sages posed the question: Why is the soul made fully accountable rather than the senses and the organs, the perpetrators of the offence?

The Midrash teaches: In the time to come, the Holy Blessed One will say to the soul: 'Why did you disobey all the mitzvot?' And the soul will answer: 'It is the body which disobeyed all the mitzvot. Since leaving it, after I was separated from the body, how have I sinned?' The Holy Blessed One will then ask the body: 'Why did you sin?' And the body will reply: 'It is the soul that sins. Since it left me, have I committed any sin?' God will bring them both together and will judge them as one.

This may be compared to the case of a king who had an orchard, with grapes and figs and pomegranates that ripened early. The king thought to himself: If I place a watchman who can see and walk around, he will himself eat of the early fruits. So what did he do? He placed there two watchmen, one blind and the other lame. They watched over the orchard and would sit there and smell the early fruits.

One day, the lame man said to the blind man: 'I can see fine early fruits in the orchard. Let me climb on your back and we can pick and eat the fruit.' So the lame man got astride the blind man and they ate the fruit and returned to sit where they had been. After some days, the king came and looked for the early fruits but found none. He said to the lame man: 'Who ate them?' The lame man replied: 'Do I have legs that I can move about?' So the king said to the blind man: Did you eat them? The blind man replied: 'Do I have eyes to see and pick the fruit?' The king placed the lame man astride the blind man and said to them: 'Just as you stole the early fruits and ate them, both of you, so I will judge both of you together.

The Holy Blessed One, acts the same way, bringing the soul and inserting it into the body, then judging them both together. (Lev. Rabbah 4:5)

That is not a mitzvah

Why does the Torah call an act of a sinning soul by the name "mitzvah"? Rabbi Levi Yitzhak of Berdichev says: This is to teach us how indecent is pride in God's presence. A person who commits an offence and knows it, makes penitence. But what about a person who performs a positive mitzvah and is proud of it, boasts about it in the town, in the market-places and in the thoroughfares? Such a person becomes full of pride and arrogance, as though saying: 'I have enriched the Holy One'. This, then, it not a positive mitzvah but an offence, a sin, a crime.

Rabbi Nahum of Chernobyl used to say: I am more fearful of the mitzvot that I have kept and enjoyed than I am of the offences I have committed.

In the case of a ruler who sins ... unwittingly ... he shall bring his offering.... (Lev. 4:22-23)

Without bias

"Rabban Yohanan ben Zakkai said: Happy is the generation whose ruler brings an offering for his unwitting sin" (Horayot 10b).

Rabbi Yisrael Lipkin of Salant taught. "What special merit does a generation have when the ruler of its time brings an offering for an unwitting sin? As is known, a person does not consider it a duty to bring such an offering. This is particularly so with a ruler who is elevated above the people and is often arrogant, since everything is permitted to a ruler and there is no-one to question what this ruler's actions.

That is why Rabban Yohanan ben Zakkai teaches us that, when the ruler of the people brings an offering for a sin, and does not hide any failures - this testifies as to the greatness of the generation. The people did not flatter the errant ruler but pointed out the offence, assisting the ruler to do penance. Such an insightful generation is worthy of all praise because it is not only influenced by their leader but exerts an influence on their leader too, ensuring that all travel the right path.

Understanding the other person

Rashi reads 'asher' (in the case of) as being connected with the word 'ashrei' (happy), and comments: "Happy is the generation whose ruler gives thought to bringing an atonement sacrifice even for an inadvertent sin. It is that much more certain that such a ruler will regret any willful sins"..

175

But would it not be better for a generation to have a ruler who did not sin at all? Rabbi Menahem David of Amshinov answers: "No, it would not. A ruler who had never sinned would be unable to forgive the sins of another. Such a person would not understand and would not feel the broken heart of the sinner, and would distance and reject those who sinned.

If a soul sins in that he hears the voice of swearing. (Lev. 5:1)

It depends on you

Rabbi Yitzhak of Vorky suffered much anguish in his youth because of his wife, who caused him much grief. But he suffered in silence. Later, however, when he saw that his servants were also tortured by her, he was unable to make up his mind as to whether he should put up with this also or whether he should forgive and be silent about his own suffering but not about the suffering of the servants. In the end, he traveled to his teacher, Rabbi David of Lelov to ask for his advice.

Rabbi David heard what he had to say and responded: "What are you telling me? Say it to yourself!"

Rabbi Yitzhak did not understand what his teacher meant until, some time later, he came across a teaching of the Baal Shem Tov: If a person causes harm in deed, he has suffers because of his animals and servants. If he causes harm in his speech, he suffers because of his wife and other. And if he causes harm in thought, then he suffers because of his children. If a person is worthy and rectifies these three aspects: thought, speech and deed, then everything is turned around for good.

He then understood that everything depended on him.

When a person sins ... by dealing deceitfully with his fellow in the matter of a deposit (Lev. 5:21)

Restitution for Robbery

In the final section of Vayikra (Lev. 5:20-21), the law is given regarding a person who does harm to the property of another (robbery, denying receipt of a deposit and so on) and commits perjury regarding the matter, but who later confesses the sin. The punishment of such a person is twofold: restoration has to be made with the addition a quarter of the capital value, and a guilt offering must be brought to atone for the theft.

On this point, we read in the Mishnah: "If a person robs another to the extent of a perutah [a small coin] and takes a false oath [that he did not do so] and then admits his guilt, he has to personally convey it to the wronged party [even to] Media" (Bava Kama 9:5).

The intention of the Mishnah is to emphasize that a robber cannot find atonement until full restoration of the stolen amount is made directly to the owners, even if they have traveled to a country as distant as Media.

The question is why did the Mishnah not say: "he has to personally convey it to the wronged party even to a remote country"? Why does the Mishnah specify Media?

The Gaon of Vilna, explained: It is said in Isaiah (13:17): "Behold, I will stir up the Medes against them, who shall not regard silver; and as for gold, they shall not delight". We can deduce from the words of the prophet that, in the land of Media, silver and gold are of no importance. That is why the Mishnah says "he has to convey it to him personally even to Media". This teaches us that even if the person robbed lives in a rich country where money is of little value, the robber is not cleansed until full restitution is made.

... or anything else about which he swore falsely .... (Lev. 5:24)

A cunning trick

There was the case of a certain man who deposited a hundred denarii with Bar Telamion. When he came to claim them back from him, Bar Telamion said to him: 'Whatever you deposited with me, I have already delivered into your hand.' The claimant said: Swear to it. What did Bar Telamion do? He took a cane, hollowed it out and put the denarii inside it and began to lean on it. When they arrived at the synagogue, Bar Telamion said to the claimant: Hold this stick in your hand while I take the oath for you. Then he said: I swear by the Master of this House, whatever you deposited with me, I have returned to you. The claimant took the stick and threw it to the ground in anger at the false oath. The denarii began to scatter and he began to pick them up. Bar Telamion said to him: Go on, pick them up, then. They are yours that you are picking up.... (Lev. Rabbah 6:3)

Parashat Tzav

Adonai spoke to Moshe, saying: Command Aharon and his sons, saying: This is the ritual of the burnt offering; It is the burnt offering, because it is to remain burning upon the altar all night until the morning, and the fire of the altar shall be kept burning on it. (Lev. 6:1-2)

The Law of the Sacrifices

The main purpose of the sacrifices was to bring people closer to God. The sacrifice itself is not the main thing but the confession of wrong doing and the repentance for the offence which accompanied the sacrifice.

At what point did the sacrifice fulfill its role? When it succeeded in joining the heart of the person offering it and in purifying the soul from the sin which had adhered to it. The sacrifice thus opened a gate before the sinner and created a path to a new life, clean of all wrong doing and crime.

But a danger lay in wait for a person who could deviate from the central idea in the sacrifice ritual and distort its true purpose. The person offering the sacrifice could disregard the inner significance of the sacrifice. Such a person might erroneously think that the very act at the altar atones for the wrong doing. Such a person would continue sinning without inhibitions, would destroy, and steal without any morals, thinking in blind and ignorant confidence that the sacrifice would atone for all sins.

A sacrifice which does not shake up the person offering it, which does not generate an upheaval of the heart, is nothing more than an act of foolishness. Rabbah expressed this idea: "To come near to listen is better than to give the sacrifice of fools; for they consider not that they do evil" (Eccl. 4:17). Go close and listen to the words of the sages: sinners should bring a sacrifice and repent and not be like the fools who bring sacrifices but do not repent ... for they do not know if they are offering (the sacrifice) for the good or for the bad. Exclaimed the Holy Blessed One: "They do not distinguish between good and bad, yet they bring a sacrifice before Me?!" (Yalqut Shimoni, Eccl. 4).

The Holy Blessed One does not need the sacrifice, only the sincerity of the heart of the person offering the sacrifice. "For My thoughts are not your thoughts, nor are your ways My ways" (Is. 55:8).

If ordinary mortals own some articles, they are happy – but only so long as the articles are whole. If they breaks, however, people have no use for them. But what are articles of value for the Holy Blessed One? It is people's hearts. The Holy One has no use for haughty people, as it is said: "Everyone who is proud in heart is an abomination to Adonai" (Prov. 16:5). If the person's heart is broken, then the Holy One says: This is Mine, as it is said: "Adonai is near to the broken-hearted" (Ps. 34:19). (Midrash Hagadol, Vayeshev 38).

Rabbi Yehoshua ben Levi, taught: "Come and see how great are the low of spirit in the esteem of the Holy One since, when the Temple stood, a person brought a burnt-offering and received the reward of a burnt-offering, a meal-offering and received the reward of a meal-offering; but the one whose mind is lowly, it is as though such a person had offered every one of the sacrifices; as it is said: 'The sacrifices of God are a broken spirit.' (Ps. 41:19) (Sotah 5b).

The priest shall dress in linen raiment ... and he shall take up the ashes. (Lev. 6:3)

Everyday concerns

Rabbi Simhah Bunim of Peshischa said: The Torah commanded the high priest that, when he enters the Holy of Holies on the Day of Atonement, he should change his clothes and that his first task should be "terumat hadeshen" (removal of the ashes). Why was that? When the holiest person in the Jewish People enters the holiest place of all, the innermost sanctuary, on the holiest day of the year, he is, at that moment, totally immersed in the world of spirituality and sanctity.

Mundane matters, worldly concerns, could well be forgotten by him. He might forget, for example, that he should pray for the livelihood of Israel. That is why he is commanded to change his clothes, to put on workday garments and to engage in the simplest of all daily tasks - so that he will remember the concerns of the Jewish People, their daily needs.

The fire shall be burning always upon the altar; it shall never go out. (Lev. 6:6)

The Spiritual Altar

King David said: "that I may dwell in the house of Adonai all the days of my life, to behold the beauty of Adonai, and to frequent His temple" (Ps. 27:4). There is an apparent contradiction here. "Dwell" has a sense of permanency about it but "to frequent" implies multiple visits.

King David's desire was to dwell in the house of Adonai on a permanent basis all the days of his life but since permanent dwelling can lead to habit and routine, he further requested "to frequent". A person who comes to visit frequently has a taste of something new each time. And so King David's request was to be a permanent resident in the house of Adonai but with a level of constant renewal as though he were frequenting, as though he were coming to visit God's temple for the first time.

Peace, peace to the near and to the far

A divine spark flickers in every Jew and never goes out. The leader of the generation - the priest, prophet or rabbi - has only to fan that spark with words of enthusiasm each morning in order to alert and arouse people to observe the mitzvot between people and God - for this is what the "korban oleh" [the burnt offering] hints at - and to observe the mitzvot between people, for this is what the "korban hashelamim" [the peace offering] hints at.

If the priests do this and kindle the sparks in the hearts of the Jewish People, they may be absolutely certain that the divine fire will forever burn on the altar and will never go out....

A Perpetual Fire

The Rebbe of Lubavitch, Rabbi Menahem Mendel Schneerson, used to say: Each person has an altar inside - the heart. Always burning in the heart is a perpetual fire of the love of God, a fire that inspires people to find a point of contact with the Creator. This is a fire which cannot be extinguished. It is eternal. Often, however, it does not burn with an open flame which can be seen and felt, but in an ember hiding among the coals where, although it exists, it cannot be seen.

In the place where the burnt offering is killed shall the sin offering be killed. (Lev. 6:18)

Transgression after transgression

Our sages, of blessed memory, said: "generally speaking, a burnt offering is brought as expiation for sinful thoughts" (Lev. Rabbah 8:3). The sin offering, on the other hand, atones for sins actually committed.

Rabbi Yisrael Lipkin of Salant, founder of the Mussar Movement, taught: Reality teaches us that there is a close correlation between thinking about an offence and actually committing one. A person who thinks sinful thoughts, will, in the end, perpetrate the sin itself too. This is intimated in the above verse. "In the place where the burnt offering is killed", where people fail with sinful meditations which require a burnt offering, there "shall the sin offering be killed", there they subsequently fail with the actual sinful deeds which require a sin offering".

Then Moshe brought Aharon and his sons forward and washed them with water ... and he placed the headdress on his head. (Lev. 8:6-9)

Prophet and Priest

Moshe anointed Aharon to be Israel's first priest. Moshe brought Aharon forward and washed him from the top of his head to the soles of his feet. He dressed him in his tunic and robe and so on.

The prophet invests the priest not only with a crown of holiness, not only with the spirit, but he also determines his apparel and washes his body. He then sprinkles some of the blood of the sacrifice "on the lobe of Aharon's [right] ear and on the thumb of his [right] hand and on the big toe of his [right] foot" (Lev. 8:23).

There was not one limb of Aharon's body that Moshe's hand did not purify. There was not one item of Aharon's clothing that was not put on him by Moshe. With a sort of individual providence, Moshe watched over all the minutiae of the high priest's preparations.

But who anointed Moshe? A person is anointed to the priesthood. A person is anointed as king. But a person is not anointed to be a prophet. Thus, nothing similar was done for Moshe himself and we know nothing about his clothing. That is to say, his apparel was of no importance. All of Moshe's sanctity he received from the inner sanctum, from above and from within. Aharon needed a uniform. His garments were part of his role and part of his strength. Moshe needed no such authority. Moshe was a man of the wilderness, a man from the desert land. He took his strength from the burning bush and from Mount Horeb. He stood barefoot on God's burning soil, without anything intervening. He immersed himself in real fire and a "baptism of fire" will always be a true prophecy and a source of authority.

Aharon and his sons did all the things which Adonai had commanded by the hand of Moshe. (Lev. 8:36)

Everything according to character

Once, the Hatam Sopher turned to one of the worshippers and asked him to lead the congregation in prayer. But the latter made as though he were modest, shrugged his shoulders and declined, as one who was unfit for such great honor.

The Hatam Sopher said to him: Rashi said regarding the verse "So Aharon and his sons did all the things": This is said in their praise - that they did not turn to the right nor to the left". They did not shrug their shoulders out of humility and did not make as though they were unfit but, what they were asked to do, they stood up and did. Excessive humility - Rabbi Sopher concluded by saying - is also a form of pride.

Parashat Shmini

It came to pass on the eighth day, that Moshe called Aharon and his sons, and the elders of Israel. (Lev. 9:1)

Eternal Proof

When Rabbi Ezekiel Landa of Prague died, the leaders of the community convened to elect a successor. Names were put forward of well-known rabbis who had proven themselves to be outstanding teachers in different communities. Rabbi Yaakov, one of Rabbi Ezekiel's sons, stood up and declared with much emotion: "I consider it my duty to inform you that my father had asked before he died that his first-born son, Rabbi Shmuel, was to serve in his stead as rabbi and court president of our community".

At this, a great commotion broke out among those who were gathered there, and they were divided into two camps. Many of the community leaders expressed their opinion that it was "a mitzvah to uphold the words of the deceased" and that Rabbi Shmuel should be inducted as the city rabbi. But voices were also heard arguing that Rabbi Yaakov's testimony could not be taken at face value, as he was an interested party.

Rabbi Yaakov again asked for permission to speak, and said: Midrash Tanhuma teaches us about the first verse of Parashat Shmini that Moshe called all the elders of Israel in order to announce Aharon as high priest in their presence. "Said the Holy Blessed One to Moshe: Call the elders together and anoint Aharon, and I will give him greatness before them. This was so that the elders should not say that Aharon made himself high priest".

The question that has to be asked here is: If the elders did not believe Aharon and suspected that he might have appointed himself high priest and that it was not according to the word of Adonai, then why should they believe Moshe? From here we can learn that the elders would not have believed Aharon if he had claimed to have been appointed according to the word of Adonai, because he was an interested party. On the other hand, the elders did believe Moshe when he told them that the Holy Blessed One, had commanded him to anoint his brother, Aharon, to the priesthood. Had Moshe wished to deceive them then he would have told them that he, Moshe, was himself to be appointed high priest.

In the same way, you have to weigh things up and decide on the matter being discussed here. Had I, heaven forbid, been lying to you regarding the last will of my late father, I would have pretended that my father had appointed me to take his place in the congregation of Prague! Not many days elapsed and Rabbi Samuel Landa, the first-born son of the Gaon, Rabbi Ezekiel Landa, was inducted as the rabbi and court president of the congregation of Prague, a position in which he served to the end of his life.

Moshe said: This is what Adonai has commanded that you keep so that the Presence of Adonai may appear to you. (Lev. 9:6)

A Carriage for the Divine Presence

The Seer of Lublin said: The Children of Israel craved and yearned for the inspiration of the Divine Presence. They waited and hoped, saying: When will the sanctuary be completed and the Divine Presence come to rest? Moshe admonished them: Does the Holy Blessed One need a sanctuary? Is it not God's whole desire and wish that the Divine Presence should be within each of, in the soul and in the heart of every Jew? "This is what Adonai has commanded that you keep" - the Torah and the commandments and then, as an inevitable response, "the Presence of Adonai will appear to you". You will thus have no need for the sanctuary at all because each one of you will be a sort of sanctuary and carriage for God's Presence.

Moshe said to Aharon: Approach the altar, and offer your sin offering, and your burnt offering, and make an atonement for yourself, and for the people. (Lev. 9:7)

Don't be embarrassed

Rashi comments on this verse that "Aharon was self-conscious and was afraid to approach it. Moshe said to him: Why are you feeling self-conscious? It was for this that you were selected!"

Rabbi Moshe Leib of Sassov used to say: "Why are you self-conscious"? - It is because you are self-conscious "that you were selected". And Rabbi Yehiel Meir of Gostynin said: Since Aharon was selected for high office, quarrelsome people, rabble-rousers, began to gossip about him and pay him no respect. They said: Do you see this son of Amram who danced before the molten calf now serving before Adonai? Aharon would hear the insults and hide his face in embarrassment. Moshe said to him: Why are you embarrassed? Do you not know that this is the lot of every public figure, of every leader? All you can do is adjust to your fate for "it was for this that you were selected" - to suffer all sorts of slanderers, nags and mischief-makers....

Recognition of Human Frailty

Rabbi Simhah Bunem of Peshischa said: We read in the portion of Shmini that, on the eighth (shmini) day [after the consecration of Aharon and his sons as priests], Moshe says to Aharon: "Come forward to the altar and sacrifice your sin offering and your burnt offering, and make expiation for yourself and for the people". Moshe, our teacher, thus emphasizes to Aharon, that he should first offer a sacrifice for himself and only then make expiation for the people. There is a very important rule in Jewish law [Halakhah]: One who is not obligated to perform a particular observance cannot perform it on behalf of others.

This rule also applies for teaching the public how to observe the Torah and the commandments. One who has never seen offences and offenders is unable to extract others from the spiritual morass into which they have sunk. And only a person who has been close to the vanities of this world and has come face to face with the frailties of humanity will be able to summon up the spiritual forces necessary to mend one's own ways and those of others fully and completely....

Moshe said to Aharon: This is what Adonai spoke, saying: I will be sanctified in them that come near to Me, and before all the people I will be glorified. Then Aharon held his peace. (Lev. 10:3)

Acknowledgement of Divine Justice

The preparations for the dedication of the Sanctuary lasted for seven days. How tremendous were the expectations as the great day drew near when the Divine Presence was to take up residence in the sight of the entire people!

The hoped-for day came at last, the eighth day, and the Sanctuary was erected. The impressive ceremony reached its climax "...and the glory of Adonai appeared to all the people" (Lev. 9:23). The fire of enthusiasm kindled in all hearts and then overflowed. "...when all the people saw, they shouted, and fell on their faces" (Lev. 9:24).

Who was the captain in this stormy and tempestuous sea of the masses of people? Upon whom were everyone's eyes at this festive moment? Aharon the high priest! He lifted up his hands and blessed the people, who followed his every movement with bated breath.

And then his two sons, Nadav and Avihu, entered to serve in the worship and to offer up incense. Suddenly, as a bolt of lightening out of a clear sky, the blow fell. "There went out fire from Adonai, and devoured them, and they died before Adonai" (Lev. 10:2).

Despite this terrible personal tragedy, Aharon justified the Divine judgment: "Then Aharon held his peace". Rashi comments that "He was rewarded for his silence".

The daughter of Rabbi Eliyahu Rabinowitz-Teomim, the Chief Rabbi of Jerusalem, died in the prime of her life. A time was set for the funeral, and the members of the Hevrah Kaddisha came at the appointed hour and wished to depart for the funeral. But the rabbi had shut himself up in his room and asked to delay the start of the funeral for a short while. After about a half an hour, the Rabbi emerged from his study and the signal was given to begin the funeral procession.

Some time later, he explained the delay. He said: "Our sages commanded us that "it is incumbent upon a person to bless God for the evil in the same way as one blesses God for the good" (Mishnah Berakhot 9: 5). When I came to: "Blessed be the True Judge", I realized that, from a spiritual point of view, I was incapable of blessing the bad "in the same way" as one blesses the good. Thus, I shut myself up in my room until I succeeded in recovering for myself the feeling of joy which had accompanied me when my daughter came into the world. Only then was I able to justify to myself the Divine Justice and only then could I, out of that same feeling, bless Adonai who had judged me with true justice.

A Thundering Silence

"Aharon was silent". Rabbi Nahman of Breslau used to say about this: One can shout with a still, small voice and it can be a very loud. Anybody can do that. That is to say: one can depict the shout in one's thoughts and introduce the sound of the shout right in there with the niggun and go deep into the content of the shout without any sound until the shout emerges with a still, small voice.

Rabbi Shlomo Hacohen of Rodemsk said: What is said about Aharon shows greatness, but what is said about David shows even more greatness. In the case of Aharon, it is said: "And Aharon was silent". He accepted punishment with love silence. But, in the case of David, it is said: "So that my glory may sing praise to You and not be silent" (Ps. 30:13). Even at a time of trouble and distress, King David was able to keep up his singing.

Nevertheless a fountain or a pit, where there is plenty of water, shall be clean. (Lev. 11:36)

Who am I and what am I?

Rabbi Menahem Mendel of Kotzk used to say: "Immersion in a miqveh [a ritual bath] purifies when a person's head is completely immersed below the surface so that not a single hair remains out of the water.

The purification of Israel is achieved in the same way. When they bend their backs and subdue their hearts before their Father, Who is in Heaven, only then is the verse upheld for them: "Adonai is the hope [miqveh] of Israel" (Jer. 17:13).

Parashat Tazria

Adonai spoke to Moshe, saying: When a woman at childbirth bears a male child... or, if she bears a female child.... (Lev. 12:1-5)

The Mystery of Life

Despite the giant steps. taken by contemporary science, birth remains a vast mystery, arousing in us a holy fear. The Midrash explored this mystery through vivid images and ingenious word play:

"This is what Scripture was referring to (in the prayer of Hannah, Samuel's mother): 'There is none holy like Adonai because there is none like You, neither is there any rock like our God.' (1 Sam 2:2)

What is the meaning of 'neither is there any rock (tzur) like our God'? It means: There is no artist (tzayar) like our God. How is that? A king of flesh and blood paints a picture on the wall because he cannot do so on water. But the Holy One creates (yotzer) the embryo in his mother's insides, within the water (in the womb of the mother). In other words: There is no artist (tzayar) like our God.

Another explanation. A king of flesh and blood creates (tzar) a form on the wall but he cannot create in it a spirit and a soul. But the Holy One creates (tzar) a form within a form (creates the embryo within its mother) and places within it spirit and soul. In other words: There is no artist (tzayar) like our God" (Tanhuma Tazria 2).

If a woman conceives, and bears a male child.... (Lev. 12:2)

Against your will, you live

The Talmud states: "What does an embryo resemble while it is still inside its mother? Folded writing tablets... Rabbi Simlai said: there is no time in which a person enjoys greater happiness than in those days" (Nidah 30b).

Only when a person is born are the tablets opened and, day after day, the pages are filled in. A person's deeds "write" on the pages of life. So long as the embryo is inside its mother, however, the writing tablets are folded and lie there closed. What will be written on them? At that point, no one knows. Only at the end of a person's life will the journal's pages be full. It will contain pages of glory and splendor and pages of weakness and failure; pages of weeping; rose-colored pages and gray-colored pages. Nobody's journal remains blank.

A certain man once came to the Tzaddik, Rav Yitzhak Meir of Gur, and told him of the tortuous path he had traversed so far in life, and that he was trying to return and live as he had in his younger days, since those early times seemed more attractive to him than his present life. Rabbi Yitzhak Meir said: "It is true, as Rabbi Simlai has said, that 'there is no time in which a man enjoys greater happiness than in those days', but have you ever found a person who could return to his mother's womb? From this you must learn - that a person does not return to a place or to years past, however beautiful they might have been. A person has to move forward, ever forward!"

Against your will, you die

We read in the Zohar: A person's whose time comes to depart from this world is visited by three angels. These angels show such a person things that no mortal can see in a lifetime. This is the day on which the King of the Universe asks for the return of the deposit ... There is no greater sorrow than that of the soul when it departs from the body. But a person does not die until first seeing the Shekhinah , the Divine Presence, and then, by virtue of the passion and the yearnings which arise in the soul to be joined with the Shekhinah, the soul disengages and is separated from the body".

Adonai spoke to Moshe and Aharon, saying: When a person has on the skin of his body a swelling, a rash, or a discoloration, and it develops. into a scaly affliction on the skin of his body, he shall be brought to Aharon the priest or to one of his sons the priests. The priest shall see the affliction. (Lev. 13:1-2)

The association between the portions

In the portion of Shmini, the Torah gives a detailed list of the pure animals that may be eaten as well as a long list of animals, birds and reptiles that may not be eaten. The portion of Tazria, which immediately follows Shmini, deals with various impurities that may affect people, and with various skin afflictions.

Rabbi Yisrael Lipkin of Salant explained the connection between the portion of Shmini (which ends with a list of what is permitted and what is prohibited in food), and the portion of Tazria (which deals with the laws of afflictions): Our sages, of blessed memory, have already said that these afflictions result mainly from the sin of speaking badly of others. Let us, however, observe how the masses of the people behave with this grave sin. People are very cautious about eating forbidden foods and check excessively to ensure that not even the smallest of small worms should, Heaven forbid, enter their mouths. But they exercise absolutely no caution at all over what emerges from their mouths, in talking gossip and slander without any pangs of the heart or the conscience.

A time for action and a time for speaking

Rabbi Mordekhai of Pinchov, the student of the Seer of Lublin, was wretchedly poor. Whenever he went to Lublin, his wife would instruct him not to forget to tell the Rabbi about the terrible straits they were in and ask him for advice and a blessing. But every time, he forgot. When he met the Rabbi, he would become involved in a discussion with him over matters of Torah and forgot to mention even one word about his difficult situation.

One day, his wife finally decided to take action. The next time Rabbi Mordekhai was about to depart for Lublin, she got up and went with him. He no longer had any choice. When he went to see the Rabbi, he sat down and told him about the situation he and his family were in. Why, asked the Seer of Lublin, did you not tell me about this before? The student replied: I was of the opinion that the Rabbi knows about it through the holy spirit in him.

The Seer replied: In the portion of Tazria, the Torah tells us that "when a person has on the skin of his body a swelling, a rash, or a discoloration ... he shall be brought to the priest ... and the priest shall see the affliction". One does not have to say anything or to tell anything to the priest but just to come to him and the priest will himself see the affliction. But, when it comes to houses, it is said: "And the owner of the house shall come and tell the priest, saying: Something like a plague has appeared upon my house" (Lev. 14:35). In the latter case, in matters concerning houses, it is not enough just to come to the priest. One has to tell him about the affliction.

Love the truth and peace

The question has been posed: Why did the Torah determine that afflictions are to be examined by Aharon the priest or by one of his sons?

The sages, of blessed memory, have already noted in a number of places that the afflictions come to a person because of the sin of gossip and slander. But then many of those who engage in slander claim that they are telling the truth about their fellows. They are of the naïve opinion that they are keeping a mitzvah by exposing the truth to public scrutiny.

That is why the Torah teaches us here that the leper is to be brought to Aharon the priest to learn from him that, for the sake of peace between two people, a person may deviate from the truth. What did Aharon used to do? When he saw two people who hated each other, he would go to the one without the knowledge of the other and say to him: Your fellow came to me and asked me to make it up between the two of you! In this way, Aharon increased peace and friendship among people.

We can deduce from this that, however important truth might be in human life, peace between people is more important. This was the way of Aharon the priest throughout his lifetime. That is why the leper was brought to him, so that he could learn this good quality from him, repent of his sins and be healed of his disease.

Why are there afflictions in the world?

Although there is today no longer any practical halakhic or legal significance to the many laws dealing with impurity and purity which are detailed in this portion, the great interest in the problems mentioned here has not ceased. This is because our sages considered the afflictions and diseases mentioned in this portion to be more than just descriptions of a disease. These afflictions have symbolic significance too. The diseases and afflictions visit a person as punishment for bad deeds.

The sages said: "For seven things afflictions come into the world: for slander, for bloodshed, for a false oath, for incest, for vulgarity, for robbery and for enviousness" (Arakhin 16a). The Torah twice mentions the leprosy with which Miriam was afflicted (Num. 10:12). This was her punishment for having indulged in gossip about Moshe with her brother, Aharon. The Torah intimates that gossip is a sort of contagious disease, since slander passes the disease on from one person to another.

All the days when the disease shall be in him he shall be unclean; he is unclean; he shall dwell alone; outside the camp shall his habitation be. (Lev. 13:46)

So that they may learn a lesson

A person catches leprosy as a punishment for 'lashon hara' (slanderous talk). The Talmud explains: The slanderer is separated from other people (through the slander recounted), therefore said the Torah: 'He shall dwell alone; outside the camp shall his habitation be' (Arakhin 16b).

Rabbi Zalman Sorotzkin explained: The person who indulges in slander thinks that so-and-so is depriving him of his means of livelihood or that some other person is not showing her due respect. So the slanderer garrulously denounces one person before another and the other before the first. From hatred of an individual such a person ends up hating everyone, thinking that the whole world was created only for him or that people are stealing and destroying what belongs only to her. Such a person should be sentenced to die by plague, as the spies who slandered the Land of Israel were, but mercy was shown from heaven and the punishment was commuted to leprosy, which is as difficult to bear as death.

To cure such a person from this spiritual illness (which is the cause of the physical illness), the Torah said: "He shall dwell alone; outside the camp shall his habitation be" (Lev. 13:46). During the time of slanderers are exiled from the camp, they would surely be struck by feelings of longing for human company and would very much want for someone to come to them, to rescue them from such loneliness. Only then will they learn to assess correctly the need for proper contact with people and will desist from nitpicking and searching for others' shortcomings.

With mere words

Rabbi Yitzhak of Vorky was told that one of the people in town was spreading lies and rumors about the town people, which could damage people's reputations. Rabbi Yitzhak of Vorky called the man to him and said: My brother, so long as you are making things up about people whose character and deeds you do not know, you will be perceived as a liar. Go out and tell all the bad things in the world about me and about you, and I guarantee you that no one will protest or say a word against you, or contradict what you are saying.

Parashat Metzora

Adonai spoke to Moshe, saying: This shall be the ritual for the leper on the day of his cleansing; he shall be brought to the priest. (Lev. 14:1-2)

Words can kill

In Midrash Tanhuma, we read "Whoever indulges in gossip will be stricken with leprosy ... because gossip is worse than bloodshed. A person who commits manslaughter kills one person, but gossip kills three: the person repeating the gossip, the person listening to it and the person about whom it is said" (Metzora 2).

We read further: Rabban Shimon Ben Gamliel said to Tabbai his servant: 'Go and buy me some good food in the market'. He went and bought him tongue. Rabban Shimon said to him: 'Go and buy me some bad food in the market'. He went and bought him tongue.

Rabban Shimon asked him: 'What is this? When I told you to get good food you bought me tongue, and when I told you to get bad food you also bought me tongue!'

Tabbai replied: 'Good comes from it and bad comes from it. When the tongue is good there is nothing better, and when it is bad there is nothing worse'. (Lev. Rabbah 33:1)

The Plain Meaning of Scripture

There was the case of a certain peddler who used to go around the towns near Sepphoris, crying out: "Whoever wishes to buy the elixir of life, let him come and take it. He approached the house of Rabbi Yannai, who was sitting and studying in his room.

Rabbi Yannai looked out at him and said: "Come up here and sell some to me". The peddler said to him: "Neither you nor those like you have need of it". The Rabbi pressed him, so the peddler took out a Book of psalms and showed him the verse: Who is the man that desires life and loves many days, that he may see good? (Ps. 34:12) What does the next verse say? Keep your tongue from evil and your lips. from speaking guile. Depart from evil and do good. Seek peace and pursue it. Rabbi Yannai said: All my life I have been reading this passage but did not know how it was to be explained, until this peddler came and made it clear. (Lev. Rabbah 16:2)

Practicing what one preaches

Rabbi Meir Hacohen of Radin was famous during his lifetime as the "Hafetz Hayyim", the title of one of his books which deals with the obligation to guard one's tongue and the prohibitions on gossip. This nickname, of the man and of the book, is taken from a verse in the Book of psalms: "Who is the man who desires life (Hafetz Hayyim), and loves many days, that he may see good? Keep your tongue from evil, and your lips. from speaking guile" (Ps. 34:13-14).

The Hafetz Hayyim once said to his associates: I have an extra obligation to guard my tongue from evil. If I fail to do so, I will be guilty of the sin of robbing the public. As you know, at the present time I am gaining publicity from the sale of my book, Hafetz Hayyim, which deals in great detail with the prohibitions on gossip. If I am not myself especially cautious over this sin, it will appear that I tricked people with the sale of my book, and the money that I receive for it will be by way of robbery.

Guard your tongue

"Whoever guards his mouth and his tongue keeps. his soul from troubles" (Prov. 21:23).

The Hafetz Hayyim was walking through the empty streets of his town one winter evening. As he went on his way, a Jew from out of town stopped him and asked: "Where does your rabbi, the righteous author of the Hafetz Hayyim, live?"

The Hafetz Hayyim answered him: "First of all, he is not a rabbi and, second, he is not righteous".

The shocked Jew replied: "What are you saying? Everyone considers him to be God-fearing and absolutely righteous". The Hafetz Hayyim again answered him: "What everyone says means nothing. The world does not know him. I know him well, and I assure you honestly that that is a great overstatement and exaggeration". The Jew became very angry and slapped him across the face. The Hafetz Hayyim sincerely regretted having caused a Jew to commit an offence.

Soon afterwards, when the Hafetz Hayyim arrived home, he found the same Jew sitting in the house, waiting for him. When the Jew realized that the man facing him was the Hafetz Hayyim in person, and that he had slapped him across the face, he was very shocked and nearly fainted. The Hafetz Hayyim calmed him, spoke to him quietly and said: It is nothing. You have done nothing wrong. I justly deserved the slap across the face that I received, for I have now learned an important lesson: Not only is it forbidden to speak slanderously about others, but a person is also forbidden to speak badly of himself....

The priest shall go out of the camp; and the priest shall look, and, behold, if the disease of leprosy is healed in the leper.... (Lev. 14:3)

It depends on him

The Kabbalist, Rabbi Yitzhak Luria, taught: It is common to think that leprosy comes to a person naturally, as the result of increasing melancholy, depression and loneliness. One would have expected, therefore, that the natural medication for this illness would be that a person should live among other people, should spend time in a merry society, in order to dissipate the melancholy.

But the Torah ordered that the leper should reside alone, outside the camp, so as to prove thereby that the matter is not natural in any way but derives from the hand of the Divine Providence by which the person is punished for sins committed. A person who repents completely will be healed even while isolated and separated from people.

This is what Scripture says: "And the priest shall go out of the camp" and, nonetheless, shall realize "and, behold, the disease of leprosy is healed in the leper" - despite the isolation which, in the natural way, should increase the illness, only then will the priest understand that the healing of the disease is by no means a natural matter but "from the leper". The healing depends only on the leper. Wrongdoing caused the leprosy, and repentance resulted in healing.

A doctor's duty

The obvious question here is: Since it is written that the leper has been brought to the priest "on the day that he is to be cleansed" (Lev. 14:2), why did the priest have to "go outside the camp", to the place where the leper was living?

The answer here is that we can learn a moral lesson, not only regarding the leper, but also with respect to all the illnesses that beset a person during his or her lifetime. Just as the patient has to do everything possible to be cured of the illness, so is the doctor obliged to try, with all possible means, on behalf of the patient. As a rule, the responsibility for taking the initiative falls on the patient. It is up to the sick person to go to the physician. But, when the patient delays in coming to the doctor, for whatever reason, the doctor is forbidden to remain indifferent to the fate of the patient, but must go out to the patient to provide a remedy and medication.

If such is the case with the healing of the body, how much truer is it with the healing of the soul! If people come of their own initiative and their own free will to the rabbis to ask for spiritual healing for any sin and wrongdoing - how good and how pleasant that is! But, when the masses are neglectful in this and do not rise early to visit the rabbi, then the spiritual shepherd is forbidden to hide from this and say: "I have seen nothing; I have heard nothing!" A spiritual leader worthy of the name does not wait for people in need of spiritual help to come, but must go out to the people at any time, at any hour. And, sometimes, a leader has to "go outside the camp" and visit places of questionable morality in order to return errant children to their Parent in Heaven....

The priest shall make expiation before Adonai. (Lev. 14:31)

The Priest - Physician of the Soul

Nowadays, medical science has come to recognize that many a physical illness is at the same time a spiritual crisis. Much attention is being given now to the healing of the soul in tandem with the healing of the body. Modern medicine sees a strong connection between the body and the soul. Some illnesses of the body are only symptoms of pathological phenomena in the soul.

It is surprising that this fact was already known to our forebears. They noticed the connection between illnesses of the body and those of the soul since, as Judaism sees things, the physical and the spiritual are intertwined.

The Torah says that, when an affliction is discovered on a person's body, the person is to be brought to the priest and the priest will determine whether the patient can be cleansed, or whether isolation is required.

And so the question can be asked: Why did the Torah rule that the sick person should be brought to the priest of all people? What does the priest, the spiritual leader and guide in matters of religion and spirit, have to do with treating the affliction of the body?

Our Torah understood that bodily illnesses often visit a person as the result of a breakdown, of a spiritual crisis. Who, then, is better suited to guide the patient than the priest, the spiritual instructor and physician of the soul?

When you come to the land of Canaan, which I give to you for a possession, and I put the disease of leprosy in a house of the land of your possession. (Lev. 14:34)

You have been warned

Several of the aggadists viewed this chapter, which deals with house plagues, as a grave warning to the envious that Adonai will inflict on them plagues which will expose their disgrace before everyone: How is that? A man says to his fellow: Lend me a measure of wheat, and he says: I don't have any. Lend me a measure of barley but he replies: I don't have any. Lend me a measure of dates - and he answers: I don't have any. Or a woman says to her fellow: Lend me a sieve, but she replies: I don't have one. Lend me a meshed sieve, and she says: I don't have one.

What does the Holy Blessed One do? Inflicts plagues on the person's house so that when all the possessions are taken out of the house, everyone sees and comments: Did you not used to say: I don't have any. Look how much wheat there is here. See how much barley there is here, how many dates there are here! (Yalqut Shimoni, Metzora 14).

Parashat Aharei Mot

Adonai spoke to Moshe after the death of the two sons of Aharon, when they came near Adonai, and died. (Lev. 16:1)

Blessings

Rabbi Shlomo Rabinowitz of Radomsk once traveled through Krakow. He was asked by the local community to teach them some Torah. He agreed and said the following: Any tzaddik who does not draw down on Israel a bounty of blessing and livelihood and richness is not a tzaddik at all and is not fit to be a leader of the Jewish People.

The Talmud teaches: "Say you of the righteous when he is good (tzaddik ki tov); that they shall eat the fruit of their doings" (Isaiah 3:10). Is there then a righteous person who is good and a righteous person who is not good? One who is good to Heaven and good to people, is a righteous person who is good; One who is good to Heaven but not good to people, that is a righteous person who is not good. (Kiddushin 40a).

Rabbi Rabinowitz continued: A righteous person (tzaddik) who is not good to people means one who does not draw down for Israel a bounty of goodness and livelihood.

This was the sin of Nadav and Avihu, the two sons of Aharon who were killed by God (Lev. 10:1-2). They made do with "when they came near Adonai" (Lev. 16:1) only and did not bring down an abundance of livelihood and goodness on Israel, and therefore "and they died", for they were unsuitable to be leaders of Israel.

After he had finished speaking, Rabbi Rabinowitz suddenly turned to Rabbi Shimon Sofer, the local rabbi, and asked: "Do you know for what purpose you were appointed from heaven to serve as rabbi in Krakow?" The rabbi did not answer, wanting to know what the speaker was driving at, and Rabbi Shlomo Rabinowitz continued: "Do you think that you were appointed as the rabbi here in Krakow to judge what is forbidden and what is permitted in matters of cutlery and crockery? If so, you are mistaken. There are many teachers, in every street and every alley here, all capable of making such decisions. You should know that you were chosen to serve as rabbi in a great city such as Krakow in order to bring down on Israel abundant good, livelihood, health and all that is good".

For I appear in the cloud above the cover. (Lev. 16:2)

"And your faithfulness every night"

Rabbi Meir Shapira, head of the Sages of Lublin Yeshiva, said: sometimes people display a weakness of faith when going through difficult times. It is toward these people that Scripture here calls: "For I appear in the cloud above the cover". A person should not give up, even when difficult times are upon him. Often, when darkness covers the earth, it can seem to a person that everything is hopeless and that even the reckoned days for the coming of the Messiah have come and gone. And then, suddenly, the sun of hope shines through again and the light of salvation is seen in its full splendor. The Jew has to be educated constantly for the difficult times life might bring should remember that after the worst storms, the sun rises again....

... which abides with them in the midst of their uncleanness. (lev16:16)

It's what's inside the counts

Rashi comments: "although they are unclean, the Shekhinah dwells among them".

The story is told about Rabbi Avraham Yehoshua Heschel who journeyed to a certain city. The people there prepared two places for him to stay and gave to the rabbi himself the choice, to decide at which one he would stay. Both landlords were affluent men, who observed kashrut with great strictness. They both offered spacious accommodation suitable for welcoming such an important guest. About one of them, however, there was gossip that he was involved in crime and, knowing about it, he was abject in his own eyes, humble, and kind-hearted. The other man kept his distance from crime and was proud of it. The Rabbi from Efta chose the landlord who was the subject of the gossip and stayed over with him.

When the Rabbi's associates later asked about his accommodation choice, he replied: The one, although untainted by crime, was nevertheless a man of pride and we have learned from the Talmud that "every person in whom there is haughtiness of spirit, the Holy Blessed One declares: we cannot both dwell in the world". If, as it were, there is no room for the Holy One at this one's place, then surely there can be no room for me. As to the one in whom there is no coarseness but only some offences, it is explicitly written in the Torah: "... abides with them in the midst of their uncleanness". Since the Holy One has, as it were, can be accommodated at this man's place, I, too, stayed there.

In the seventh month, on the tenth day of the month, you shall afflict your souls. (Lev. 16:29)

Who can and who has to?

The tzaddik Rabbi Avraham Yehoshua Heschel of Apt, author of Ohev Israel (A Lover of Israel), used to say: If only I had the power, I would cancel all the public fasts we have been commanded to keep because we are weak and exhausted in this long and harsh exile. I would keep only two: the fast of the Ninth of Av and the fast of the Day of Atonement. For, on the Ninth of Av, when our temple and our glory was destroyed, who can eat? And on the holy Day of Atonement, when we are purified of all sin and wrongdoing before the Creator of the Universe, who has to eat?!

For on that day shall he make an atonement for you, to cleanse you, that you may be clean from all your sins before Adonai. (Lev. 16:30)

I am ashamed of myself

On the eve of the Day of Atonement, after the final pre-fast meal, Rabbi Naftali of Ropshitz went into his study and did not come out for the Kol Nidrei prayer. The Hassidim were all gathered in his synagogue, waiting for him. The sun had dipped below the tree line and the time had come to say the Kol Nidrei but the rabbi had not arrived. The Hassidim sent Rabbi Naftali's son, Rabbi Eliezer, after him. He went into his father's study and found him there, sobbing his heart out.

"Father", he asked him, "why are you here in your room, crying rather than in synagogue, at the prayer service?"

"Woe is me", Rabbi Naftali again broke out crying and weeping. "I am ashamed to go to the synagogue. Hassidim are standing there in their hundreds, waiting for me. They think that I am righteous and pure but I know what I am and what I have done. Throughout the year, I take upon myself before my Maker, my Creator, that I shall make full repentance and will change my ways for the better. A year has passed, and I have not made repentance. I promised before the Holy One during the Ten Days of Penitence, that I would scrutinize my actions and would sin no more. And now, here I am, on the eve of the Day of Atonement, as night falls, and I know that I have still not made repentance"... and Rabbi Naftali again burst out crying.

Atonement and Pardon

Rabbi Soloveitchik said: The Day of Atonement has two effects. First of all, it atones and then it cleanses. These two elements, of atonement and of cleansing, are the direct result of the sin, because these two elements are also to be found in the sin: sin obligates and, opposite it, is the atonement or the pardon; and sin makes impure, and opposite it, is the cleansing or the forgiveness.

A sin creates an obligation that is similar to a lien in the judicial sphere. There is no sin without punishment, whether imposed by an earthly court or by a heavenly court. "Atonement" means pardon, a concept originating in the laws of property. Just as a person can forgive another for owed property, so does the Holy Blessed One, pardon and cancel the punishment inherent in the sin.

A sin also makes a person impure, however. This is in a different realm, the metaphysical realm, in the realm of the short distance between a person and God. The sin is a flaw and damage to the inner being of a person, to the soul, which is where the Shekhinah, the Divine Presence, resides.

And Rabbi Soloveitchik continued: "You shall be clean before Adonai". God created people to be free, but this freedom that is granted does not allow them to do as they please, or to act irresponsibly. On the contrary, the person who is created "in the image of God" always remains "before Adonai". Such a person can never be free of the religious bond or the tie to God. People cannot run away from before God, because God chose each person's soul as the place in which to dwell as within a sanctuary.

Prayer comes from the heart

One Yom Kippur, Rabbi Levi Yitzhak of Berdichev was very sad and tense. This lasted from the Kol Nidrei prayer until the middle of the Ne'ilah. But just before he completed the Ne'ilah prayer, the face of the Zaddik suddenly shone and a smile of joy and satisfaction spread over it.

When the prayers were completed, the Zaddik said to his followers: "On this Day of Atonement, there was a big prosecution of the Jews in Heaven. It was as though a barrier of steel had been drawn between us and our Creator. Then, toward evening, just before the end of the Ne'ilah prayer, two women started talking together on matters concerning the holy day.

One woman said to the other: "I have every confidence that, with our prayers, we have attained a good and blessed year for all of Israel". "How can you be this confident?" her friend asked her. "How could it be otherwise?!" the first one responded, "had we been standing in front of a robber and had pleaded and wept so much before him - even he would have had pity on us".

The Rabbi paused for a moment and then added: The simple words spoken by that woman during the Ne'ilah prayer made such an impression in the upper worlds that the prosecution's case, which had been hanging over our brethren, the Children of Israel, throughout the holy day, was completely dismissed....

He shall make an atonement for the holy sanctuary, and he shall make an atonement for the Tent of Meeting, and for the altar, and he shall make an atonement for the priests, and for all the people of the congregation. (Lev. 16:33)

Repentance as Halakhah

Rabbi Avraham Yitzhak Kook was well known for his warm and heartfelt attitude towards people of all parties and streams. From time to time he would meet with the members of non-religious moshavim and kibbutzim and he would also return enchanted and enthused at the pioneering enterprise of the young people of Israel in the new "Return to Zion" movement.

A delegation of rabbis once came to Rabbi Kook and wished to complain that the Chief Rabbi was seen in the company of young people who did not observe the Torah and its religious mitzvot. Is it possible - one of the visiting rabbis challenged him - that the Land of Israel will be built and established by young men and women who deride the mitzvot of the Torah? Is this not literally tantamount to a desecration of what is sacred?

Certainly not, Rabbi Kook responded in his clear and enthusiastic voice. You can reach this conclusion yourselves! The holiest place in the Land of Israel is surely the Temple, and the holiest part of the Temple is without doubt the Holy of Holies. When the Temple was standing, nobody was allowed to enter the Holy of Holies except for the high priest who would go in there for ritual purposes just one single time a year - on the Day of Atonement. And even that he was allowed to do only after lengthy preparations and while wearing special clothes.

But while the Temple was being built, laborers and craftsmen from all strata of the people must surely have entered there, and they would not have been particularly outstanding in Torah or particularly fearful of Heaven. These many people came to the holy site at all times and at all hours, until the construction work was completed. And so it is with these young pioneers. They are building our land and it is holy work that they are doing. We should, therefore, treat them with an extra portion of affection, and be both critical and friendly at the same time.

You shall therefore keep My laws, and My judgments, by the pursuit of which you shall live; I am Adonai. (Lev. 18:5)

The reasons behind the commandments

The commandments of the Torah can be divided into two parts: the laws - those mitzvot whose reasons are obvious to everyone (such as mitzvot between people); and the statutes - those mitzvot whose reasons are unknown to us (such as the laws of Kashrut).

Rabbi Elazar ben Azariah said: A person should not say: I do not want to eat pork ... rather: I want to eat pork, but what can I do when my Creator has decreed that I should not? (Torat Kohanim, Kedoshim).

We believe that the mitzvot were given to people for their own good and so it makes no difference at all whether we know the reason and explanation of each and every mitzvah or not. On the contrary, by observing those mitzvot whose reasons are not known to us, we only prove our true faith.

Rav said: The mitzvot were only given in order to purify human beings. Does the Holy Blessed One really care if one person slaughters an animal from the front of the neck and someone else from the back of the neck? Or, does the Holy One really care if one person eats impure animals and another eats pure animals? Hence: The mitzvot were only given in order to purify human beings. (Tanhuma, Shmini)

Elsewhere the Midrash offers another reason for the mystery: "The Holy Blessed One did not disclose to Israel the rewards of the mitzvot in the Torah. Had God done so, they would have seen which mitzvah came with a large reward and would have kept it, and which mitzvah came with a small reward, and they would not have kept it. The end result would have been that part of the Torah would have been revoked. (Pesiqta Rabbati 23)

Parashat Kedoshim

Adonai spoke to Moshe, saying: Speak to all the congregation of the Children of Israel, and say to them: You shall be holy; for I Adonai your God am holy. (Lev. 19:1-2)

Sanctity of Life

There are few portions whose name paraphrases their general content, as does this portion called Kedoshim (holy). It opens with a command of holiness: "You shall be holy; for I Adonai your God am holy". It reiterates the imperative of holiness in the middle of the portion: "Sanctify yourselves therefore, and be holy; for I am Adonai your God" (Lev. 20:7), and, at the end of the portion, comes the command: "And you shall be holy to Me; for I Adonai am holy" (Lev. 20:26).

This teaches us that all the matters mentioned in the portion are matters of holiness and that they embrace all areas of life: between people and their parents, between people and their Creator, between people and their neighbors, between people and creation, between Israel and its land, between the body and soul of a person, between a man and a woman, between impurity and cleanliness - all spheres of life receive a refill of holiness. Life flows through all channels of the life of individuals and society and is sanctified by intention and direction, accord and restriction and the designation of a noble purpose for all of life and its deeds.

The portion of Kedoshim contains fifty positive ("you shall") and negative ("you shall not") commandments. Most of these concern interpersonal relationships. From this, we may conclude that a person cannot be "holy" just by observing the mitzvot between a person and God. We have learned that the Day of Atonement, for all its sanctity and grandeur, does not atone for offences committed by one person against another, in which the former harmed the person, property or honor of the other, until peace is made between them. The same idea applies in connection with the portion Kedoshim. The mitzvot between a person and God prepare people for holiness and purity; those between people consolidate and reinforce the holiness, and make it fundamental and impregnable. Without these, it would be impossible to attain a life of holiness either during the days of the year or on the Day of Atonement.

You shall not steal, nor deal falsely, nor lie one to another. (Lev. 19:11)

Incessant liar

The liar - the Magid of Helem used to say - is worse than the thief and the robber. The thief steals by night but does not steal during the day, because in the daylight hours he is afraid. The robber steals by day and steals by night, but only from individuals, not from the public, because he is afraid of the public. The liar, however, lies by day and by night, to individuals and to the public ...

Thus they said

Rabbi Nahman of Bratzlav said: There is only one truth. Many truths are a lie.

Rabbi Menahem Mendel of Kotzk used to say: Everything in the world can be imitated, except for the truth.

There is room for doubt

A scholarly, brilliant, and God-fearing Shohet (ritual slaughterer) once came to Rabbi Yisrael of Salant and expressed his desire to leave his profession because he was worried at the great responsibility it entailed, and at the possibility of inadvertently allowing something not kosher to be sold to the community.

"What are you thinking of doing instead?" Rabbi Yisrael asked him. "I will open a shop and engage in trade". the shohet answered. Rabbi Yisrael was surprised and said: "You are worried at the responsibility of ritual slaughter, which has only one negative mitzvah, that of allowing something not kosher. Yet, engaging in trade involves heeding many warnings and prohibitions: 'Do not rob', 'Do not exploit', 'Do not defraud', 'Do not steal', 'Do not deal falsely', 'Do not lie' as well as many other mitzvot, both positive and negative, entailed in weights and measures and so on. Now, that is something to be worried about ...".

The wages of a laborer shall not remain with you until morning. (Lev. 19:13)

Wages

The wife of Rabbi Sussya of Anipol, who was very poor, begged to have a new dress made for her. Rabbi Sussya could not resist her pleadings, so he borrowed some money and bought for her some cloth for a dress, and the wife gave the cloth to the tailor. Some time later, he again noticed that his wife looked sad. He asked: What is the meaning of this?

His wife then told him the following: She had indeed given the cloth to the tailor and he had sewn a dress for her as required. When the tailor brought the dress to her, however, she saw that his face was gloomy and she heard his broken-hearted sighs. So she asked him: What is this heartbreak about, and why?

The tailor answered her: I see this fine dress and I recall the anguish brought by it to my daughter. Some time ago, my daughter became engaged and the date of the wedding was approaching. The groom saw that his about-to-be father-in-law was sewing a fine-looking dress and he was sure that I was making it for my daughter. When he learned that it was not so, he became very angry and he no longer looks favorably on me or on my daughter. My daughter saw this and her heart is broken. She is afraid that he might cancel the betrothal. And do I have a heart of stone? The pain of my daughter is my pain also and the whole world is uncomfortable for me.

When I heard that, I immediately said to the tailor: Here, I give the dress to you as a present for your daughter, the bride. I am not a bride about to enter the wedding canopy and my Sussya will not divorce me if I do not have a fine dress ... The tailor took the dress and left. I did a good deed, but see how pitiful I am, wearing worn-out clothes as always. I am embarrassed to be seen among people.

Rabbi Sussya said to her: Forget about embarrassment. Righteous people have nothing to be embarrassed about. You should be happy and pleased that you were able to overcome your urge to wear a beautiful dress and preferred to give it as a gift to that poor bride. But, tell me, have you paid the tailor his wage?

His wife looked at him in astonishment and asked: Is it not enough that I gave the dress to the tailor? Do I also have to pay him? Certainly, answered Rabbi Sussya, that poor tailor labored for you for a whole week, just for you, in order to earn a wage. He relied on the income from this dress to provide for his household for the whole week. If you do not pay him, then you are depriving him of his earnings. The gift is one thing. His wage is something else entirely.

In righteousness shall you judge your neighbor. (Lev. 19:15)

When in Rome ...

We read in the Midrash: "Alexander of Macedonia went to visit the king of Katzia, who showed him much silver and gold. Alexander said to him: I did not come here to see your silver and your gold, but to see your leaders and your laws. While they were sitting there, two men came in to have their case adjudicated by the king. One said: I purchased a ruin from this man and dug it out and found a treasure underneath it. I said to him: Take your treasure. I bought a ruin from you; I did not buy a treasure. The second man said: Just as you are afraid of the punishment for robbery, so am I. I sold you a ruin with everything in it, from the bottom of the earth to the top of the sky.

The king summoned one of them and said to him: Do you have a son? Yes, he said. He summoned the other and asked him: Do you have a daughter? Yes, he said. Then the king ruled: Let the two of them marry and the treasure shall be theirs. Alexander expressed his surprise and the king asked him: Did I then not adjudicate well? Yes, you did, he replied. Then the king of Katzia asked him: Had this case come before you in your country, how would you have handled it? Alexander replied: I would have cut off the head of this one and of that one, and the treasure would have been confiscated by the royal treasury!

The king of Katzia asked him: Does the sun shine for you? Yes, he replied. Does rain fall on you? Yes, he replied. The king was silent for a while, then asked: Do you perchance have cattle in your country? Yes, replied Alexander. Then, said the king to him, it is by the merit of the cattle that the sun shines for you and that the rain falls on you. (Tanhuma, Emor)

You shall not spread gossip among your people. (Lev. 19:16)

The prohibition applies to the individual and to the general public

What is the meaning of 'among your people'? The Baal Shem Tov said: This is to tell you that you should not say derisive and slanderous things about the Jewish People as a whole. As a rule, even great people are careful and guard their tongues from slandering individuals, but they often permit themselves to slander a particular group of people. That is why it is said: "You shall not spread gossip among your people". "Your people" includes Israel, the whole of Israel, and any part of the whole - and one must not speak of them badly or slanderously nor relate anything to their detriment.

Do not stand by the blood of your neighbor. (Lev. 19:16)

Saving souls

To desert a person at a time of danger, to leave such a person alone, is tantamount to killing him. Rambam wrote: Anyone who can save [another] but does not do so transgresses against 'Do not stand by the blood of your neighbor'. Anyone who sees another drowning in the sea, or being attacked by bandits or by a wild animal, and could save him but does not do so ... violates what is written in the Torah: 'Do not stand by the blood of your neighbor'. (Mishneh Torah, Hilkhot Rotzeah, 1:14)

You shall not avenge, nor bear any grudge against the children of your people. (Lev. 19:18)

Inspects kidneys and heart

What is 'avenging' and what is 'bearing a grudge'?

Rashi writes: If one person says to another: 'Lend me your sickle,' but the second person replies: 'No!' Then, the next day, the second person says to the first: 'Lend me your hatchet,' but the first person says: 'No, I am not going to lend it to you just as you would not lend me your sickle.' - that is avenging.

What is 'bearing a grudge'? If one person says to another: 'Lend me your hatchet,' but the second person replies: 'No!' Then, the next day, the second person says to the first: 'Lend me your sickle,' so the first person says: 'Here it is; I am not like you who would not lend a hatchet to me.' - this is called bearing a grudge, retaining hostility in the heart even though no avenging action is actually undertaken.

We learn from this that one who retains hostility, even while lending what is asked for, even while repaying bad with good, nevertheless violates a negative commandment of the Torah just as surely as the person who takes actual revenge!

When you come into the land, you shall plant all kinds of trees for food. (Lev. 19:23)

The importance of planting trees in the Holy Land

What were the Children of Israel commanded to do as they entered the Land? - "You shall plant all kinds of trees for food"! This is the only way that one can bond with one's homeland with unbreakable ties of love.

Our sages taught: "The Holy Blessed One said to Israel: Although you will find the Land of Israel replete with all that is good, you should not say "We will sit and not plant". Rather be prudent and plant, as it is said: "You shall plant all kinds of trees for food". Let no man say: "I am old and do not have many years left to live. Why should I wear myself out? When you came into the Land, you found trees which others had planted. You, too, must plant for your children" (Tanhuma Kedoshim 5).

In the Wilderness, our ancestors lived a life of idleness: the manna came down to them from Heaven and water flowed from the rock, providing all their needs. Things changed the moment they entered the Land. The time for miracles was over. The time for hard, exhausting work began. Our sages explained this point with the following parable: A mother hen, when her chicks are small and thin she gathers them together and places them under her wings and keeps. them warm. She digs and pecks before them in the refuse. But, once they have grown up, if one of them wishes to approach her, she pecks at it, as though saying to it: "Go and dig in the refuse for yourself". So it was with Israel. When they were in the Wilderness, the manna descended and the well flowed and the quail was aplenty, the clouds of glory surrounded them and the pillar traveled before them. But once they had entered the Land, Moshe said to them: "Let each and every one of you take a hoe - go out and plant". (Lev. Rabbah 25)

Sanctify yourselves, therefore, and be holy. (Lev. 20:7)

A Multifold Holiness

It is not difficult for the angels to be holy because they live in an atmosphere of holiness and are carried aloft by constant holiness. For a person to be holy, however, is no easy matter. Much devotion is required to reach this level.

Rabbi Menahem Mendel of Kotzk explained the verse: "And you shall be men of holiness to Me" (Ex. 32:30) as: You shall be holy people to Me, in that you shall sanctify your mortal deeds, for this is the main holiness required of humanity. The Master of the Universe has no shortage of angels but holy people are in short supply and our world has need of them. Thus: "Sanctify yourselves, therefore, and be holy" - a double sanctity and also a double reward.

Parashat Emor

Whosoever he be ... that brings an offering, whether it be any of their vows, or any of their freewill-offerings. (Lev. 22:18)

All are Permitted

The Sages deduced that the Hebrew word "Ish" (a man) included non-Jews who made vows and freewill-offerings like the People of Israel. (Nazir 65a)

Rabbi Shimshon Raphael Hirsch wrote: The Book of lev. begins with "When any of you brings an offering unto Adonai" (Lev. 1:2). This teaches us that every person - not just one of the Children of Israel - is permitted to bring offerings if one has a spiritual need to do so.

So it happens that, with this one word, our verse expresses a great idea - which Isaiah's prophesy uses an entire verse to express: Even them [the aliens] will I bring to My holy mountain, and make them joyful in My house of prayer; Their burnt offerings and their sacrifices shall be acceptable upon My altar; For My house shall be called a house of prayer for all peoples (Isaiah 56:7).

No animal from the herd or the flock shall be slaughtered on the same day with its young. (Lev. 22:25)

Cruelty to animals

Rambam wrote: "It is forbidden to slaughter it and its young on the same day - one should be careful not to slaughter both of them, that the mother should not see its young being killed. For this would be a great cruelty to animals. There is no difference between the pain felt by people and that felt by animals in this matter, because a mother's love and her pity for her young is not a matter of intelligence but of the instinct which most animals have, as do human beings" (Guide for the Perplexed, Part 3).

We also read in the Talmud: The sufferings of Rabbi were caused by a certain incident, and departed likewise. 'They were caused by a certain incident' - What was it? A calf was being taken to the slaughter. It broke away, hid his head under Rabbi's skirts, and cried in terror, as though saying: 'Save me!' Rabbi said to it: 'Go, for this were you created.' Thereupon they said [in Heaven]: 'Since he has no pity, let suffering come to him.'

'And departed likewise' - How so? One day Rabbi's maidservant was sweeping the house; seeing some young weasels lying there, she made to sweep them away. 'Let them be,' said he to her; 'It is written, 'and his tender mercies are over all his works.' (Ps. 145:9). Thereupon they said [in Heaven]: 'Since he is compassionate, let us be compassionate to him.' And he was relieved of his sufferings. (Baba Metzia 85a)

You shall not profane My holy name, that I may be sanctified among the Children of Israel - I, Adonai, who sanctify you. (Lev. 22:32)

Sanctification of the Name

Both last week's portion and this week's portion deal with laws, rulings and mitzvot in all spheres of life: that of the individual and that of the community, family and sexual life, work life and agriculture, the relationships. between people (rich and poor, borrower and lender, purchaser and vendor, lessee and lessor), the relationship of people to the fauna and flora, man's relationship to God and the various ways of worship, and all the ways that lead a person to the supreme objective of Judaism, which is contained in the short imperative: "You shall not profane My holy name, that I may be sanctified among the Children of Israel".

The sanctity that the Torah advocates is not religious but moral. If a person lives a life of righteousness and integrity, in love and humility, so that all who see will praise this person and want to follow the same path - such a person is one who sanctifies God's name. A person like that is a sort of lighthouse for all those who have trouble finding the right path in the sea of life. The image of such a person illuminates and warms everyone who are in the vicinity.

These are the set times of Adonai, the sacred occasions which you shall celebrate, each at its appointed time. In the first month, on the fourteenth day of the month, at twilight, there shall be a passover offering to Adonai. (Lev. 23:4-5)

Hospitality of a great person in Israel

Rabbi Yosef Haim Sonenfeld was one of the great rabbis at the end of the 19th. Century. Most of his life he lived in a small apartment in Old Jerusalem and his modest home was wide open to passers-by.

One Passover eve, some tourists came to the Rabbi's home. The leader of the group said to the Rabbi, with an apologetic tone: 'Our Teacher, our Rabbi! We arrived in the country only this morning and we are looking for a suitable place to make the Passover Seder as required. Could we perhaps. sit at the Rabbi's table for Seder Night?'

'What a question?!' responded Rabbi Yosef Haim in a cordial tone. 'All of you will this night be welcome guests in my home'.

'But Rabbi', the guest exclaimed, 'we do not want to cause you any special financial expenditure on our account. We will pay you generously for everything'. And, as he spoke, he pulled out a wad of bills from his wallet and offered it to the Rabbi.

Rabbi Yosef Haim took the bundle of bills from the man and immediately called to his wife and said to her, in the presence of the guests: 'Take this money, which I have just received from the guests who will be with us this evening, and buy with this money all that you need for conducting the Seder'.

The satisfied guests departed from the Rabbi's home. At the Seder, they ate and drank from the Rabbi Yosef Haim's table as it should be. The next day, too, they ate the festival meal at the Rabbi's table. During the intermediate days of the Festival, Rabbi Yosef Haim came to where the guests were staying and placed before them the money he had received from them on the eve of the Festival. Seeing the astonishment on the faces of the tourists, the Rabbi explained: Am I suspect in your eyes for having taken, Heaven forbid, a reward for observing the mitzvah of hospitality!?

'But then why did the Rabbi take the money on the eve of the Festival?' asked one of the group. 'I wanted you to enjoy my full and pleasant table as one eating and drinking of his own', replied Rabbi Yosef Haim with a smile.

You shall take on the first day the fruit of good trees, branches of palm trees, and boughs of thick trees, and willows of the brook. (Lev. 23:40)

The Reward for Mitzvoth

The Vilna Gaon, who used to content himself with the most meager portions from one Shabbat eve to the next, was ready and willing to sell not only the cloak off his back but also his place in the next world for the sake of strict observation of the mitzvot.

One year, during a draught, there were no etrogs to be found. Messengers were sent from Vilna to towns on the Italian coast where they could normally find etrogs – but they returned empty handed. This caused a stir in town: A community with no etrog? The city's elders assembled together at a meeting and decided: As far as the community was concerned, what would be would be. But the Gaon could not be left without an etrog. They sent a special messenger out and ordered him to find and bring one etrog for the Vilna Gaon even if it cost a great deal of money. The messenger set out and traveled from country to country, exerted himself and exhausted himself, - but did not find one. On his journey home, he happened upon an inn, and found that the innkeeper had a beautiful etrog of the finest quality. He implored the man to sell him his etrog, but the innkeeper refused. He offered him a great deal of money, but the man was adamant in his refusal. The messenger decided to tell him that the etrog was required for the Vilna Gaon.

The innkeeper heard his words and said: "For the Vilna Gaon, I am prepared to give him my etrog for nothing, but on condition that the Gaon's portion in the next world for the mitzvah of the etrog this year will be given to me alone".

The messenger began to bargain with him, he offered him an enormous amount for the etrog, but the innkeeper was adamant. He also had to perform the mitzvah of the etrog, and if he gave up the mitzvah for the Gaon, then the Gaon also had to give up and agree that this mitzvah of the etrog would be in his name.

It was hard for the messenger to come back to Vilna without the etrog, so he agreed to these terms.

When he returned to Vilna holding the etrog, the heads of the community envied him for having been the messenger for this mitzvah-to find an etrog of the finest quality for the Gaon. But the messenger himself was troubled. The Gaon would have to know about the condition before he made the blessing over the etrog, and how was he going to brace himself before the holy Gaon and tell him that he had bargained with his portion in the next world?

On the eve of the Festival, he thrust himself into the Gaon's room and told him the whole story. The Gaon listen and with a beaming face told him: We do not know the reward for a mitzvah. But it is clear to me that it is worth giving away all of my portion in the next world if only I can perform the mitzvah of the etrog according to halakhah.

And you shall bind them together

'The fruit of the citrus' tree symbolizes Israel: Just as this etrog has taste as well as fragrance, so Israel have among them such as possess learning and good deeds. 'Branches of palm trees' also applies to Israel: Just as the palm tree has taste but no fragrance, so Israel have among them such as possess learning but no good deeds. 'Boughs of thick trees' also symbolizes Israel: Just as this myrtle has fragrance but no taste, so Israel have among them men who possess good deeds but have no learning. 'And willows of the brook' also applies to Israel: Just as the willow has no taste and no fragrance, so Israel have among them such as possess neither learning nor good deeds. What, then, does the Holy Blessed One, do to them? To destroy them is impossible! But, says the Holy One, let them all be tied together in one band and they will atone for one another. (Lev. Rabbah 30:12)

Shoemakers' Crown

When the Baal Shem Tov explained Simhat Torah to his followers for the first time, he told them as follows: It is the custom of Jews to lose much of Simhat Torah in sleep. On the Sabbath and on festivals, it is usual to sleep longer. This is even more so on the Simhat Torah festival, when one is tired after dancing the "hakafot" with the Torah scrolls held aloft and the eating the festival meal. The angels have no work. They rise early on Simhat Torah as every other day, but, without the souls of human beings, they cannot worship the Creator.

So what do they do? They go to the Garden of Eden and see there many things but do not understand how they got there, such as heels, soles and laces of shoes, even whole sandals. They are surprised and ask: What are these things doing here? We thought that in the Garden of Eden one would find a tzitzit, tefillin, even a torn tallit - but sandals?

So they to and ask the angel Michael. And Michael says to them: These articles came here from the dancing of Jews with Torah scrolls in their hands. Just as there is an angel in Heaven who makes crowns for his Maker from the prayers of Jews, so I make a crown from the soles and the shoes which were worn out on the feet of Jews dancing at the Simhaht Torah festival, rejoicing in the joy of their Torah. (Lev. Rabbah 25)

The Blessing of Enjoyment

Rabbi Mordekhai of Neskhiz was very poor and every day of the year he tried to ration his meager meal so that he could save each and every prutah to buy an etrog of the finest quality for his Sukkoth.

One year, the day after Rosh Hashanah, he was traveling to Brody to buy an etrog with the ten sheqalim that he had saved up. On the way, he saw a Jew standing and crying. Rabbi Mordekhai approached him and asked him why he was crying. The Jew replied: "I come from the next town, and I am a water carrier. I had a wagon and a horse and barrels to bring water from the well, which is in the field, to our town, and with this I used to eke out a living for the members of my household. But misfortune has struck. On my way to town, my horse fell and died, and here I stand and I cannot move from here. How am I going to provide a living for my family?

Rabbi Mordekhai took out his wad of money and gave it to the water carrier.

Rabbi Mordekhai returned to his home with no money and no etrog, but he happily prayed:

"Thank you, Blessed God, for finding me an etrog that cannot be equaled in its fine quality. This year it will not be my portion with all my fellow Jews in the town. Some will celebrate with a good etrog and some with an etrog of the finest quality, and I shall celebrate God with the horse - I shall make the blessing over the horse ...".

Parashat Behar

You shall count for yourself seven shabbatot of years, seven times seven years; and the space of the seven shabbatot of years shall be for you forty-nine years. (Lev. 25:8)

Self-scrutiny

Why this long-windedness? Details, calculations and a general total? The Supreme Wisdom here gives an intimation with advice to each person to undertake a soul-searching of all the days and years of one's life.

A parable is told of a poor man who used to go begging from door to door. Once, he journeyed to a different city, where he was not known, and there bragged about being rich. But there was a person there from his own city who knew him, and proved to him the folly of his ways. He addressed him as follows: You have always been in the habit of collecting donations penny by penny and of filling your pockets with small coins. You think you have much and that you are rich. Try and exchange the pennies for larger coins, for silver dinars, and the total you will have will come to a very small amount and you will not be thought of as rich.

So it is with a person who does the reckoning of his days and years in this world. Such a person reaches seventy or eighty years and begins to think that humans are citizens and permanent residents in this world. However, if such a person were to count in units of shmittah years, the total will be very small, just ten or eleven. Then a truer picture will emerge. Such a person is a lodger here rather than a permanent resident and must realize how weak and insubstantial human life is. This precisely is the intention of the poet: "Adonai, let me know my end, and the measure of my days, what it is; that I may know how frail I am" (Ps. 39). The psalmist is not asking in order to know what a person has but to appreciate what a person does not have - "that I may know how frail I am".

Consider this: the Jewish People does not count as do other peoples and our reckoning is not as theirs. The norm in this world is that a person is assessed according to wealth, or valued according to material possessions. What do people say about such a person? - "So-and-so is worth so much". Time is also viewed by them as money, as change. The Children of Israel, however, are not like that. Their accounting is made in terms of righteousness and their reckoning is one of integrity. A person is assessed in terms of Torah, mitzvot and good deeds.

And the Jewish People know that time is of the highest worth. It cannot be weighed against money nor can it be compared to gold. That is why we calculate the years, keep a tally of the weeks and count the days and hours. Years are calculated in terms of jubilees and shmittah years, these being years in which there are no things and acquisitions, no measuring of land and negotiations over everything, years in which all are equal, whether miserable paupers or the rich and wealthy. Weeks are counted from Passover to the Revelation on Mount Sinai, to the Giving of the Torah, on the Festival of Shavuot. And days are counted to the coming of the Messiah for "I wait daily for his coming" (Rambam' Thirteen Principles of Faith). And hours, too, are counted. Although the world to come is something good, Torah and good deeds in this world are better, as we have learned in our Mishnah: "More beautiful is one hour spent in repentance and good deeds in this world, than all the life of the world to come" (Pirke Avot 4:17).

And as to the verse in this week's portion: "And you shall count for yourself ...". - for yourself, for your benefit and for your good. A person does not count money and material possessions since, in the end, all success in these matters is left to others and nothing is taken from the whole of material existence except for the calculation of the mitzvot and good deeds which a person counts and accrues.

You shall return every man to his possession, and you shall return every man to his family. (Lev. 25:10)

"And he shall turn ... the heart of the children to their father" (Mal 3:24)

Rabbi Shmuel Mohilever, one of the founders of religious Zionism, once said at a public gathering in Bialystok: "The harsh and lengthy exile to which Israel is subject shatters family cohesiveness and breaks it apart. These times cause children to leave their parental homes and abandon their ancestral heritage. With our return to the Land of Israel, however, and with our re-integration into the heritage of our ancestors, we are assured that children will return not just to their Land but also to the heritage of their forbearers. This is intimated in the verse: "you shall return every man to his possession, and you shall return every man to his family". With our return to our ancestral land and to our former possession, we shall also return to our families and to the spiritual heritage of our forbearers.

You shall not wrong one another. (Lev. 25:14)

Financial Wrong and Verbal Wrong

Rashi explained that this verse refers to financial wrongs, while the identical verse 17 refers to verbal wrongs. In other words, one should not vex. or annoy one's friend, and one should not offer advice that is not fitting simply because it is advice that advice-giver finds useful.

How do we know from the Torah that verse 14 refers to financial wrongs and verse 17 refers to verbal wrongs?

This is how: In verse 14 it says, literally, do not wrong your "brother". Siblings know each other very well. They know each others' verbal mannerisms and cannot be deceived with words alone. In verse 17, when it says "You shall not harm your friend", the Torah is warning about verbal harm, since one does not know one's neighbor as well, and it is very possible to deceive a person with flattery and sweet talk.

Ultimately this is a matter of the heart, that one should not think one thing and say another thing.

Losing Face

Rabbi Elazar of Mitz wrote in his "Book of the Pious": Just as there is a Verbal Wrong (that is, saying something that might cause pain or anguish to another), so there is wrong with the Evil Eye, when one casts a mean glance toward a friend. Even though one does not harm another with these deeds or words, but only with intangible hard-heartedness and selfishness, it is forbidden to act this way, because this is included in the prohibition against bringing harm to another person.

Furthermore, he wrote, Verbal Harm, where one abuses or insults another, is worse than Financial Harm because Financial Harm touches only the pocket, and it is possible to bring reparation, while a Verbal Harm brings pain to the heart of another, which is not possible to repair. Even if one tries to appease the other, how can one cure a broken heart?

You shall live on the land in security. The land shall yield its fruit...and you shall live upon in security. (Lev. 25: 18-19)

A Double Promise

Why does the phrase "in security" appear twice? The Ketav Sofer explained that there are two distinct dangers that loom over a nation. When a nation is in crisis, and faces hunger and deficiency, it often also faces the threat of internal turmoil and rebellion, since bitterness and pain are rampant among the people. On the other hand, when there is plenty, and harmony rules, there is external danger – from its neighbors who become jealous, and tempted to conquer a land that is blessed with such wealth.

This is therefore the meaning of the double promise: First "And you shall dwell upon the land and the land shall yield its fruit, and you shall eat your fill" - that there will be abundance, and of course there will be peace and quiet; and second, at the same time, even though the land will excel in abundance and wealth, there will be no sign of danger from their neighbors abroad, "And you shall dwell upon it in security".

If your brother has become poor, and his means fail with you; then you shall relieve him; though he may be a stranger, or a sojourner; that he may live with you. (Lev. 25:35)

Stretch Out Your Arm

To what can we compare this? To a burden on a donkey. If the package is sitting on the back of the donkey, one person can steady it. However, if it falls to the ground, even five people cannot lift it up. The difference between these two situations is that when the package is just beginning to fall, it only requires a steady hand to straighten in out so that it will regain its stability. This is not the case when it has already fallen down, in which case it requires a huge effort to lift it up. So Scripture warns us not to wait until a poor person who is struggling falls down to the ground. If that happens it will be very difficult to lift this person back to a position of stability.

Rabbi Moshe ben Hayyim Alshikh points out that most of the verses in the first part of chapter 25 contain plural verbs. But when the Torah comes to teach about giving assistance and support to the poor, the language shifts to the singular: "If your kinsman is in straits...". When a homeless poor person turns to the community for help, the response is all too often: "Better that you should turn to such-and-such, who is very rich and can help you more than I can". This is why the Torah turns to each and every Jew and demands: It is your personal obligation to help your fellow Jew, and you may never be exempt from giving help to the needy by shifting the responsibility to someone else.

Rabbi Shlomo Makerlin taught: In order to help someone, one must be willing to go into the mud up to one's neck. If you want to raise someone who is sunk in the mud, you have to go down into the mud and push from there. You cannot pull such a person up from above.

The Reward of Mitzvot

The story is told of a Hasid and his righteous wife who lost their wealth. He became a day laborer.

Once, as he was plowing in the field, he met Eliyahu, of blessed memory, in the guise of an Arab. Eliyahu said to the Hasid: You have six good years. Do you want them now, or at the end of your life? The Hasid replied: You are a sorcerer. I have no answer for you. Just leave me in peace. Eliyahu returned to him three times. On the third occasion, the Hasid told him, "I will go and consult with my wife".

He went to his wife and told her: A certain man came to me and pestered me three times, and posed this question: You have six years. When do you want them – now or at the end of your life? He asked her: What do you think? She replied: Take them now. So the Hasid went and said to Eliyahu – Bring the good years to me now. Eliyahu said to him: Go home right now, and by the time you reach the gates of your house you will see a blessing on your home. When he arrived home his sons were digging through the dirt, and discovered enough coins to support the family for six years. They called to their mother and told her the good news. By the time the Hasid came home, his wife told him what had happened. Immediately the Hasid offered thanks to God and was very pleased.

What did the righteous wife then do? She said to her husband, since the Blessed Holy One has showered us with kindness, and has bestowed upon food for six years, let us occupy ourselves with Gemilut Hasadim during these years. Thus she did. Everything she gave, day by day, she told her youngest son to write it down. He did so.

At the end of six years Eliyahu came, of blessed memory, and said to the Hasid: "The time has come for me to take back what I gave you. Said the Hasid to Eliyahu: When I took it, I only took it on my wife's advice. So, when I return it, I must return it with my wife's consent. He went to his wife and said to her: The old man has returned to take back what is his. She said to him: Go tell him: If you find people more faithful than we, give your treasure to them. The Blessed Holy One agreed with them, and saw how much kindness they bestowed upon so many, and added even more blessings upon them.

Generous Giving

Giving alms to the poor and to those struck by fate is an elementary human commandment. It is our duty to help everyone who is in distress and to ease their suffering.

Our sages greatly praised those who perform charitable deeds for their fellows and who give generous alms to the poor. Throughout the generations and in all places of exile, the Jewish People has been noted for establishing public welfare institutions, the purpose of which was to act charitably toward those in need.

Those who depend on charity are miserable souls, and we are told to be particularly cautious when giving them charity. It is preferable for a person not to give charity at all rather than to give it in a way that insults the recipient. We should try to help the poor generously and wholeheartedly so that the recipient of the aid will not be hurt or embarrassed.

The Talmud relates the following story: Mar 'Ukba had a poor man in his neighborhood into whose door-socket he used to throw four zuz every day. One day the poor man thought: 'I will see who does me this kindness'. On that day Mar 'Ukba was delayed at the house of study and his wife [who, because of the late hour had gone to meet him] went with him. As soon as the poor man saw them approaching the doorway he went out after them, but they fled from him and ran into a swept furnace (a large oven from which the hot coals had just been removed). Mar 'Ukba's feet were burned. His wife said to him: Put your feet over mine. Mar 'Ukba was hurt [that his wife was miraculously immune from the heat]. She said to him: I give Tzedakah from inside our home, and thus provide more immediate pleasure to the poor [whereas when money is given, pleasure is delayed]. And what was the reason for all that? (Why did Mar 'Ukba and his wife run into the hot furnace?) - Because the sages said: 'It is better to throw one's self into a fiery furnace than to publicly put someone to shame' (Ketubot 67b).

Charitable Giving is an Investment for the Future

"Our Rabbis taught: King Monobaz (the son of Queen Helena, from a royal family which converted to Judaism, immigrated to the Land of

Israel and helped the Jews in the great war against the Romans) gave away all his own treasure and the treasures of his ancestors in drought and famine years. His brothers and his father's household came and accused him, 'Your fathers saved money and added to their family's treasures, and you are squandering them?!'

He replied: 'My fathers stored things in a place which can be tampered with (from which it is possible to take, to steal), but I have stored them in a place which cannot be tampered with. My fathers stored something which produces no fruits, but I have stored something which does produce fruits (for the fruits of charity are in this world while the principal remains for the world to come.) My fathers gathered treasures of money, but I have gathered treasures of souls. My fathers gathered for their heirs and I have gathered for myself. My fathers gathered for this world, but I have gathered for the future world" (Bava Batra 11a).

Everyone is obliged to give charity

By nature, a person does not tend to disburse his money to the poor, and so it is said that one needs spiritual training for the act of charity, just as a person needs physical training for the body. When a person first starts a course of physical training, each and every exercise is difficult but they gradually make the body more flexible and strengthen the muscles. It is the same with spiritual training. A person has to become accustomed to giving charity from time to time and these "exercises" will, in the end, train the soul so that it will always be ready for acts of charity and loving-kindness.

Since everyone has to become accustomed to performing good deeds, the poor person is not exempted from the mitzvah of charity. The rule has already been laid down: "Even a poor person who subsists on charity should give charity" (Gittin 7b). If this were not so, then, as the years pass, the poor person's heart could turn to stone. Thus, the poor person is also required to be kind to others and, helping others spiritually if not materially. Rabbi Levi said: If you have nothing to give the poor [console them with kind words] and say: 'My soul goes out to you because I have nothing to give you'. (Lev. Rabbah 34:15)

234

Parashat Behukotai

If you walk in My laws and keep My commandments and do them. (Lev. 26:3)

"And you shall study it day and night" (Joshua 1:8)

Rashi comments: "If you walk in My laws" - one could think that this refers to fulfillment of the commandments, but the verse continues "and keep My commandments". How, then, can one explain "If you walk in My laws"? - that you should laboriously study the Torah.

The story is told of a certain student who complained to the Hafetz Hayyim, saying: Rabbi, for years now I have toiled in the study of Torah and I have not yet attained its goal of seeing something good, of properly understanding a page of Gemara with commentaries. That being so, how am I going to end up?

Student! - the Hafetz Hayyim answered him - Where did the Holy Blessed One command us to be geniuses? All we were commanded was: "And you shall study it day and night" - "that you should laboriously study the Torah". We have to work at it whether we become scholars or not.

Furthermore, what is the meaning of the word "scholar" (lamdan)? The reference is not to someone who knows how to study but to one who actually sits and studies. In the same way, a thief is one who actually steals, not one who is proficient in the laws of stealing ...

The "Hafetz Hayyim" further explained: the main "walking" in the laws of the Torah is the labor, and that is what we were commanded to do. In this way, one can also understand what it says in the Talmud, the words we say at the conclusion of the study of each tractate: "We labor and they labor, but we labor and receive a reward and they labor and do not receive a reward" (Berachot 28b). This would appear to need some sort of explanation. Have you ever seen a tailor sew a garment or a shoemaker make shoes without being paid for it? Is it possible that a man could work and labor in business or on behalf of his fellow, and not be recompensed?

This is how it is: The custom in the world is that if someone hires a laborer to sew a garment, or to make a pair of shoes, and the laborer toils at the job all day and all night and does not complete the sewing of the garment or the shoes, no payment will be forthcoming. For such a craftsperson to ask for payment would be foolish! The client wants the garment or the shoes and, even if the laborer toiled at it for a whole week, the client will not pay until the job is complete. The reward is not for the labor but for the finished product, and there is no value to labor without a result... .

But this is not the way things are with the study of Torah. We are commanded to labor and toil in the Torah. One who studies Torah is rewarded for the labor, even if the learning is unsuccessful. This is meaning of what is said in the Talmud: "We labor and receive a reward" even if only for just the labor, while "they labor and do not receive a reward" other than for a finished product.

Such is the way of Torah

Rabbi Israel Baal Shem Tov taught the following parable: A certain man entered a shop where confectionary and all sorts of sweetmeats were being sold. The shopkeeper allowed him to taste a little of everything without charge. When the man realized this, he was extraordinarily pleased with himself and thought: How fortunate I am that I can walk around a shop full of good things and take into my mouth of all the food.

After he had wondered around the shop and tasted a bit of everything, he repeated his steps. and began, a second time, to taste each and every one of the sweetmeats in the shop. Then the shopkeeper said to him: - I allowed you a first taste so that you could appreciate the nature of the foodstuffs and whether they suited your palate or not. You cannot, however, taste and then come around and taste again. A repeated tasting is eating, and for eating you have to pay.

The moral of the story is: Many people go down to the orchard of the Torah to learn good qualities. At first, the learning is easy and the Torah student immediately sees the light in it. "If one comes to be cleansed, one is helped" (Shabbat 104a). The student is allowed a taste. But if one wishes to go deep into the orchard of the Torah, one has to labor and toil extensively.

You shall dwell in your land safely. And I will give peace in the land. (Lev. 26:5-6)

It is a sign

"And I will give peace in the land" - It is said (Ps. 120:7): "I am for peace; but when I speak, they are for war". What is the meaning of the words "but when I speak"? Would it not have been sufficient to have said: "I am for peace but they are for war"?

Rabbi Shmuel Eliezer Taube of Lodz explained: True peace is when there is neither place nor need to explain the predilection and desire for peace, when it is something so obvious that there is no need to talk about it at all. But when it is necessary to deal with peace and to discuss it the whole time, when peace conferences are convened and leagues for peace are founded, when talk of peace is on everyone's tongue - this is a sign that their direction and their scheming are for war and that peace is endangered. This is the meaning of "I am for peace" - the peace sentiment is within me, in my nature, but "when I speak", when the atmosphere is replete with talk about peace, this is a sign that "they are for war".

Peace at home within

One could ask: Once Israel has been assured by the Almighty that they will dwell safely in their land, why did the Torah have to add: "And I will give peace in the land".? Is it possible to live securely in the Land of Israel without peace?

Jewish scholars explain: The Scriptural assurance "And I will give peace in the land" does not refer to achieving peace from the attacks of external enemies but to peace within, peace between all factions of the people, peace between one person and the next.

The sages in the Talmud commented: Why was the First Temple destroyed? Because of three things which prevailed there: idolatry, immorality (adultery) and bloodshed. But then why was the Second Temple destroyed, considering that in its time the people occupied themselves with Torah, mitzvot, and acts of charity? Because at that time, baseless hatred prevailed throughout the land. That teaches you that groundless hatred is considered as grave as the three sins of idolatry, immorality, and bloodshed together. (Yoma 9b).

Our sages further noted: "In the generation of [King] Saul there were many scholars but, nevertheless, they did not gain victory over their enemies. This is because there were informers among them and disputes. And then we find that in the generation of [King] Ahab they were all idolaters but, nevertheless, they gained victory over their enemies. This is because there were no informers among them but peace reigned in the camp of Israel. (Jerusalem Talmud, Peah, Chapter 1).

We find this same concept in the opening verses of the portion of Behukotai. The Holy Blessed One, says to the Children of Israel: "And I will give peace in the land" - I promise you that in the future peace will reign between one person and another of the Jewish People, and then, "Nor shall the sword go through your land. And you shall chase your enemies, and they shall fall before you by the sword" (Lev. 26:6-7).

I will walk among you and I will be your God and you shall be My people.
(Lev. 26:12)

Mutual Dependency

This week's Torah reading starts with the blessings the People of Israel can expect if they follow God's laws and keep the commandments. What is the nature of these blessings? Economic and military advantages! "You shall eat your fill of bread ... and you will pursue your enemies ... and you will live securely in your land". But the idealistic peak of the blessings is at their end: "And I will walk among you and I will be your God and you shall be My people".

This closeness to God is depicted in a more concrete fashion in a legend quoted in the Midrash: To what can the matter be likened? To a king who came to his tenant-farmer and the latter hid from him. The king said to the tenant: Why are you hiding from me? I am the same as you are. And so the Holy Blessed One, will walk among the righteous and the righteous will tremble before Him. And He will say to them: "Why do you tremble before Me? I am as one of you" (Yalqut Shimoni, Behukotai 26).

This legend expresses a daring opinion. Had it not been written, it would have been impossible to say it. According to this opinion, there is a mutual dependency between God and Israel. Just as the people is in need of the proximity of God, so, as it were, the Holy One also needs the proximity of the people. Were it not for Israel, God's existence would not be known in the heart of people, for the People of Israel, from the time of Avraham to our own generation, spreads the knowledge of God in the world.

Even then, when they are in the land of their enemies, I will not reject them and I will not spurn or destroy them. (Lev. 26:44)

Looking back

The following is recounted in the Zohar: Rabbi Hiya the Great went to visit the scholars of the Mishnah in order to learn from them. He went to Rabbi Shimon Bar Yohai and saw a screen there. Rabbi Hiya was surprised but said: I will listen to what he has to say from here [from behind the screen].

He heard him say: 'Make haste, my beloved, and be like a gazelle or a young deer' (Song of Songs 8:14) - all that Israel ever wanted of the Holy One is this, as Rabbi Shimon said: Israel's desire is that the Holy One not walk and not be distant but that God make haste like a gazelle or a young deer.

What is the reason? Said Rabbi Shimon: No animal in the world behaves as does the gazelle or the young deer. When it takes off, it goes a little way and then looks back to the place where it had come from. It always turns its head and looks back.

And so said Israel: Master of the Universe! If we are the cause for Your removing Yourself from among us, may it be Your will that You do so like the gazelle or young deer who runs off but turns back to look at the place it left. And this is as it is written: "And even then, when they are in the land of their enemies, I will not reject them and I will not spurn or destroy them'"..

Speak to the people of Israel, and say to them, If a man shall make a special vow to give to Adonai the estimated value of persons ... (Lev. 27:2)

What is a vow?

A vow is the term for a commitment, which a person takes on willingly, to take some action or to desist from doing something. This commitment stems from a religious feeling or comes from a personal need. There are two types of vows: vows of holiness - where a person undertakes to make a donation to the Temple (in our days to the synagogue), to give charity to the poor or for any other good purpose; and vows of denial - where a person is promising to avoid things that are permitted by law.

The people, it seems, were in the habit of making vows, particularly at times of trouble and tragedy. Our portion deals with the person who makes a special vow to dedicate property: livestock, houses, lands, slaves, children and even one's self. All the vows can be redeemed with cash, as is detailed in the portion.

A person making a vow is a sinner

Our sages, of blessed memory, expressed their opposition to vows, particularly to those of the second category. They said: "A person who vows is placing a collar (a chain of iron) on the neck" (Jerusalem Talmud, Nedarim 9:5). And so did Rav Dimi, the brother of Rav Safra, say: "Anyone who makes a vow, even one who keeps. it, is called a sinner" (Nedarim 77b). This is because it was feared that the person making the vow might not be able to keep it. What the Torah has forbidden should suffice a person and there should be no need for people to add further prohibitions to those in the Torah.

With respect to any of the vows which a person has taken on and later regrets doing so, the priest-scholar, the spiritual leader of the generation, can interpret the vow and its conditions and release the person from them. To this end, the leader has to find an "opening of regret", that is to say, to determine that, had the person making the vow known, at the time of making the vow, a certain thing which has only now become known, then no vow would have been made in the first place.

Breach of Vows

The punishment for one who breaches vows and promises is grave. It is related in the Midrash: It once happened to a certain young woman, who was good-looking and adorned with silver and gold, that she was going to her father's house but lost her way and found herself in an uninhabited area. Half the day had gone and she was thirsty when she noticed a well with a rope for a bucket hanging from it. She took hold of the rope and slid down it, After she had drunk of the water, she tried to climb back up but was unable to do so. She cried and shouted out. A young man passed by the well and heard her calling. He went over to the well and said to her: Are you a human or a spirit? She replied: I am a human being. He asked her: What is your nature? And she told him the whole story. He asked her: If I pull you up from the well, will you marry me? And she said that she would. He pulled her up and wanted to lie with her immediately. She asked him: From what people are you? And he said: From Israel and I am from such-and-such a place and I am a Cohen. She said: The Holy Blessed One chose you and sanctified you from all Israel and yet you seek to behave like an animal, without a ketubah and without a marriage ceremony? Follow me to the home of my parents, who are from such-and-such family, important and well connected Jews, and I will become betrothed to you. They pledged their betrothal to each other with an oath. She asked: Who will be the witness (to the oath)? A certain weasel was passing by near them and so she said: Let this weasel and this well be witnesses - and they both went their separate ways.

That young girl kept her vow and she refused everyone who wanted to marry her. When they started to pressure her to get married, she began to behave as though sick with epilepsy and she would tear her clothes and those of anyone who touched her until people kept away from her.

But the young man returned to his own city and abandoned his vow. He married another woman and they had two sons, one of whom fell into a well and died, while the other was bitten by a weasel and died. His wife asked him: Why is it that our sons are dying in such strange manner? And he told her the episode with the girl. She divorced him and said: Go to your portion, which the Holy One has given to you.

He went to the city and asked about her. He was told: She is crazy. Whenever someone wants to marry her, she does such-and-such to him. He went to her father and told him the whole story and said: I accept whatever fault there is in her. Witnesses were called. He went to her and she started to behave as was her custom. He told her the episode of the weasel and the well. She said: I, too, have kept my word. She was immediately restored to sanity and married him and they merited many children and grandchildren" (Yalqut Shimoni 2:834).

Numbers

Parashat Bemidbar

Adonai spoke to Moshe in the wilderness of Sinai, in the Tent of Meeting.
(Num. 1:1)

"When you went after me in the wilderness, in a land that was not sown" (Jer. 2:2)

The wilderness was a wonderful school for us. It was there that we learned to be God's People. From this verse our rabbis learned that one of the three things in which the Torah was given is the wilderness, as it is said: "From the wilderness (to) Mattanah [='gift' in Hebrew]" (Num. 21:18). (Num. Rabbah 19:33)

Here, in this wilderness, our ancestors were put to the test ten times. The first generation that the Holy One brought out of Egypt did not pass these tests, for they were very difficult and the people were unable to rise up to the challenge. They failed at Masa and Meriva, and that generation all died in the wilderness, where they lay, supine in the dunes, awaiting the great shofar call from God. (Baba Batra 74a). But a second generation arose in this wilderness - who accepted the Torah and learned it from Moshe and Aharon as well as from the obstacles over which the early generation has stumbled - and they grew into a free people, great in Torah, a people who had not experienced the taste of slavery. They were born into an atmosphere which was all Torah, freedom and liberty. And this was the generation which God chose to bring into the Land.

Why was the Torah given in the Wilderness?

What is the reason for the Torah having been given in the Wilderness? So that the Torah can be likened to the Wilderness. Just as the Wilderness belongs to everyone and has no owner, so the Torah has no owner. The Torah belongs to all those who study it.

But what is the reason that the Torah was given specifically in an arid and desolate wilderness, where snakes, serpents and scorpions abound, and where we knew that they were without clothing and without food and even without water? (As it is said: And their clothes grew with them for they had no change of clothing, and the manna was their food and they drank water from the rock).

The reason is to teach us that the Torah has to be accepted in faith and trust. At the time of the giving of the Torah, the Children of Israel had left Egypt and entered into an arid wilderness. They had no food but the manna, which came to them through the merit of Moshe. They had no shade but the pillar of cloud, which shaded them, through the merit of Aharon. And they had no water but the well through the merit of Miriam. Nevertheless, they accepted the Torah. In the same way, the Torah should be accepted every day and every hour, despite all obstacles, without preparations, either material or spiritual.

Let anyone who wants to take, do so

The giving of the Torah was marked by three things: fire, water, and wilderness. This was to indicate that, as these things are freely available without charge to all humanity, so also are the words of the Torah free. Again: Just as wilderness is ownerless, so one who is not open to acquiring and imparting knowledge to all like the wilderness cannot acquire wisdom and Torah. (Num. Rabbah 1:7)

You shall number all those in Israel who are able to bear arms, from the age of twenty years up, in their hosts. (Num. 1:3)

When your enemy falls

Other ancient peoples often felt hatred for their enemies, rejoiced in their downfall, and treated prisoners of war cruelly. Our Torah, however, teaches us a humane attitude towards our enemies and prisoners: "Do not rejoice when your enemy falls and let your heart not be glad when he stumbles" (Prov. 24:17).

The reason for this is clear. All people were created in the image of God. Furthermore, maltreating an enemy and prisoner only increases hatred and wars. All cruelty and hatred have a damaging, negative impact on a person's soul. From hating an enemy, one learns hatred in general.

Our sages opposed all forms of hatred. This included hatred for an enemy. And so we find in the Torah commandments which, demand of us that we restrain ourselves - specifically at a time of war.

Before engaging in a war, we are commanded by the Torah to offer peace terms to a town: "When you approach a town to fight against it, you shall offer it peace terms. If it responds peaceably to you and lets you in, then all the people therein shall pay tribute to you and serve you" (Deut. 20:10-11).

Offering peace terms can result in great military harm because the advantage of surprise is thus lost. Nevertheless, the Torah demands this of us in order to prevent unnecessary bloodshed. In this, the army of Israel indeed differs from every other army in the world.

They registered by families, by the house of their ancestors. (Num. 1:18)

My parents were simple folk

At the engagement party which Rabbi Israel of Rizin prepared for his grandson and the daughter of Rabbi Tzvi Hirsch of Rimanov, he recounted for his future in-laws, and the guests who had gathered, his family genealogy. (According to the tradition commonly held among the Hassidic communities of Eastern Europe, the family of the Rabbi of Rizin was connected to a respectable family tree, going back to King David).

The Hassidim swallowed every word coming out of the mouth of their revered rabbi. When he had finished, he bent down towards Rabbi Tzvi Hirsch of Rimanov and said: And now, dear in-law, tell us about your family genealogy!

Rabbi Tzvi Hirsch astonished the honored guests with the following account: I freely admit that I do not have a family tree full of rabbis and tzaddikim. My parents were simple but honest folk who earned their living through hard manual labor. When my parents died, I was a youngster of some ten years in age. Because of our dire economic straits, I was put to work as a tailor's apprentice. That tailor taught me two things: "Don't tangle with what is new and try as far as possible to repair the old". Ever since then, those words of the tailor have served me as a guiding light throughout my life..

The Children of Israel shall encamp, each man with his division and under his flag. (Num. 1:52)

Symbol

Come and see how great is the power of a symbol! What is a flag? A piece of cloth at the top of a pole. The cloth, in itself, is worth nothing, just a piece of rag. The pole, in itself, is nothing but a pole, one piece of wood among many - but, when they are joined together, the cloth to the pole, the pole to the cloth, it becomes a banner. This is a flag, which is such a large, important and respected symbol in every nation and culture, every movement, organization and order.

This passion for the flag, the symbol of freedom, existed deep in the hearts of our ancestors, even during their sojourn in Egypt, but it only took on shape when they left there. Our sages, of blessed memory, gave this romantic point of view a concrete expression in the following legend: "When the Holy Blessed One revealed the Divine self upon Mount Sinai, twenty-two thousand chariots of angels descended too ... and they were arrayed under separate standards ... When Israel saw them arrayed under separate flags, they began to long for flags too, and said: Would that we could be arranged under standards like them ... Said the Holy Blessed One: How eager you are to be arranged under standards! As you live, I shall fulfill your desire. The Holy One immediately showed Divine love for Israel and said to Moshe: "Go and make flags for them and, as they have desired, arrange them under their flags" (Num. Rabbah 2).

Each under his standard, under the banners of their ancestral house. (Num. 2:2)

Roots

Rabbi Yehudah Leib of Gur used to say: The meaning of this is that every Jew should try, as much as possible, to act in ways similar to, and as reminder of, the deeds of ancestors. Acting this way will prevent a person from being cut off from the ancient roots from which the nation acquires all of its life, spirit, and existence. The standard of the children must always be according to the banners and guidelines of our ancestors....

Parashat Naso

When a man or a woman commits any wrong toward a fellow man ... and they confess the wrong they have done.... (Num. 5:6-7)

Reciprocal Guarantee

From the beginning of the verse, we learn that the Torah, in this section, is addressing the individual, as it says: "a man or a woman", but then it continues "and they confess", using the plural form. Why?

If we study the text thoroughly, however, we will realize that the change from the singular to the plural here is not coincidental. The Torah wants to teach us an important rule that "All Jews are responsible for each other". This is why an individual is forbidden to say: "It is enough that I have saved my soul" but must also make repentance for the sins of others. If done sincerely, a person undertaking such a communal repentance can acquit and protect the community if they fall into sin and transgression. It was with a clear intent that the early sages set our prayer of confession in the plural form: "We have sinned ..."., etc. The same is true with the prayer said on the Day of Atonement: "For the sin we have committed before You" - in the plural form. Our concern with the confession has to be for the fate of the whole house of Israel, and not just for our own soul.

... they confess the wrong they have done .... (Num. 5:7)

The earth is Adonai's, and all that fills it (Ps. 24:1)

Confession is a basic requirement of complete repentance in all cases of wrongdoing. Why, therefore, is the commandment for confession stated in the context of the sin of stealing rather than elsewhere?

Rabbi Yehudah Leib of Gur answered: To tell the truth, every wrong-doing is one of stealing. God gives people life-force and strength so that they will do the Divine will. If a person uses that strength and that life-force to act contrary to the will of the Creator, then that person is stealing God's possession. The mitzvah of repentance and confession thus rightly belongs here.

If any man's wife goes astray and is unfaithful to him. (Num. 5:12)

The causes for unfaithfulness

The details of the matter dealing with the unfaithful wife take up an entire tractate in the Talmud - the tractate of Sotah. There we read (1:2): "What do they do to the suspected adulteress? They bring her up to the great court, which is in Jerusalem, and the judges admonish her [to admit that she was unfaithful] in the same way that they admonish witnesses in capital cases. They say to her: My daughter! Much[sin] is caused by wine, much by frivolity, much by immaturity, much by bad neighbors [That is, there may be some excuse for what you have done]. Confess your guilt and so make unnecessary the ordeal for the sake of God's great name, which is written in holiness so that it may not be obliterated by the water. And they relate to her matters which neither she nor any of the family of her father's house is worthy to hear [about people in the past who confessed their guilt] (Sotah 1:2).

In other words, in order to make it easier for her to confess, she is told about people who sinned and confessed, such as: the case of Judah and Tamar, his daughter-in-law, the case of Reuben and his father's mistress, and the case of Amnon and his sister, all of whom confessed their wrongdoing without being humiliated into doing so.

The members of the court tried to persuade her to confess, if she had been unfaithful to her husband, and so not have to drink of the "bitter water". They did this in the same way as they warned witnesses in capital cases, that they should tell the truth lest an innocent man be executed because of what they said. And so with the suspected adulteress, it would be better for her to confess rather than to put herself in any danger.

They spoke to her softly and tried to find some merit in her deeds because there might have been reasons, which led her to the act of unfaithfulness. Perhaps. she did it because she had drunk too much wine, or out of an excess of frivolity, perhaps. because she was still very young, and perhaps. because she had come under the influence of wicked neighbors. If one of these was the reason, they requested that she not be humiliated into admitting what she had done and then she would not have to drink of the "bitter water".

If a man or woman shall clearly utter a Nazirite vow to consecrate him or herself to Adonai. (Num. 6:2)

Rules his spirit and controls his soul

On the one hand, our sages, of blessed memory, said: A nazir is a sinner, guilty of sins against the soul, because a nazir afflicts the self through abstention from wine (Nedarim 10a). On the other hand, they said (Nazir 6b): A nazir is called holy.

These two opinions appear to contradict each other. How can a Nazir be both sinner and holy? Both opinions represent the Divine truth. Physical self-mortification is not the way of the Torah. The Holy Blessed One created good trees, among them the fruit of the vine, so that people could enjoy themselves. One should be able to rule over one's spirit and exercise control over one's soul; In general, a person should make an effort to be limited by what is permitted until custom becomes second nature and the golden median is instinctively followed. Then what the Torah forbids will suffice and the person will happily drink wine in the correct measure.

If, however, one sees that the evil inclination is taking over, one must force one's self in the opposite direction, building a fence around a fence, walking the right path and avoiding being swept away in the forbidden current. Consequently, a nazir is a sinner who reached the point of having to indulge in self-infliction because of an inability, in the first instance, to exercise self-control.

The Golden Path

Why does the section about the nazir in the Torah follow immediately after the section about the suspected adulteress? In order to teach that a person should not tend to extremes, neither as an adulteress who went astray from the good path and turned to the worst things possible, nor as the nazir who abstains from wine, and who unnecessarily afflicts the self. On the contrary, a person should always direct all thoughts and actions to the middle golden path.

This method was also acceptable to Rambam. He wrote: This is so that a person should not say: 'Since jealousy, lust, and honor are bad and shorten one's life, I will remove myself as far as possible from them and adopt the opposite extreme' to the point where he eats no meat, drinks no wine, does not marry or live in pleasant accommodation or wear attractive clothes. This, too, is a bad way to go and it is forbidden to follow it. Anyone who takes that road is called 'sinner' (Hilkhot deot, chapter 3).

Accordingly, the sages ruled that a person should not deny abstain from things other than what the Torah has prohibited, and should not place restrictions on the self through vows and oaths about things that are permitted. The sages said that a person should not undertake a voluntary fast. About matters such as these and those that follow from them, Solomon commanded and said: "Do not be too righteous; nor make yourself too wise" (Eccl. 7:16).

One person overdoes while another does not do enough

Rabbi Avraham Yehoshua Heschel of Apt had no patience at all for those who engaged in self-mortification and fasting. On one occasion, he came to a township on a day when a public fast had been declared because of the lack of rain. Rabbi Heschel did not pay attention to this fast. Instead, he went into the hostel, prayed and sat down at the table to eat.

When the inhabitants of the town heard of this, they were shocked and said to him: Rabbi, it is forbidden to eat today! This is a public fast day here in our community! We desperately need rain!

For what do you actually need rain? He replied pleasantly. Is it not so that the field will give crops. and that there will be a good harvest and you will have a means of livelihood? And what are you doing about it? You proclaim a fast and thereby show the Master of the Universe that it is possible to manage without any livelihood, without eating and drinking. Is this really the answer? The path to take is the opposite of this: to eat more and to drink more. Then the Master of the Universe will see that your needs are many and will surely not deny you Divine beneficence....

Speak to Aharon and to his sons, saying: Thus shall you bless the Children of Israel. (Num. 6:23)

All are equal

Rabbi Yisrael of Mudezitz used to say: The Torah bids the children of Aharon, the priests: "Thus shall you bless the Children of Israel" - you have to bless the Children of Israel as they are. The priests should not show preference to the great and important members of the community, nor to the righteous or the pious. The whole intention of the Torah here was that the priests should bless, in equal amount, every Jew standing in front of them and so the sublime value of the unity of Israel will be demonstrated in the mitzvah of the priestly blessing.

May Adonai's face shine upon you and may God be gracious unto you. (Num. 6:25)

A free gift

Rashi interprets "and may God be gracious unto you" as meaning "May God grant you good grace". After first being blessed with "May Adonai cause his face to shine upon you" which, according to the sages means the light of the Torah and the light of the Divine Presence (Num. Rabbah), what special "good grace" is still required?

The "good grace" with which a person is blessed is Divine grace, because it is private and unique. Not every person is capable of understanding the special uniqueness of 'grace'. Sometimes the nature and spiritual character of different people may be the opposite of each other, and then a mountain grows between them and they do not understand each other. Graciousness is a matter of preference and each person has a unique personal preference. This is the meaning of "and may God be gracious unto you" - "May God grant you good grace" - that people should understand the special, individual grace in you and in every other Jew.

May Adonai lift up God's countenance upon you. (Num. 6:26)

Meeting Glances

"Adonai lift up God's countenance upon you" - this is the high point in the threefold benediction. Not only will God keep you, make the Divine face shine upon you and be gracious to you, but also "Adonai lift up God's countenance upon you". Rashi, in his commentary, explains that this expresses the following idea: May God suppress the Divine anger. "And may Adonai grant you peace" - in your heart, in your surroundings, in your land and in your world.

Our sages, of blessed memory, felt uneasy with this benediction. In their opinion, the promise that "Adonai will lift up God's countenance upon you" stood in contradiction to the qualities of the Holy One about whom it is stated: "For Adonai your God is the God of gods, and Lord of Lords, a great God, mighty and awesome, Who favors no person [lit. – 'who will not lift up countenance']" (Deut. 10:17).

The Tosafists, however, saw no contradiction. This is what they wrote: "The plain meaning of Scripture is directed at the countenance of people, so that a person should not be favored because of greatness or wealth or age. On the contrary, "Adonai will lift up God's countenance upon you" refers to the countenance of the Divine Presence, that Adonai might show you a radiant countenance.

In other words: we have here two items of evidence, two aspects, two modes of lifting up a countenance - that of a person lifting up the face toward the heavens, of lifting the eyes on high, as it is written: "Lift up your eyes on high" (Is 40:26) out of a desire for God's proximity, out of a yearning of the soul, a craving of the heart, out of a silent prayer of "her lips. moved, but her voice was not heard" (1 Sam 1:13) and, from on high, God lifts the Divine countenance "Adonai looked down from heaven upon the children, to see if there were any who understand, and seek God" (Ps. 14:2).

People lifts up their countenance and seek Adonai, while Adonai lifts up the Divine countenance and seeks us in return. When the two glances meet, the glance of a person in prayer meeting with the light of Adonai, so that the prayer is accepted and heard - at that moment - the benediction will come true.

Parashat Beha'alotkha

Aharon did so ... as Adonai had commanded. (Num. 8:3)

Aharon did not change himself

Rashi comments on this verse: "[This is said in order] to tell the praise of Aharon, that he did not change [anything from the instructions given]".

What is Scripture telling us? Is it even conceivable that Aharon might not have done as Adonai had commanded? And what is Rashi telling us? - "to tell the praise of Aharon, that he did not change". Is it not as certain as anything could be that Aharon would not have deviated by a single hair's breadth from what he had been commanded by Adonai through Moshe?

Rabbi Meir of Premislan, however, used to say: Scripture teaches us: Although Aharon had reached the highest rung in being the high priest, nevertheless, he did not change his ways in sacred matters but remained, as previously, involved with others, mixing with the people, bringing peace between people, and peace and love between spouses. He would intermingle with the people and bring them closer to Torah and the mitzvot. As Rashi put it: "to tell the praise of Aharon, that he did not change", that is to say: he did not change himself after ascending to such a high post!

This is how the candlestick was made; it was of beaten gold, its shaft, its flowers, were hammered work; according to the pattern which Adonai had shown Moshe, so he made the candlestick. (Num. 8:4)

They were united

In 1925, Rabbi Saul Yedidya Elazar, the Rabbi of Modezhitz, visited the Land of Israel for the first time and was received for an interview

257

by the Jewish statesman and philosopher, Sir Herbert Samuel, who was then the British High Commissioner.

During the conversation, the High Commissioner said to the rabbi: You should try to introduce some peace between the quarreling [political] parties in the Jewish community of the country!

The rabbi replied to the British High Commissioner: Our sages, of blessed memory, tell us that when the Holy Blessed One commanded Moshe to make the candlestick, Moshe found it difficult, until God showed Moshe precisely how to make it. "And this is how the candlestick was made, it was of beaten gold". 'Mikshah' (beaten) implies 'mah kashah' (how difficult) it is to make, for Moshe was greatly vexed by it. Seeing that he found it difficult, the Holy One said to Moshe: 'Take a talent of gold, cast it into the furnace and take it out again, and the candlestick will assume shape of its own accord' (Num. Rabbah 15:4). These words of our sages appear surprising. Although the Holy One is the teacher and Moshe is the pupil, Moshe found it too difficult to comprehend the work of making the candlestick!

This matter - continued the rabbi raising his voice slightly - is not to be understood literally. The candlestick was "of one piece of pure beaten gold" so as to symbolize the perfect unity of the entire people. "Its shaft" refers to the simple folk; "its flowers" refers to the important members of the community. The tremendous task facing Moshe, then, was one of uniting all sections of the people into one unit and even the nation's chosen teacher found this difficult, until he received assistance from on high. And now, too - the rabbi concluded - we can attain Jewish unity only if God will infuse us with spirit from on high that will annul the inclination for divisiveness that is latent within us.

It was always so; the cloud covered it, appearing as fire by night. (Num. 9:16)

And your faithfulness every night (Ps. 92:3)

Come and see what Rabbi Moshe Avigdor Amiel says: This verse is an eternal sign for the fate of the Jewish People throughout the generations: "It was always so; the cloud covered it". Whenever dark clouds gathered above us and the gloom could be felt, just then, when all options appeared to have been exhausted, and there was no hope and no recovery, then, at the height of the darkness - "it appears as fire in the night", the light of the glory of Adonai is revealed and disperses the heavy clouds hanging over the camp of Israel.

The rabble in their midst had a gluttonous craving. (Num. 11:4)

Rabble

The Tabernacle had been set up. The people's army had been established. Levites and priests were serving as intermediaries between the people and the Tabernacle. The tribes with their camps. and standards were ready for the journey, with a pillar of cloud to guide them by day and a pillar of fire to guide them by night, shading them by day from the heat of the desert sun and warming them in the cold desert night. The admonitions of a prophet can be as a rain-giving cloud, soaking in dew and consolation, or they can be as a scorching flame of fire. A people can be as lucid in soul and mind as the light of day or the night can be in their soul, despair eating at their hearts. Hence the pillar of cloud and pillar of fire. The people are not just one erring on the way in the wilderness but "a people who err in their heart" (Ps. 95:10). It is because they err in their heart that they are punished with wandering in the wilderness.

There is a people's army, physically ready for the march of conquest; the Tabernacle and the Ark are there to assist and support spiritually. There is the golden Menorah, which is pleasing to the eye and trumpets that delight the ear. There is rule and order when camping and when journeying, at times of peace and during battle. There is a battle cry for the military campaign: "Advance, O Adonai! May Your enemies be scattered and may those who hate You flee before You!" And there is a song of respite, for physical and mental rest: "Return, O Adonai, to the myriads of thousands of Israel" (Num. 10:35-6). That being so, why did the people not move off on the journey to enter the Land? Who was procrastinating? What was delaying them?

It was the rabble who had a "gluttonous craving", not, this time, for a golden calf but for a real calf. They were worse than calf-worshippers - says Dr. Israel Eldad - for the latter's intention was to the gods while the former were thinking not of God, nor of an alien god, but of a real calf. The likes of such in our generations have been worshippers of gold.

Moshe's promises that he would lead the people to a land flowing with milk and honey went unheard. They were demanding to be given meat, here, of all places, in this wilderness! All the sufferings of Egypt had vanished from their memories. The wounds from the whips. on their backs had healed, and they demanded to be given meat. Moshe says: "You shall be holy" and they respond: "Fish". Moshe proclaims: "A special people" and they demand: "Water-melons". Moshe assures them: "If you walk in My ways ...". and they cry for "onions and garlic". Moshe entreats: "I will be your God and you will be My people", and they respond with: "Meat, meat ...".

The man Moshe was very humble, more than any other men which were upon the face of the earth. (Num. 12:3)

Humility

A well-known rabbi once asked Rabbi Naftali of Ropshitz: "Could you please tell me how you have won the hearts of the people who come to you in their many thousands? I am greater in Torah than you are, so why do they not come to me?" "To tell you the truth", replied Rabbi Naftali, "this is also surprising to me, but it would seem to me that the reason why they come to me is because I have never asked why they come. Perhaps. they do not come to you because you do ask this question....

Humility is not a quality that can be commanded

Rabbi Michel of Zlotzov was once asked: All the mitzvot are commanded in the Torah except for humility, which is equivalent to all the other qualities. The Torah simply praises one person [Moshe] who is more humble than any other. What is the meaning of this silence?

The Rabbi replied: A person attempting to be humble in order to uphold a mitzvah would never attain the world of true humility. The very thought that it is a mitzvah to be humble contains a satanic temptation. The person would become arrogant to the point of considering oneself to be scholarly and righteous and God-fearing and with all the other good qualities and fit to be appointed over the people. In truth, however, this thought comes from arrogance and pride and is not one of the qualities of Hassidim.

His heart is not haughty, nor his eyes lofty (Ps. 131:1)

Rabbi Yisrael Lipkin of Salant used to say: "Come and see how the Holy Blessed One testifies about Moshe Rabbeynu, saying that he was "more humble than any other person". This is a distinguished description, the likes of which we do not find being said about anyone else in the whole of the Bible.

Significantly, Moshe was not then in the twilight of his life but at the height of his career as the leader of the people, with another thirty-eight years of leadership still ahead of him. Yet, even after Moshe heard these words of praise from the Holy One, his heart was not haughty nor his eyes lofty. This is the most supreme level of humility, the like of which "no other man on earth" has attained.

Wholeness of Qualities

No one has perfect qualities unless they are also graced with the quality of humility. We read in the Talmud: "This house - if it did not have a doorstep, it would appear as though defective, as though in ruins. And so you, too, even if you are perfect in all the qualities, if you have no humility, you are deficient" (Kallah 3).

A person whose conduct is modest is acceptable not only to fellow people, but also to the Creator. The sages told a parable: "A mortal who has a vessel is happy with it, so long as it is whole. If it breaks, who wants it? And what is the vessel of the Holy Blessed One? It is a person's heart. If the Holy One does not want haughtiness, as it is said: "Everyone who is proud of heart is an abomination to Adonai" (Prov. 16:5). If the heart breaks, then the Holy One says: This is Mine, as it is said: "Adonai is close to the broken of heart" (Ps. 34:19). (Midrash Hagadol, Vayeshev 38)

Humility nests in the heart

The Baal Shem Tov once told the following story: There was once a great minister who, although he had attained wealth and greatness, was not satisfied with his life. He was always nervous and any slight mishap, anything gone wrong, would cause him serious suffering and often bring him to the point of depression. Sometimes he would regret the loss of his money and at others the passing of his days. He would recall an insult someone hurled at him, and then he would remember that "All men are false" (Ps. 116:11). Every small ache would cause him immeasurable sorrow, and, because of his constant anxiety, his life became insufferable. He consulted with doctors who gave him medicines to remove the terror and grief from his heart, but they were of no help. He asked sages for their advice and they gave him more medication.

Once, an old beggar came to him and saw that the minister was very sad. The old man asked him the reason for his sorrow. The minister spoke to him about his fears and the old beggar said to him: I will give you a remedy. You must realize that pride is the source of your trouble. You imagine, in your pride, that the whole world is yours and that you deserve all that is good in the world. You also wish that eternal life were at your beck and call. But you also well know that in the end you will die and so you know no spiritual rest. You must know that you will not be cured of your illness of fear until your learn the quality of humility and act humbly. If you do not seek greatness and satisfaction the whole time, you will be happy with what you have and will no longer know sadness. But remember and observe to remove pride from your heart and conduct yourself with humility.

The minister heard what the old man said and decided to follow his advice. From then on, he no longer sat, as had been his wont, in his carriage on his journeys out of town. He would walk behind it on foot and the carriage would be driven in front of him. At the same time, the minister would reiterate the quality of humility and say: I am humble; I am humble; and the proof of this is that I am walking behind the carriage.

Some time later, the beggar met him on the road and saw how things were. He said to him: Minister, this is not the way to acquire the quality of humility, with the carriage being driven ahead of you and you walking behind it, congratulating yourself on your humility. On the contrary, sit in the carriage humbly, and let humility be, not in your words and your thoughts, but engraved in your heart. For this - a heartfelt humility - is the most difficult of all ...

Parashat Shelah Lekha

Adonai spoke to Moshe, saying: Send men, that they may spy out the land of Canaan, which I give to the people of Israel. (Num. 13:1-2)

What was the sin of the spies?

In an earlier generation, Avraham emigrated from Ur of the Chaldeans, when Adonai commanded him: "Get out from your country" (Gen. 12:1). He did so unconditionally, unhesitatingly, without many questions and without receiving assurances that this land, which was designated for him, was a land "flowing with milk and honey". But his descendants, having witnessed the greatest of miracles with their own eyes: the exodus from Egypt, the crossing of the Red Sea, the victory over Amalek and the Giving of the Torah on Mount Sinai, were still not ready, despite all these miracles, to go into the land without being sending spies to check out the road for them.

The spies who were sent to scout out the land were not merely intelligence and spying personnel but "all those men were chiefs of the people of Israel" (num13:3). They were the chiefs of the tribes, the chosen representatives of the people, and it was specifically these people whom Moshe picked as spies so that no-one would say that "simple people caused us to fail". They came from all the tribes of Israel so that no one could blame another tribe - with the exception of the tribe of levy, from which no one was sent to scout out the land. This was so that no one would be able to say: This person is from Moshe's own tribe and he is influenced by Moshe and is, therefore, not objective. How was it then that these "princes of the congregation and eminent people" descended to such a low level that they slandered the Land of Israel, to the point at which it was said about them: "The only intention of the spies was to disgrace the Land of Israel" (Midrash Tanhuma)?

It was these same spies who brought of the fruit of the land with their very own hands and who testified: "We came to the land where you sent us, and surely it flows with milk and honey; and this is its fruit" (Num. 13:27). How, then, did it happen that these same spies could so damage the good reputation of the country?

These spies failed their mission. With their return to the camp, they did not lie to the people nor did they tell them things that never were. What they did was much worse. Their account was a half-truth and they slandered the Land. They demoralized the people and planted the seeds of defeatism among them. And all this derived from their lack of faith in Adonai's power. They left the people with doubt and presented them with a distorted picture, as they cast light and shadow over the Land of Israel. The people were bewildered and confused; fear entered their hearts and doubt gnawed at their thinking: Where is Moshe leading us? What military adventure is he planning for us? The spies do tell some good things about the country but, at the same time, they speak disapprovingly of it - only so that they will be believed, that they will not be suspected of bias and lack of objectivity.

"We came to the land where you sent us, and surely it flows with milk and honey; and this is its fruit. The people who live in the land, however, are strong" (Num. 13:27-28) -- Such is the way of those who utter slander; they begin by speaking well of one and conclude by speaking ill. (Num. Rabbah 16:17)

And the spies succeeded in their undertaking: they tell of the Land that it "is a land that eats up its inhabitants" (Num. 13:32), and so the people did not want to go there and death in the Wilderness was decreed upon them. In vain, did Yehoshua the son of Nun and Caleb the son of Yephunneh try to encourage the people: "The land, which we passed through to spy, is an exceedingly good land" (Num. 14:7). The people no longer believed them. The redemption and the entrance to the Land of Israel require a spiritual affinity, a willingness to accept absorption pangs with love. Otherwise, it is not a question of redemption and there is no "going up" to the land but simply a migration.

Endless Trouble

The people cried bitterly over their punishment for the sin of the spies. Immediately after this unjustified weeping, they moved on to anger and sought to harm Moshe and Aharon: "And the whole people threatened to pelt them with stones" (Num. 14:10). They sought, as it were, to harm the Divine Presence: "Rabbi Hiyya bar Abba said: This teaches that they took stones and hurled them against the One who is above". [reading 'them' as including the Holy One] (Sotah 35a).

However difficult it might be to release a slave from imprisonment from Egypt, it is seven times harder to release the slavery from out of the slave's soul. The spirit of the people was not yet ready to depart from Egypt.

All those men were chiefs of the people of Israel. And these were their names.... (Num. 13:3-4)

Attitude not relationship

Since this whole undertaking ended in devastating failure, why was it important to give the names of the spies and even the names of their fathers? To teach us that they were publicity-drunk and, that at every possible opportunity and occasion, they would proclaim themselves and their fathers and brag that they were preeminent. And so it was that they fell into the trap of speaking ill of the Holy Land and their end was bitter.

The story is told about a certain man who came to Rabbi Ezekiel of Kozmir. The Rabbi noted that the man was behaving arrogantly and overbearingly and asked: Who is this man? Is he perhaps. great in Torah or in commerce? He was told: He is a common person but well-related. He is proud of his family's genealogy...

Rabbi Ezekiel said to them: Let me give you a parable. What is this like? It is similar to an overloaded cart which sinks in the mire of slime and sludge and the horses can no longer get it moving from its place. What did the cart-owner do? He went and brought a crow bar, lifted up the cart with its load and moved it on to firm ground. A policeman who was watching noted that the crow bar did more work than did the horses. He argued from minor to major and thought: If one crow bar can do that, then four crow bars will do that much more. He went and

267

placed a cart on four crow bars, one in each corner, and waited for it to move off....

So it is with genealogy - Rabbi Ezekiel concluded his parable - one good ancestor can place a person on the right track but anyone who thinks that travel based solely on an ancestor's merit, is no more than gullible and simpleminded.

They spread lies about the land they had scouted. (Num. 13:32)

Love of the Land

According to Rabbi Akiva Yosef Schlesinger, the sin of the spies has been hanging over the heads of Israel from then until now. He writes in his book "Heart of the Hebrew": The only purpose of the punishment of exile, which has been decreed against us to this very day, is to correct the sin of the spies and their slander against the Land which, to this day, has not been uprooted from the hearts of Israel, as it is said: "They (those who came out of Egypt) rejected the desirable land" (Ps. 106:24). There will be no redemption until this sin is uprooted from us, until we display befitting love for the Land of Israel, until we try and make every effort to redeem it from the hands of foreigners ...

Pardon, I pray, the iniquity of this people. (Num. 14:19)

Patriarchal Merit

Rabbeinu Bahya Ben Asher asks: Why does Moshe not mention patriarchal merit here in his prayer? At the sin of the Golden Calf, Moshe appealed to God by saying: "Remember Your servants, Avraham, Yitzhak, and Yaakov" (Ex. 32:13). This appeal was instrumental in canceling the evil decree against the members of his people. It would stand to reason that Moshe would use this same argument again.

The answer, Rabbeinu Bahya tells us, is that Moshe believed that patriarchal merit would stand Israel in good stead for any sins they committed against the Holy One. But when the Children of Israel rejected the land designated for them and spoke rebelliously about the land of the patriarchs, Moshe's resolve weakened and he had doubts as to whether those who were rejecting the inheritance of their ancestors would benefit from invoking the ancestral merit ...

In this wilderness shall your carcasses drop. (Num. 14:29)

There is no pardon

Rabbi Yisrael Elhanan Spektor of Kubana said: Come and see how great is the sin committed against one's own people. We see that the Holy Blessed One forgave the generation of the Wilderness for a number of grave sins: they sinned with the Golden Calf - but they were pardoned; they sinned when they grumbled and asked to eat meat voluptuously - but they were pardoned; and when, subsequently, Israel sinned in the dispute of Korah- they again earned pardon for their grave sin. It was only for the offence of the spies, who slandered the Land and sought to take the people back to Egypt, that Adonai did not pardon Israel but decreed for all those who had come out of Egypt that "in this wilderness shall your carcasses drop".

We can learn from this that repentance is of benefit to a sinner for all the transgressions in the world – both those between a person and God and those between people - with the exception of sins perpetrated against one's own People - for that there is no atonement and even total remorse is of no help to the sinner.

Seek not after your own heart and after your own eyes, following your lustful urges. (Num. 15:39)

Procurers for crime

We read in the Jerusalem Talmud: "It has been taught: Rabbi Levy said: The heart and the eyes are two procurers. The Holy Blessed One, has said: If you give me your heart and your eyes - then I will know that you are totally Mine" (Berakhot 1:5).

269

It would seem that things should have been in the reverse order. First, the eyes see, then they entice the heart into desiring something wrong. Should the verse not have said: "that you seek not after your own eyes and after your own heart"?

Rabbi Moshe Alsheikh noted, however, that a person's eyes are not always under one's control. Sometimes things are things without any a priori intention to see them. That is why one is not cautioned or punished for a first glimpse. So what is one cautioned and punished for? For a second, longer, look, for observation of licentiousness, where the heart entices the eyes and attracts them into looking and observing. Thus, the heart is the primary culprit, and the eye only the secondary one. That is why it is said: "that you seek not after your own heart" first and, subsequently, "after your own eyes".

Parashat Korah

Now Korah... and Datan and Aviram ... and On, the son of Pelet, and certain of the people of Israel, two hundred and fifty princes of the assembly, regularly summoned to the congregation, men of renown. They gathered together against Moshe and against Aharon, and said to them: You take too much upon you, seeing as all of the congregation is holy, every one of them, and Adonai is among them. Why then do you raise yourselves up above the congregation of Adonai? (Num. 16:1-3)

The Rebellion

Korah was smart. He saw that the time was ripe. He noted that bitterness had accumulated in the people and was building up. He could scale those mounds of bitterness and compete, if not against Moshe directly, then at least against Aharon.

This was the first opposition that arose against Moshe out of a pure lust for power. Prof. Israel Eldad remarks: It was no longer a matter of water or bread or meat. It was not fear of an enemy and war. But this was an archetype of the struggle for control. The desire to rule was the main reason and everything else was no more than an excuse.

The guise for the rebellion was ideological. A rebellion in the name of equality versus dictatorship. A rebellion in the name of 'people power' verses an authority that the rulers have taken for themselves. These issues are explicit: "all the congregation is holy, every one of them". The principle of equality with the emphasis on "and Adonai is among them" is using Moshe's own words: "You shall be holy; for I Adonai your God am holy" (Lev. 19:2). If that is so, then no one person has a greater portion in God and all are equal in holiness for God dwells amongst them all. "Why then do you raise yourselves up above the congregation of Adonai?" This is the protest against authority. "Raise yourselves up" - you may arrogate power to yourselves but who elected you?

271

On this occasion, it is not a mixed multitude or some rabble going wild. It is more dangerous this time. It is a group of notables, chiefs and levites, central figures who harness the bitterness of the masses to their chariot, mouthing the egalitarian slogan. Scripture emphasizes: "two hundred and fifty princes of the assembly, regularly summoned to the congregation, men of renown". These three descriptive phrases mark the gravity of the rebellion and state that the rebels are respected by the people. "Princes of the assembly" - elected by the assembly to be the heads of the tribes; "Regularly summoned" - Moshe himself had promoted them to serve in the Tent of Meeting; and, in general, "men of renown".

It is not surprising that, among the rebels, led by Datan and Aviram and On, the son of Pelet, are three princes from the tribe of Reuben. This tribe is bitter. They were the first-born of the House of Yaakov but the leadership has now been given to the tribe of Levi.

And so all the elements came together: Jealousy within the tribe of Levi, by one family that another has been chosen for the priesthood; jealousy by the tribe of Reuben that it had been downgraded from its natural leadership position; and the bitterness of the people, desperate and scared at the outcome of the mission of the spies and the fate they fear awaits them. Korah then uses them all in his own bid for leadership.

Denigration of others

"Now Korah took". What did he take? Rashi says: "He lured the heads of the Sanhedrin among the people with fine words". That is, he took their hearts.

Why do you raise yourselves above the congregation of Adonai? (Num. 16:3)

Searching for pretexts

Rabbi Menahem Mendel of Kotzk taught: All those who take issue with the righteous invent things, which are the opposite of the nature and character [of the righteous]. And so it was in the case of Moshe our Teacher. The Torah testifies about him that he "was a very humble man, more so than any other man on earth" (Num. 12:3), yet Korah and his band could find nothing else to complain about than that Moshe was proud, accusing him and Aharon: "Why do you raise yourselves ... ?"

Always the same

Rabbi Naphtali of Ropshitz used to say: This is the way of the argumentative and of those who instigate disputes - whatever a righteous person does, they will always find something to complain about, some fault. If the righteous person lives apart from the world and spends all day and night on Torah and worship, then they say that the world derives no pleasure or benefit from this person. If, on the other hand, such a person is involved with the people and deals with communal needs, then they argue that this person is wasting time on public affairs and does not study.

Moshe used to study Torah in his tent, which was outside the camp. They found fault with him because he was not inside the camp and was not involved in communal affairs. Aharon, the priest, was involved in communal affairs, pursuing peace within the community and showing an interest in the fate of each and every person. They found fault with him, too, arguing that, as he was "holy to Adonai", he should not be involved in public affairs but should spend his whole time studying ... This is how it has always been with the various Datans and Avirams and still is ....

Moshe sent to call Datan and Aviram, the sons of Eliav; but they said: We will not come up. Is it a small thing that you have brought us out of a land that flows with milk and honey, to kill us in the wilderness, that you also make yourself a ruler over us? (Num. 16:12-13)

He did not put himself out enough

Rabbi Simhah Bunam of Pasischa says: Why was Moshe our Teacher not successful in imposing peace in the camp of Israel? Because he did not exert himself to go to Datan and Aviram. He did not try to persuade them with conciliatory, peacemaking words. Rather, he sat in his tent and sent people to call them to come to him. He thus cut off the path to peace.

Moshe was very angry, and said to Adonai: Do not respect their offering; I have not taken one ass from them, nor have I hurt one of them. (Num. 16:15)

I had need of no one

We read in the Midrash: Rabbi Levi said: What is the greatness of Moshe in that he did not take animals by force from the people? Moshe said: When they were traveling on one journey after another, I never said to even one of them: Take this vessel in your hands [and carry it for me]. Take this vessel on your ass [and have it carry it for me]. But I did my own carrying and my own loading. Said Rabbi Yudan: Great is the generation when it applies itself to public needs - from whom could the ass have been taken if not from the public? But, in the case of Moshe, we find: "And Moshe took his wife and his sons, and set them upon an ass" (Ex. 4:20) - Moshe's own ass and not someone else's. (Midrash Shmuel, 14:9)

How to avoid anger

Rashi comments on this verse: "He was very aggrieved". Moshe our Teacher was perfection in character and in good deeds and, under no circumstances, could he come to the point of actual anger against another person. Even when Datan and Aviram hurt him with their behavior and speech, in the presence of many of Korah's people, Moshe did not actually become angry but was "very aggrieved".

It is told about Rabbi Menahem Mendel of Lubavitch that his whole life he was careful not to show the slightest sign of anger. Sometimes, when people annoyed him and he sensed that his anger was rising, he would ask for someone to bring him a copy of the Shulhan Arukh. And he would say: Our sages, of blessed memory, said: "One who becomes angry is as though he had worshipped idols". It follows, therefore, that I am now facing a serious question – of no less importance than issues of "prohibition and permission". I cannot allow myself to become angry until I have first thoroughly learned the book of laws and have seen whether permission is granted for a person to be angry at another. He would then study the Shulhan Arukh and become deeply involved in the laws there, until his sense of wrath and anger completely subsided ...

Adonai spoke to Moshe and Aharon, saying: "Stand back from this community that I may consume them in an instant!" But they fell on their faces and said, "O God, Source of the spirit of all flesh! When one man sins, will You be wrathful with the whole community?" (Num. 16:20-22)

Examine the heart

When all of Moshe's efforts to settle the dispute were to no avail, the order came: "Stand back from this community that I may consume them in an instant!" But this time, too, the dedicated leaders stood in the breach and prayed for the people. Our sages give us details of the prayer in a legend quoted in Midrash: "And they fell on their faces and said, "O God, Source of the spirit of all flesh! ... and they said to Him: Sovereign of the Universe! In the case of a mortal king, if ten or twenty of his subjects rebel against him and rise up and curse the king or his messengers, what does the king do? He sends his army there and makes a massacre of them, killing the good with the bad, because he cannot know who rebelled or who did not rebel, who showed honor to the king and who cursed him. But You know the thoughts of every person and what the hearts counsels. You understand the inclinations of Your creatures and You know who has sinned and who not, who has rebelled and who not and You know the spirit of each and every one of them. Hence it is said: "O God, Source of the spirit of all flesh! When one person sins, will You be wrathful with the whole community?" So the Holy Blessed One said to Moshe and Aharon: "You have spoken well. I shall make it known who has sinned and who not". (Num. Rabbah 15:11)

It came to pass that, on the next day, Moshe went into the Tent of Testimony; and, behold, the rod of Aharon for the house of Levi had budded, and brought forth buds, and put forth blossoms, and yielded almonds. (Num. 17:23)

Seek peace, and pursue it

Rabbi Solomon Kook (the father of the late Chief Rabbi of Israel, Rabbi Avraham Yitzhak Kook, of blessed memory) once visited a certain community and found a great dispute raging between the worshippers and the officers of the synagogue. When the rabbi, who was a great scholar and a messenger from the Holy Land, arrived, they welcomed him pleasantly, showed him great respect and asked him to impose peace among them.

Rabbi Kook responded willingly and mounted the bimah. In his public address, he referred to the dispute of Korah and his congregation and asked: Why did Aharon's rod yield almonds and not some other fruit?

The almonds contain a hint of the outcome of the dispute. Almonds come in two varieties: bitter and sweet. The first type is sweet at the beginning and bitter at the end. The second type is bitter at first and sweet at the end. So it is in matters of disputes and peace. The first type is just like a dispute, for sweet is the contention, the battle, and the opposition, but the end is very bitter. Peace is the opposite. At first, it is bitter and difficult to concede - and the evil inclination burns and does not make it easier to be conciliatory. But in the end, when a person listens to the good inclination, and concedes a bit for the sake of peace, how good and sweet it is for all concerned.

The words of the rabbi went straight into the hearts of his listeners and he was successful in bringing peace to the community.

Parashat Hukat

This is the ordinance of the Torah ... Speak to the people of Israel, that they bring you a red heifer without blemish. (Num. 19:2)

Against the accusers

We read in the Talmud: Rav 'Ulla was asked: To what extent is a person obligated by the commandment of honoring parents? - He replied: Go forth and see what a certain gentile, Dama son of Netinah by name, did in Ashkelon. The Sages sought to buy from him jewels for the ephod, at a profit of six-hundred-thousand [gold denarii] - but as the key (to the chest of precious stones) was lying under his father's pillow (and his father was asleep), he did not trouble him (did not wake him up).

The following year the Holy Blessed One gave him his reward. A red heifer was born to him in his herd. When the Sages of Israel went to him [to buy it], he said to them: I know you, that [even] if I asked you for all the money in the world (in exchange for the red heifer) you would give it to me. But I ask of you only the money which I lost through my father's honor. (Kiddushin 31b)

What is the connection between honoring parents and the red heifer? Rabbi Avraham Mordekhai of Gur taught: When that gentile performed this great act, an accusation arose in the heavens, and the quality of justice said: This gentile was more careful in the observance of this mitzvah (of honoring one's father) than Your people Israel. Accordingly, the Holy One arranged for there to be a red heifer in that gentile's herd so that he would himself admit the praises of Israel and would give them a warm recommendation, welcoming them by saying: "I know you, that [even] if I asked you for all the money in the world (in exchange for the red heifer) you would give it to me". This is a great statement of defense for Israel that they disperse their capital and their wealth for the observance of the commandments. Even for this commandment of the red heifer, which has no reason and is legislation without logic, they are prepared to give in cash "all the money in the world" in order to observe it.

Remove Satan from before us and from behind us

Rashi commented: "The reason why Scripture uses the term hukah - enactment - is because Satan and the nations of the world taunt Israel, saying: What is this commandment and what is the reason for it? It is an enactment, a decree from before God and you may not query it".

The question arises: Why does Rashi double the taunting question of Satan and the nations of the world: "What is this commandment?" and "What is the reason for it?". And, in Rashi's answer to Satan and the nations of the world, we find a double response: "It is a decree from before God" and "You may not query it".

Rabbi Meir of Premislan replies: Satan, the destroyer, and the evil inclination, attack anyone seeking to keep a mitzvah: before the mitzvah is kept and after it has been kept. When a Jew intends to observe a commandment, the evil inclination attacks with the would-be pious question: "What is this mitzvah?" What is the special value of this mitzvah that you wish to observe it now? Can you not find greater and more important mitzvot?

Even when a person does manage to turn away from Satan, and manages to observe the commandment, the evil inclination is not finished. It comes back with words of praise, saying to the person: "What is the reason for it?" - Do you know the high quality of this mitzvah which you have just observed? This is a great mitzvah. There is none greater! In this way, the evil inclination tries to tempt the keeper of the mitzvah into pride, which is one of the most despicable traits, and to give rise to a sense of satisfaction at what has been done so far. This is to kill the aspiration and desire to observe the additional mitzvot ordained for us.

To these two questions of the evil inclination, Rashi offers two fitting answers. To the would-be pious question before the observance: "What is this mitzvah?", the decisive reply is given: "It is a decree from before God". It is the command of the Creator, and, therefore, I wish now to keep this mitzvah specifically. And to the question that the evil inclination puts after observance of the commandment: "What is the reason for it?", an incisive answer is given: "You do not have the right to query it".. Do not query the achievement you have reached by observing the commandments and do not nurture within yourself a sense of pride and satisfaction at what you have already achieved. On the contrary, give thought the whole time to observing additional commandments out of a constant striving to excel in characteristics and in good deeds.

Atonement for sins

Rashi comments on this verse: "The red heifer comes and atones for the sin of the golden calf". To that, Rabbi Yitzhak of Vorke said: The sin of the golden calf derived from a lack of faith. The mitzvah of the red heifer was given as a counter-balance; it is an enactment, a decree without a reason, and its observance is a matter of pure faith.

Fresh water shall be added to it in a vessel. (Num. 19:17)

Flowing water

Rabbi Meir Shapira of Lublin: Israel are likened to water. By its nature, water spreads out and covers vast areas, causing wildernesses to flourish, moving mountains and removing obstacles and creating paths - even when there are large obstacles in its way. When is this? When the water is in a fluid state. But when it is frozen, it has no strength.

Israel is the same. With enthusiasm, everything can be attained but in a state of deadlock and nothing moves, and nothing can be achieved.

There was no water for the congregation; and they gathered themselves together against Moshe and against Aharon. (Num. 20:2)

The Waters of Contention

The sages, of blessed memory, tell us about the buffoons of the generation of the "Waters of Contention" and how they would bait Moshe:

"Moshe and Aharon walked along and the whole of Israel followed them. Some of the people would see a stone and they would stand around it. They would approach the stone and say: Do you not know that Ben Amram (Moshe) used to be a shepherd for Yitro? And shepherds understand water. He wants to lead us to a place where there is water and say to us: 'Look, I have produced water for you'. And so he would mislead us? Were it so (were he able to perform miracles) let him produce water from this stone" (Yalqut Shimoni, Hukat).

We also read in the Midrash: "'Moshe lifted up his hand, and with his rod he struck the rock twice'. He struck it once and the rock started to drip a small quantity of water, drop by drop. They said to him: Ben Amram, is this small amount of water for babies on the breast or for those weaned of milk? He immediately rose to their bait and struck the rock a second time and a large quantity of water emerged and flooded everything in sight" (Tanhuma, Hukat).

Unforgivable error

The recurring problem of the grave lack of water resurfaces. For the first time in his life, Moshe does not know how to cope with a threatening crisis. As the voices of protest grow, he shuts himself away in his tent. He falls on his face (Num. 20:6) and no longer has the courage to face the people. But then God commands him: "Take the rod" - Return to your younger days, when, with the help of your rod, you coped with one crisis after another.

God commands him to speak to the rock and bring water out of it (Num. 20:8). Moshe, however, does not fully comprehend the command. Rather than showing the force of outstanding leadership, he lets his anger take over: "Listen, you rebels!" he addresses the people. And then he immediately makes another, unforgivable, mistake. Instead of speaking to the rock, as God had told him to do, he hits it with his rod.

This is the reason for the dreadful punishment: "You shall not lead this congregation into the land" (Num. 20:12). Moshe, after starting out by reprimanding the violent Hebrew in Egypt: "Why do you smite your fellow?" (Ex.2:13), ends by smiting the rock! Moshe, the man who had known how to cope with serious crises, flees and falls on his face. Moshe, the shepherd, who had led his flock firmly yet in a respectful way his entire life, castigates and seriously reprimands the people. And judgment is passed on him that he cannot, and will not lead the people into the land. Moshe hits the rock twice (Num. 20:11). Anyone can make a mistake once in a moment of anger, but he repeated the error of his ways and so it was decreed that he may no longer be a leader.

Aharon, too, is punished. Even though he was not an active participant this incident, he, too, is punished and forbidden to enter the land. He was not a party to the first striking of the rock but, after it, he could have told Moshe that he had made a mistake and demanded that he stop doing so immediately. After the rock had been smitten a second time, Aharon was no longer free of responsibility and could not argue "I did not know". By not protesting, he became an accomplice and was punished accordingly.

The sages tried to explain the punishment of Moshe and Aharon in a number of ways. The gravity of the words of the Holy One when he charges Moshe and Aharon should also be noted. "Because you did not trust Me enough to affirm My sanctity in the sight of the Israelite people" (Num. 20:12). "You disobeyed Me" (Num. 27:14). "Because you did not keep faith with Me among the Children of Israel ... because you did not sanctify Me among the Children of Israel" (Deut. 32:51).

From the verses in the Bible, it can be understood that the sin of Moshe and Aharon was double. The first was in that they said to the people: "Shall we get water for you out of this rock?" (Num. 20:10). It would have been appropriate for them to have said: "Shall God get water for you ... " They led the people to think that Moshe and Aharon, in their wisdom, would be able to get water for them from this rock. We have to remember that Israel had just left Egypt, a land of sorcerers and magicians and of witchcraft. Israel might certainly have thought that Moshe and Aharon were themselves capable of extracting water out of the rock for them. If this were so, then because of this erroneous perception, the whole of the Torah would become a fraud. All the educational work done by Moshe and Aharon had to be directed against this perception of putting people in the place of God and of seeing people - magicians or sorcerers - as capable of providing people with food to eat and water to drink. That is why the verse is directed against Moshe and Aharon: "Because you did not sanctify Me among the Children of Israel" (Deut. 32:51).

Take the rod, and gather the congregation together, you, and Aharon your brother, and speak to the rock before their eyes; and it shall give forth its water, and you shall bring forth to them water out of the rock ... Moshe lifted up his hand, and with his rod he struck the rock twice; and the water came out abundantly, and the congregation drank, and their beasts also. (Num. 20:8 - 11)

The Holy Blessed One is extremely strict with the Righteous

From the Scriptural verses, it can be understood that Moshe and Aharon sinned in that they did not do as commanded by Adonai. Moshe our Teacher did not speak to the rock to obtain water from it, as he had been commanded, but he struck the rock. With the act of hitting the rock with his rod, Moshe disclosed a lack of sufficient faith in the power of the Creator of the Universe, as though his speaking to it were not enough and there had to be a demonstration of force....

Moshe our Teacher had never disobeyed Adonai, so why did he not do as commanded on this occasion? Furthermore: Is it conceivable that Moshe was not perfect in his faith to the point at which he doubted whether water would come forth from the rock through speech and that it was, therefore, necessary to strike the rock? And there is another question which also has to be addressed. If Moshe our Teacher sinned, why was his prayer of regret not accepted? Why were the gates of repentance locked?

There had actually been a previous occasion upon which Moshe had extracted water from a rock. It happened when the Children of Israel left Egypt, at the start of their wanderings in the Wilderness. The people were thirsty for water and then Moshe was commanded to strike the rock. Now, when he is again commanded to take his rod in his hand, he was of the opinion that, this time also, he was to extract water from the rock by the power of the rod, that is to say: miraculously.

Moshe should, however, have known that something had changed meanwhile. Upon their departure from Egypt, the Children of Israel were bogged down in the materialism of Egypt and needed signs and wonders to awaken in them the sense of faith. They had to see with their own eyes "And Israel saw the great work which Adonai did in Egypt" (Ex. 14:31).

But on the second occasion, as they now drew near to the Land of Israel, Moshe should have known that the Land of Israel was not being given to the people through miraculous means but through the power of faith and the power of love of the Land. Moshe our Teacher should have recalled that he was here given an opportunity to sanctify the Name of Adonai in the sight of the whole people. Since he did not do so - he was punished. "Because you did not believe Me to sanctify Me in the eyes of the Children of Israel, therefore you shall not bring this congregation into the Land which I have given them" (Num. 20:12).

Moshe made a serpent of bronze, and put it upon a pole. (Num. 21:9)

The serpent of bronze

There were three serpents: First was the serpent of creation. It did not yet bite nor did it give off venom, but this serpent of the creation story was more dangerous - it talked. It had the poison of words. And since Adam and Eve were as innocent as children, naive and easily persuaded - they were at the mercy of this evil. At the mercy of the evil inclination.

The second serpent was that of Moshe's rod. The rod turned into a serpent. Moshe took it by the tail and it changed back into a rod. In the hands of a prophet, the serpent is helpless; it is no more than an agent, it must do the bidding of the prophet. The evil inclination is at the mercy of man.

The third is the desert serpent. The snakes and the serpents that bit Israel. Adam and Eve sinned because of a serpent. The serpents in the Wilderness harmed the Children of Israel because of their sin. Adam and Eve had their appetite aroused following the seductions of the serpent. The Children of Israel were harmed by serpents because of their gluttonousness.

The serpent no longer has the prestige and importance it had had in the creation story, where it was the initiator. It is now no more than an agent. In the Garden of Eden, the serpent had control over humanity. With Moshe, humanity has control over the serpent. In the wilderness - the people determine the outcome. The power of the serpent, of the evil inclination, depends on the weakness of humans.

Against whom is Moshe to fight? Against the power of the serpent or against the weakness of people? The serpent, the evil inclination, harms people with cunning and shrewdness. It comes from a concealed, hidden place. Moshe made a serpent of bronze and placed it atop a pole, in a place that is raised up and exposed. "If a serpent had bitten any man, when he looked at the serpent of bronze, he lived" (Num. 21:9). The denunciation of this dark, cunning and shrewd force is its weakness. When people see it exposed, they will recall the maliciousness of its venom and the result of its seductiveness. Its exposure is the antidote to its bite.

We cried unto Adonai. (Num. 20:16)

The strength of a cry

Rabbi Nahman of Bratzlav says: A cry in a person's heart is, in itself, an expression of faith. This is because, although a person may be beset with doubts and heretical thoughts and great difficulties, if a cry rings out, then, presumably, there is in this person's heart a spark and a point of the great faith. If, Heaven forbid, there no longer was even a spark of faith, this person would not have cried out at all. The very cry is proof of faith.

Rabbi Nahman further said: The prophet Hosea says: "I will betroth you to Me in faithfulness; and you shall know Adonai" (Hos. 2:22). First, one has to believe in Adonai, blessed be the Name, and subsequently one merits understanding God with one's intelligence.

When the congregation saw that Aharon was dead, the whole House of Israel wept for Aharon for thirty days. (Num. 20:29)

True love

Moshe was admired but Aharon was loved. This great love encompassed all strata of the community and, at this tragic hour, received this most beautiful expression: " Only the men mourned for Moshe because he was a true lawgiver and would admonish them. But, his entire life, Aharon never said to anyone, man or woman: "You have sinned". Rather, he would pursue peace ... [one day] when Aharon was on the road, he met a certain bad man and greeted him. The next day, the man was considering committing an offence but said: 'Oy! How will I be able to look up afterwards and see Aharon. I am ashamed because he greeted me' - and the outcome is that that man desists from the offence" (Yalqut Shimoni, Hukat 20).

Parashat Balak

Balak son of Zippor saw all that Israel had done to the Amorites ... and he sent messengers to Balaam son of Beor in Petor ... Come then, put a curse for me upon this people. For I know that he whom you bless is blessed indeed, and he whom you curse is cursed. (Num. 22:1-6)

What was Balaam's character?

This Balaam who went to curse Israel, what was he like? Was he really a prophet as he testified about himself? Or was he one of the sorcerers of his time, as he is called in the Book of Yehoshua?

If we peruse the Bible, we will find that the prophets of Israel never sought out prophecy. On the contrary, they fled from it. They tried to rebel against this burden imposed upon them, against that prophesying that they did not ask for and did not seek - but that "attacked" them against and notwithstanding their will.

In contradiction to the prophets of Israel, Balaam searches for prophesy, even pursues after it and tries to bring it down reluctantly by magical means, with seven altars and an offering of a bull and a ram on each altar, going off to seek omens and meditating on his own.

And did he succeed through these magical means? Our sages, of blessed memory, are divided on this point: "And Adonai put a davar [a word or a thing] in the mouth of Balaam (Num. 23:5). R. Eleazar said: This was an angel [sent to curb his speech]. R. Yonatan said: It was a hook" (Sanhedrin 105b).

Rabbi Eleazar was of the opinion that Balaam was guided from on high to bless the people of Israel. God opened the eyes of that wicked person so that he would have the sense to bless, not curse. Rabbi Yonatan, on the other hand, was of the opinion that Balaam was drawn to the blessing, as a fish caught with a hook in its mouth, struggling and trying to return to the lake, to the sea from which it had been pulled.

287

The hook, however, was firmly in place and did not allow him to do what he wanted.

None of Balaam's preparations for receiving some inspiration made any impression on High: "And God manifested to Balaam (Num. 23:4) - God said to him: Villain! What are you doing? He said: I have set up the seven altars ...". This is like the case of a money changer who falsified his weights. The market owner came and sensed what he was doing. He asked him: What do you think you are doing? You are falsifying the weights! And the money-changer replied: I have already sent a gift [a bribe] to your home. Balaam acted in like manner. The Holy Spirit said to him: Villain, what are you doing? And he replied: "I have set up the seven altars ...". (Num. Rabbah 20:18)

As Balaam looked up and saw Israel encamped tribe by tribe. (Num. 24:2)

Modesty

What did Balaam see? The Midrash answers: He saw that the openings of their tents were arranged not facing each other [their modesty was such that they arranged it so that no-one could see into his fellow's home]. And he said: These people are fit for the Divine Presence to dwell among them.

Balak the son of Zippor saw all that Israel had done to the Amorites. And Moab was very afraid of the people, because they were many. (Num. 22:2-3)

To his credit

Of the 54 portions of the Torah, five are named after people: Noah (the second portion in the Book of genesis); Yitro (the fifth portion in the Book of exodus); Korah, Balak and Pinhas (all portions in the Book of Numbers).

Scripture explicitly testifies with respect to Noah: "Noah was a just man and blameless in his generations" (Gen. 6:9). Yitro, Moshe's father-in-law, merited having a special section in the Torah because of his advice to Moshe: "You shall choose able men out of all the people" (Ex. 18:21-23). The sages state that Korah and his band were knowledgeable in Torah (Sanhedrin 110a). Pinhas, the son of Elazar, sanctified the name of Heaven because he was zealous for Adonai in the sight of all Israel (Num. 25). But with respect to Balak, the question has to be asked: Why did this king of Moab, who sought to restrict Israel's movements, merit having a portion of the Torah named after him?

The sages explain that, as a reward for the forty-two sacrifices which Balak, king of Moab, offered, he merited that Ruth should issue from him and from her issued Solomon (Sotah 47a). According to this tradition, the merit of his great descendants, the most important kings in Israel, Solomon and his father David, was to his credit. This is how it happened that the name of this gentile monarch, who did not hide his hatred for the Jewish People, was perpetuated in one of the fifty-four portions of the Torah.

Moab said to the elders of Midian, Now shall this horde lick clean all that is about us. (Num. 22:4)

Know Your Enemy...

This seems strange. Why would the Moabites, at a time of danger, turn to the elders of Midian, a country far away from them, rather than seek help from the Edomites who were close to their border, to the east and the south?

According to the sages, the Moabites knew that Moshe had lived for some decades in Midian and so they contacted that distant land, to the south of Edom, saying to themselves: Let us ascertain from them what the characteristics are of this leader who is now threatening the borders of Moab. The sages, of blessed memory, note that the elders of Midian told the Moabites: 'The power of the leader of Israel is in his mouth.' [i.e., prayer and intercession]. The Moabites thus decided to ask for the help of Balaam, the magician, whose power was also in his mouth. (Num. Rabbah 20:4)

Rabbi Samson Raphael Hirsch suggests that there was another logical reason why the Moabites passed over the land of Edom and contacted Midian in the remote south. The land of Midian lies to the east of the Red Sea, relatively close to Egypt. The Midianites would have maintained trading relations with the larger country of Egypt. Thus the Moabites, who were frightened by the approach of the tribes of Israel, thought that they would surely be able to learn who were these awe-inspiring Israelites, who had lived in Egypt for a number of generations, and who had now smitten the powerful Sihon, king of the Amorites, and Og, king of the Bashan, with one stroke.

Adonai opened the mouth of the ass. (Num. 22:28)

His power is only in his mouth

When the nations of the world heard that Moshe's power was in his mouth, they did not realize that the reference was to his power in prayer but thought that it lay in speeches, that he was a big talker and an excellent orator. They immediately hired the services of the Balaam, a famous orator, to out-speak Moshe. One against the other.

And so: "Adonai opened the mouth of the ass" and, in so doing, God made them realize that an ass could also be an excellent speaker.

Balaam said to the angel of Adonai, I have sinned; for I knew not. (Num. 22:34)

Their distress was also his

Rabbi Hayyim of Tzanz asked one of the rabbis who was among his admirers why he was not showing any interest in the bitter fate of a certain person, one of the residents of that rabbi's city. The latter replied: "I knew nothing at all of his unfortunate situation".

Rabbi Hayyim rebuked him and said: Of Balaam it is written "I have sinned, for I knew not". This appears problematic, for, if he didn't know, how could he have sinned? The conclusion must be that not-knowing is itself a sin. A rabbi who is a leader has to know about every injustice and discrimination, about every problem and distress, of the residents of his city. A rabbi has to feel and sense things of this sort. Otherwise, that is a blemish and a sin.

He has not seen iniquity in Yaakov, nor has he seen perverseness in Israel; Adonai his God is with him. (Num. 23:21)

It is good that I see

Rabbi Levi Yitzhak of Berdichev said: A person who is loyal to God and to God's holy people does not seek iniquities in Israel. On the contrary, such a person searches for a reason to praise the Jewish People and each individual of this people. If "he has not seen iniquity in Yaakov" this is a sign that "Adonai his God is with him" and that the fear of God is in this person's heart.

Rabbi Levi Yitzhak continued: "He has not seen iniquity in Yaakov, nor has he seen perverseness in Israel". When the transgressions of Israel ascend to the Heavens above, Adonai does not see them and takes no note of them. This is not the case when their merits ascend, for God then associates with them. This is the meaning of the verse: "Adonai his God is with him". - that the Holy Blessed One associates with Israel when they do good deeds.

People, on the other hand, can so easily make a mistake and imagine that someone has sinned when the truth of the matter is that there is no sin at all. This only underlines how important it is that people be cautious and be on guard, achieving excellence by following the advice of: "He has not seen iniquity in Yaakov".

Parashat Pinhas

Therefore, I grant him a covenant of peace. (Num. 25:12)

The way a person should choose

Zealotry and peace - says Rabbi Avraham Shmuel Binyamin Sofer - are two poles, two extreme qualities that are contrary to each other. Since Pinhas blatantly proved that he is an ardent zealot when the circumstances so require, the Holy Blessed One blessed him with "peace". This is to advise and inform that even if one must, in an emergency situation, use zealotry, nevertheless one should quickly return to a firm and sure base - peace, for peace is the foundation and secret of all blessing and of all success.

True Peace

Rabbi Menahem Mendel of Kotzk taught: The world erroneously thinks that peace means leniency and submission to the strong and aggressive, but the truth is that peace attained from inner weakness is not sustainable. On the other hand, real peace is the peace derived from a lengthy struggle without disclosure of any weakness. Only such a peace, born out of suffering and pain, will stand firm as a rock and will never fold.

Measure for measure

How can one differentiate between zealotry originating in the sanctity of the heart and purity of thought and zealotry which brings in its wake the spirit of defilement, impurity and selfishness?

The Baal Shem Tov taught: The Torah teaches us about two types of zealot, both of whom apparently were zealous for the honor of Israel: Korah and Pinhas. About Korah and his band, it is said: "And they envied Moshe in the camp, and Aharon the holy one of Adonai" (Ps.

106:16). What was their zealotry? "They gathered themselves together against Moshe and against Aharon, and said to them: You take too much upon you, seeing all the congregation are holy, every one of them, and Adonai is among them. Why then do you lift up yourselves above the congregation of Adonai?" (Num. 16:3). Their zealotry was on behalf of the whole nation but, nevertheless, we know how they ended up: "The earth opened her mouth, and swallowed them up" (Num. 16:32).

On the other hand, we find Pinhas, the zealot. He was also zealous for the honor of the nation when he saw a prince of the tribe of Shimon having relations with a foreign girl, not one of the daughters of his people, and what was his reward? Was not the word of Adonai to Moshe: "Pinhas, the son of Eleazar, the son of Aharon the priest, has turned My anger away from the people of Israel, with the zealotry with which he was zealous on My behalf among them ... I give to him My covenant of peace"?

The phrase "among them" appears to be superfluous, apart from which the whole episode is surprising. Did not the sages say that: "In all the measures [of punishment or reward] taken by the Holy One, the Divine act follows the principle of 'measure for measure' (Sanhedrin 80a)? What sort of 'measure for measure' is this - for Adonai to give a "covenant of peace" to Pinhas as the reward for his zealotry, which was expressed in a particularly non-peaceful act?

Scripture itself gives us the true answer, with the over-emphasis on "with the zealotry with which he was zealous on My behalf among them". One whose zealotry for the honor of the Children of Israel comes from the source of holiness and for the sake of Heaven remains "among them", within the Children of Israel and does not separate from the community. This type of zealotry does not disturb the unity of the nation - and such a zealot was Pinhas. Knowing the value of peace and unity, he remained within the community and was zealous for Adonai "among them". That is why the Holy Blessed One gave him a covenant of peace, a fitting reward for his act of zealotry.

The zealotry of Korah, on the other hand, did not derive from a pure place, as it is said (Num. 16:1): "And Korah took". Rashi comments on these words: "He took himself to one side, taking himself out of the community for the purpose of the dispute". Such zealotry leads to division and segregation, and a spirit of impurity rests upon it. Scripture says of such zealots: "Depart, I beg you, from the tents of these wicked men" (num16:26). Zealotry causing division and dispute, that is the zealotry of Korah and his band, those who, as it were, wrap themselves in a tallit as blue as the heavens themselves, and make a pretense of being God-fearing, but anyone who cares for his soul will stay far away from them and their ilk.

The daughters of Zelophehad ... came forward and stood before Moshe, Elazar the priest, the princes, and the whole community, at the entrance of the Tent of Meeting, and said: "Our father died in the wilderness ... and left no sons. Why should our father's name be lost to his clan just because he had no son! Give us a holding among our father's kinsmen!" (Num. 27:1-4)

Equal rights

The episode of the daughters of Zelophehad is reliable testimony regarding the respect accorded to the women of Israel, even in the early period of our people's history. Other nations at that time related to women with disregard, and they would not have dared even to imagine demanding their rights from a society which so discriminated against them. And here is the Torah, devoting a whole chapter to the five daughters of Zelophehad who "came forward and stood before Moshe, Elazar the priest, the princes, and the whole community". And what did they demand? Equality of rights with the men - "Give us a holding among our father's kinsmen!"

The five girls consulted together and came to the conclusion that discrimination against women was human doing and was not part of the order which the Creator of the world had set. "The daughters of Zelophehad came forward" - since the daughters of Zelophehad heard that the Land of Israel was to be divided by tribe and not to women, they gathered together to take advice. They said: "The compassion of the Almighty is not as that of mortals! Mortals have more compassion for males than for females but the One, who spoke and caused the world to come into existence, is not like that. God's compassion is for males and for females. The Divine mercy is for everyone, as it is said: "Adonai is good to all, and His mercy is upon all His works" (Ps. 145:9). (Sifrei Pinhas 293)

In their fight for equality, the daughters of Zelophehad recorded a glorious page in the annals of human history and they did not give up until they had achieved a complete victory.

So Moshe brought their cause before Adonai. (Num. 27:5)

Bribery

Why did Moshe not himself adjudicate in the case of the daughters of Zelophehad?

It has been said that "a woman tends to cry easily" - and Moshe was concerned lest the tears of the daughters of Zelophehad influence him and work as a sort of bribe.

It is related about the Rabbi of Sochaczew that a certain widow came before him as a litigant and broke into tears. The Rabbi stood up and announced: I am leaving this case as I am not fit to adjudicate it, because tears count as a bribe.

Let Adonai, the God of the spirits of all flesh, set a man over the congregation. (Num. 27:16)

Know how to say "No"

Rashi comments: "Moshe said to the Holy Blessed One: Master of the Universe, You know the mind of each and every one, and You know that they are not similar to each other. Appoint a leader over them who will be tolerant of all".

What did the Holy One reply? "Take Yehoshua the son of Nun, a man in whom is spirit" (Num. 27:18). Rashi comments: "in whom is spirit"

- as you requested - a man who will be able to accommodate himself to the spirit of each and every one".

Rabbi Tzvi Hirsch Levin explained: A good and suitable leader has to blend together two qualities: A true leader must always be involved with people, being of soft temperament and conciliatory, tolerant of all, bearing iniquity and overlooking wrongdoing.

What does this refer to? It refers to the leader's personal and private matters. In public affairs, however, a leader must always be the firmest of all, strong in opinions, one "who knows how to oppose the spirit of each and every one". A true leader must not be subservient to the masses or be dragged after them. A true leader must have the courage to "go against each and every one", to oppose anyone when necessary and to ignore the spirits - the spirit of the time and the spirit of the place.

Leader and not led

A true leader is ahead of the people, does not adopt the taste of the masses and does not follow their spirit, but leads them instead. A true leader raises the level of the people and does not descend to theirs.

However, things will change with the arrival of the Messiah: "With the [approaching] footsteps. of the Messiah ... the face of the generation will be as that of a dog" (Sotah 9:16). Rabbi Israel Salant used to say that it is the nature of a dog always to run ahead, before his master. When the dog reaches a cross-roads, however, he looks back to see which direction his master is interested in taking. And with the approaching footsteps. of the Messiah, "the face of the generation", that is to say, the leaders of the generation, will have the attribute of the dog. They will appear to be leading the people but, in truth, the path will not be one of their choosing and they will not be directing the people who follow them. On the contrary, they will glance behind them to see what direction the people of the street are taking, where the wind is blowing, and they will always go in the direction of the masses, who are their masters ...

Let Adonai, the God of the spirits of all flesh, appoint someone over the community. (Num. 27:16)

Someone over the community

We read in the Midrash: As people's faces are dissimilar, so, too, are their minds dissimilar; each person has a unique mind. You may know that this is so from the request Moshe made of the Holy Blessed One as the time of his death came near. Moshe said to God: "Sovereign of the Universe, the mind of each and every individual is revealed and known to You. The minds of Your children are not similar to each other. Now that I am taking leave of them, I pray You to appoint over them a leader who will bear with each one of them, as it is written: "Let Adonai, the God of the spirits of all flesh, appoint someone over the community". It does not say 'the spirit' but 'the spirits'. (Num. Rabbah 21:2)

Moshe's chief concern as he prepared to take his leave from the world was not for his family or for his personal affairs. What preoccupied his thoughts was his people, who would now remain without a leader. Out of concern for the appointment of his heir, he turns to God in prayer.

Moshe pushes for the appointment to be made immediately, but this was not because he saw no suitable candidate for the position. On the contrary, says Rabbi Menahem Mendel of Kotzk, he clearly saw a man who seemed to have all the qualities of a "natural" heir. This was Pinhas, who had just demonstrated exemplary leadership, involving daring and imagination, when he acted quickly and killed the sinners, thereby removing God's anger from His people.

The action of Pinhas the zealot even obtained the approval of God, but it was this that scared Moshe, the experienced leader. He liked Pinhas and, without doubt, approved of his courageous deed but, at the same time, he did not see how this zealot, who, at a time of crisis, decided to take the law into his own hands, could be the leader of his people. He asks God to state the name of the leader who will come after him and goes on to list the qualities he would like to see in Such a leader.

A real leader is not a zealot who measures everything against one single criterion but a person who is capable of relating with tolerance to all opinions. "appoint someone over the community" - a person who will be above petty, partisan considerations.

Who shall go out before them and come in before them, and who shall take them out and bring them in. (Num. 27:17)

After me

What qualities did Moshe seek for his successor? A leader who will "go out before them". In Midrash Sifrei it is said: "Not in the way that the kings of the nations rule, sitting in their palaces and sending their soldiers to war, but such a one as will lead them out and lead them back in again".

For many years, the Israel Defense Forces has prided itself on the fact that the order to go into battle or on a dangerous mission was not "Forward!" but "After me!", with the commanding officer always going "before them", before the troops.

Moshe adds the request that his successor should be one "who will lead them out" to war "and who will bring them back again" (from the war). He well knew that taking people out to war is not the same as bringing them back home. The latter task is much more difficult than the former and a true leader has to be capable of performing both of them.

Parashat Matot

Moshe spoke to the heads of the tribes of the Children of Israel, saying: This is what Adonai has commanded: If a man makes a vow to Adonai or takes an oath imposing some prohibition upon himself, he shall not break his word but must do all that he has said. (Num. 30:2-3)

Model and example

The portion of Matot starts with laws of vows and oaths, as told by Moshe "to the heads of the tribes of the Children of Israel". The obvious question is: why does the Torah note that this set of laws was told "to the heads of the tribes". Were not all of the mitzvot told first to the heads of the people before they were put related to the Children of Israel?

The Hatam Sofer replies: It is customary in the world that the "heads of the tribes" - the leaders and various activists - vow and make various promises to the people, sometimes even swearing to keep what they have said but, in the end, they do not keep all that they promised and even do things which are contrary to what they had originally said. The unfortunate reality is that public leaders, who are called upon to serve as models and examples to the masses with their deeds and their moral fiber, they, of all people, are destined to change things without batting an eyelid and of nonchalantly going back on promises given under oath to the members of the people. This is why the Torah here calls specifically to each of the heads of the tribes: "he shall not break his but must do all that he has said".

What is a vow?

A "vow" is an obligation that a person takes on freely to either perform some action, or to avoid doing something, or to forbid oneself things that are permissible. This obligation derives from religious feeling or a private need.

There are two types of vows: vows of holiness - where a person undertakes to make a donation to the Temple (in our day to the synagogue), to give charity to the poor or for any other good purpose; and vows of denial - where one takes on extra strictures and forbids oneself things that are permitted law.

Our sages, of blessed memory, expressed their opposition to vows, particularly to those of the second category. They said: "One who vows is as one who placed a collar (a chain or iron) around the neck" (Jerusalem Talmud, Nedarim 9:1). And so did Rav Dimi, the brother of Rav Safra, say: "Anyone who makes a vow, even one who keep it, is called a sinner" (Nedarim 77b). This is because it was feared that the person making the vow might not be able to keep it. What the Torah has forbidden should suffice a person and there should be no need to add other prohibitions to those in the Torah.

With the same enthusiasm

The father of Rabbi Simhah Bunem of Pashischa said: A person who makes a vow will surely keep it and not break the promise given. The vow, however, becomes a mitzvah since "he must do all that he has said". The keeping of the vow has to be with the same desire, the same enthusiasm as the person had at the time of making the vow. As a rule, promises are given out of desire and enthusiasm but the keeping of them is done coldly, as though the person were being forced by a demon. It is hard to keep the fire of enthusiasm burning.

Adonai spoke to Moshe, saying: Avenge the people of Israel of the Midianites; afterwards shall you be gathered to your ancestors. (Num. 31:1-2)

Ready for death

Scripture stipulates the timing of Moshe's passing from the world on his taking revenge against the enemies of Israel. Seemingly, Moshe could have delayed the act of revenge and so lengthened his own life. A leader of Israel and a true shepherd, however, does not so act.

Many legendary tales depict Moshe's pleadings before the Creator of the Universe to extend his life and not to take his soul. And now, here, his life is in his own hands. He is able to postpone the war and lengthen his days - but Moshe rises above himself and reveals to us his spiritual greatness: "Said to him the Holy Blessed One: Moshe! If you want to live for many years, even a thousand years, Israel will not see their enemies, and Midian will not be conquered by them. Moshe immediately grasped this and said: Sooner or later, everything dies. Better it be that Israel see their enemies and that Midian be conquered. From this, we learn praise of Moshe for he said: So that I should live, will I delay the revenge of the Children of Israel against Midian? Immediately [in the next verse], we read: "And Moshe spoke to the people, saying: 'Arm some of yourselves for the war, and let them go against the Midianites, and do Adonai's vengeance in Midian' (Num. 31:3). Although Moshe knew that his death would be delayed pending the war against Midian, he did not delay, but hurried to do what he was bidden with joy" (Yalqut Shimoni, Mattot 31).

Avenge the Children of Israel on the Midianites; then you shall be gathered to your people. (Num. 31:2)

What was the purpose of this revenge?

The same Midianites against whom Moshe was commanded to take revenge before his death were the second people whom Israel had met up with on their way from Egypt to the Promised Land against whom they had to seek vengeance. They were commanded to wipe out the memory of Amalek and to take vengeance against Midian. But is "vengeance" not an indecent term? How, then, can the Torah command that vengeance be taken? Is the command in the spirit of the Torah, about which it is said: "Her ways are ways of pleasantness and all her paths are peace" (Prov. 3:17)?

If we compare Amalek to Midian, we find that both these people had one common goal - the destruction of Israel. Amalek planned a physical annihilation and Midian a spiritual one. But the Egyptians also sought to conspire against the Jewish People and to destroy them by killing all male newborns. Nonetheless, it is said: "You shall not abhor an Egyptian" (Deut. 23:8). Why, then, in the case of Midian, were the Children of Israel commanded to take vengeance?

It is true that the Egyptians fought against Israel, and most cruelly so. But this stemmed from the fear "Lest they increase in num. and, should there be a war, they may join our enemies and fight against us" (Ex. 1:9-10). At least they had some reason for what they did. They acted out of fear and were punished with the drowning in the sea. There is, therefore, no further need for revenge. The various Amaleks and Midians in the world, on the other hand, who conspire against Israel and wish to put an end to the existence and survival of the Jewish People, have no reason other than pure hatred for its own sake - "[they] cut down all the stragglers in your rear, when you were faint and weary" (Deut. 25:18) - for them there is no forgiveness, no expiation.

Moshe was angry with the officers of the army, with the captains over thousands, and captains over hundreds, who came from the battle. (Num. 31:14)

Forcefulness

Go and see, say the sages of Israel, how Moshe, "the most humble of men", who many times acted with forgiveness and tolerance, knew, when necessary, how to raise his voice and how to use harsh words to reprimand "the captains over thousands, and captains over hundreds" who returned victorious from the battlefield. Moshe our Teacher thus disclosed a rare quality and the mindset of a leader who is not afraid to stand alone facing many and who grants no favors to courageous heroes when circumstances so dictate. It has to be understood that a leader cannot always show humility and tolerance vis-à-vis people; sometimes a leader has to behave with great forcefulness and admonish the errant members of his people so as to bring them back to the straight and narrow.

---

*We will build sheepfolds here for our cattle, and cities for our little ones.
(Num. 32:16)*

With the help of Adonai

The story is told of a rich tourist, a well-known Zionist, who called on
Rabbi Yaakov Moshe Harlap in Jerusalem and apologized before him:
Our Rabbi, it is well known in Heaven and earth that I desire, with my
whole heart and soul, to settle in the Land of Israel, but what can I do?
My many business affairs, large and complicated as they are, preclude
me from doing so.

Come and see - the Rabbi answered him - the Torah tells us: "The
sons of Gad and the sons of Reuben came and spoke to Moshe, ... and
said: We will build sheepfolds here for our cattle, and cities for our
little ones ... But we ourselves will go ready armed before the people of
Israel". In his reply to them, Moshe our Teacher says: "Build cities for
your little ones, and folds for your sheep; and do that which has proceeded out of your mouth".

The sons of Gad and the sons of Reuben spoke first about sheepfolds
before cities for their little ones. Moshe, however, reverses the order and
puts "cities for your little ones" before "folds for your sheep". Why did
he do so?

Moshe's thinking was: So long as you are concerned about your wealth,
and your proprietary assets are more important to you than your children and you place the security of your herds before that of your children, you are not worthy that we should place any trust in you that you
will uphold your promise to "go ready armed before the people of Israel". Therefore, do this first: "Build cities for your little ones" and only
after that "folds for your sheep", and then you and I can be certain that
you will "do that which has proceeded out of your mouth".

So it is - the Rabbi concluded - that a person may be concerned about
losing money and not worry about losing children. Such a person's
money is of no help and such children do not return to their roots.

Rabbi, the rich tourist responded, that is what I shall do. I shall try to liquidate my affairs in the Diaspora and settle soon, God willing, in the Land of Israel.

Don't say, the Rabbi replied, "God willing". Because Adonai surely wants God's children to make aliyah and come and live in the Holy Land, to build it and be built up in it. What you should say is: "If Adonai will help me", and the God of Avraham will assist you in carrying out the Divine will, and "if one comes to cleanse oneself, such a person is to be helped" (Shabbat 104a).

But we ourselves will go ready armed before the people of Israel. (Num. 32:17)

Pioneers

There are no "pioneers" in the Bible but those who go first to war, at the head of a fighting people - every pioneer, every pathfinder is first while not everyone who is first is called a "pioneer". "Pioneering" is a state that exists only for those who leaves behind them a house and an inheritance and peace of mind, and stands in the front lines, with all the inherent danger of such situations. A pioneer is not someone who lacks something but one who has put it to one side in order to fulfill a role for the sake of the people and who does not return home until after the task has been completed.

When the land shall be subdued before Adonai; then afterwards you shall return, and be guiltless before Adonai, and before Israel. (Num. 32:22)

The Desired Order

One of the students of the Hafetz Hayyim was appointed to serve as the rabbi in one of the townships. of Lithuania. Since the man was young and inexperienced in the rabbinate, he asked his great teacher to instruct him as to how he should conduct himself with the members of his congregation.

The Hafetz Hayyim said to his student: In the portion of Mattot, Moshe our Teacher calls to the children of Reuben and Gad, and says to them: "You shall be guiltless (without sin) before Adonai, and before Israel". Every rabbi and teacher should inscribe these words on the heart and should behave according to them always. First and foremost, the rabbi has to be a symbol and example, and teach the members of the community Torah and commandments, and fulfill all obligation toward Heaven, as it is written: "You shall be guiltless before Adonai". Afterwards, the rabbi must fulfill all obligation toward other people.

If, however, one should want first to please the members of the congregation and only after that to fulfill one's obligation toward Heaven - that person will fail in both and the members of the congregation will not be pleased....

Parashat Masei

These are the journeys of the Israelites, who had left Egypt in organized groups. under the leadership of Moshe and Aharon. (Num. 33:1)

The moral

The Parasha opens with a summary list of the Israelites' forty-two stations over forty years: from Rameses in Egypt to Avel Shittim in the West Plains of Moab. In most cases, the text does not detail the events of the Israelites' various journeys, and the most common expressions in this Portion are: "They left ... and they camped...".

Rambam explains why the Torah listed all the places where the Israelites stopped in the desert: God knew that in the future people might doubt the veracity of the account of these miracles, in the same manner as they doubt the accuracy of other narratives; they might think that the Israelites stayed in the wilderness in a place not far from inhabited land, where it was possible for people to live [in the ordinary way]; that it was like those deserts in which Arabs live at present; or that they dwelt in such places in which they could plow, sow, and reap, or live on some vegetable that was growing there; or that manna came always down in those places as an ordinary natural product; or that there were wells of water in those places. In order to remove all these doubts and to firmly establish the accuracy of the account of these miracles, Scripture enumerates all the stations, so that coming generations may see them, and learn the greatness of the miracle which enabled human beings to live in those places for forty years" (Guide to the Perplexed, part 3, chapter 50).

They departed from Kivrot-Hatta'avah [literally: the graves of lust], and camped in Hatzerot [literally: courtyards]. (Num. 33:17)

Temporary Housing

Rabbi Yitzhak of Vorka said: You can have no better advice for overpowering the evil inclination, for breaking and burying hatta'avah [lust]. If you desire to journey from "the graves of lust", then you must yourself observe "and camped in Hatzerot". Always remember that this world is but a courtyard [hatzer] before the house, a corridor to the parlor. No-one stays in the courtyard, in the corridor, but one prepares oneself there in order to enter the parlor....

Then you shall appoint for yourselves cities which shall be cities of refuge for you; that one who commits unintended homicide, who kills any person unintentionally, may flee there. (Num. 35:11)

Rapidly and without hindrance

To make it easier for the person committing manslaughter to flee from pursuers, Israel was commanded to institute road signs with instructions on what route to take on such a flight.

Said Rabbi Abin: "Every mile, there was a tower and, on every tower, a sign, and the sign would point and show them the way to the cities of refuge" (Midrash Shohar Tov 25).

Furthermore, the sages insisted that a person who killed unintentionally be enabled to escape to the cities of refuge, rapidly and without upset. They required, therefore, that wide roads be paved to make such a flight easy: "Our Rabbis taught: The width of a private path [used by one person into his field] is four cubits [about 1.80 meters]; that of a path from one town to another [and for the exclusive use of the inhabitants of the two towns] is eight cubits [about 3.60 meters, enough for two wagons to pass each other]. The width of a public road [used by people of more than two towns] is sixteen cubits [about 7.20 meters], and the road to a city of refuge is thirty two cubits [some 14.40 meters]" (Bava Batra 100a).

In other words, if a tragedy occurs and someone is killed by mistake, every effort is to be made so that the avenger of the dead person's blood will not be able to hurt the one who unintentionally killed. So there were cities of refuge, cities in which those being pursued could be safe. And so the halakhah, Jewish law, determined that the courts in Israel must mark the roads leading to the cities of refuge, must keep them in good repair and make them wide, removing from them all obstacles and hindrance. The road must traverse not hill nor valley nor river, but a bridge must be built so as not to delay the passage of one fleeing there.

All these things, it must be emphasized, are done with respect only to someone who commits homicide unintentionally: "If a person kills another with willful intent and then says: 'I killed unintentionally' and flees to cities of refugee - the Holy One says: Even if he enters [the Temple precincts] and flees to My altar - kill him!" (Tanhuma Masei 12).

Cities of Refuge - the domain of the tribe of Levi

In addition to the purpose of saving the person who killed unintentionally from the avenger of the blood of the person killed, the leaders of the people were also required to educate the people to maintain the sanctity of life. For that reason, the cities of refuge were located specifically in the areas set aside for the cities of the levites, rather than in the areas of other tribes which had more extensive land areas. The intention of the Torah was to ensure that the priests and the levites understood their great responsibility to educate and teach the people.

Our sages, of blessed memory, did not make do with safeguarding the person who committed manslaughter unintentionally from the avenger of the blood of the person killed, but also ensured that the former would obtain an inner, spiritual strengthening and not fail again with similar actions. In addition to the exile from one's home and city imposed on the killer - which in itself atones for any sin – such a person also had to learn from the local residents, in the company of those levites in whose areas the cities of refugee were built.

Accidental killing

There are different types of killing. There are cases where a person decides to kill another for motives such as jealousy or hatred. Such a person carefully plans the murder in a premeditated fashion. This is called murder with malice intent.

But there are many cases where a person is killed as a result of an accident, a mishap, and where the killer did not hate the victim, and possibly did not even know the victim. The Torah itself provides such an example in its interpretation: "[This is not true, however,] if [the killer] pushes down [his victim] accidentally and without malice, or throws any object at him without planning to kill him. Even if it is a stone that can kill, if he did not see [the victim] and it killed him by falling on him, [he is not a murderer], since he was not an enemy and did not bear [his victim] any malice" (Num. 35:22-23).

With their entry into the Land of Canaan, the Israelites are commanded to set aside six cities: three east of the Jordan, and three west of the river, to which an individual who has killed a human being unintentionally, without premeditation can escape from the relative of the deceased wishing to avenge the blood that was spilled.

The killer would be able to take refuge in these cities, and remain safe from the blood avengers until the time came to stand trial for the homicide.

He must remain in his city of refuge, until the death of the high priest. (Num. 35:28)

Righteousness shall go before God

This verdict of exile would, at first glance, appear to be discriminatory. One such killer could be confined to the city of refugee ten, twenty even thirty years while another, similar, killer might have to spend just two years, or one year, or even two days, perhaps. just only one day there. Where, then, is the justice?

Rabbi Mordechai Hacohen taught: Scripture is talking about someone who commits manslaughter inadvertently, who killed without meaning to do so. It is a tragedy, but what happened to the victim, happened. What one should deduce from this is that had the Torah laid down a punishment of a fixed time, so many years of imprisonment, for everyone who kills another without intending to do so, would this not result in a perversion of justice? Not all those who kill unintentionally are equal. There is inadvertency out of criminal negligence and there is inadvertency out of indolence. There is near-criminal inadvertency and there is near-unavoidable inadvertency.

Hence the Torah determined: "and he shall live there (in the city of refuge) until the death of the high priest". Before the Almighty everything is known, and the extent of the inadvertency in each crime and wrong doing is overt and known to God, who administers punishment in fair measure.

The efficacy of prayer

We learn in the Mishnah: "Therefore, the mothers of (high) priests used to provide food and raiment for them (the unintentional killers who were imprisoned in the cities of refuge) so that they would not pray for the death of their sons [the high priests]" (Makkot 2:5).

And so what if the killers did pray for the death of the high priest? Did the high priest also direct his thoughts toward them and pray that he would not die but live? The point here is, however, that one can deduce from it how great is the prayer of every Jew, even the simplest of the simple, to the extent that sometimes the prayer of a killer serving a sentence in the city of refuge is of even more weight than the prayer of the high priest who goes to the very heart of matters in his prayer.

Moreover, you shall take no ransom for the life of a murderer, who is guilty of death, but he shall surely be put to death. (Num. 35:31)

Murder - an unforgivable crime

Rabbi Zalman Sorotzkin said: The reference here is not to a bribe to sway the trial of the murderer but to the taking of a "ransom" - with the concurrence of the blood avenger - for a sublime purpose: to provide for the small orphaned children of the victim. Lest one say: Since it is not possible to bring the dead person back to life and to restore their provider to the orphans, what is the gain in putting the murderer to death and leaving the orphans to starve from hunger? Would it not be preferable to receive from the murderer a ransom payment and use that to provide for the children?

Hence, Scripture warns: "You shall take no ransom for the life of a murderer" because the murderer is a villain with respect to the whole human race and not only against the victim alone.

So you shall not pollute the land [with unbecoming flattery]... And you shall not defile the land in which I dwell; for I, Adonai, dwell among the People of Israel. (Num. 35:33-34)

Double warning

Some people so love the Land that they say that everything that is done in the Land, even the ugliest of deeds, is good and beautiful and beneficial. On the other hand, there are zealots who so love the Torah and are so zealous on its behalf that they deride the sanctity of the Land and say that criminals and the secular have defiled it...

The Torah warns against both these attitudes. "So you shall not pollute the land [with unbecoming flattery]" - You shall not call everything done in it "holy", irrespective of whether it is good or bad. "And you shall not defile the land" - You shall not say that the Land is impure, because I am living in it, "And you shall not defile the land which you shall inhabit, in which I dwell". God always lives in the Land, among the people of Israel. Rashi commented: "even when they are unclean".

So how can a person defile with his own mouth the Land in which the Divine Presence dwells?!

An entire world

Rabbi Moshe Feinstein explained the link between "defilement" and "the land" as follows: All governments are very strict about bloodshed, and in all of the non-Jewish nations' laws, murderers are sentenced to harsh punishments. Nevertheless, there is a fundamental difference between the Torah's view on this prohibition and the gentiles' legal attitude to the matter.

Gentile nations consider murder as something which undermines and ruins civilization, as reflected in the saying, "[Pray for the peace of the government;] except for the fear of that, people would have swallowed each other alive" (Avot 3:2).

Following this line of reasoning, they allow themselves to kill anyone who they think is ruining civilization, believing that in this way they are setting the world right again. It is for this reason that wars break out in the world, as well as the fact that no attention is paid to the transient life of the critically ill nor the life of the elderly.

In contrast, our Torah adopts an entirely different approach when prohibiting murder. The Torah's prohibition is grounded in the importance of human life. Consequently, even if civilization does not need a particular person, it is forbidden to kill that person. This prohibition applies to everyone to the same extent, so that the ban on killing applies equally to the most important person and to somebody who is feeble-minded, as well as to someone who has only a few hours left to live.

From this we may conclude that when an individual kills another person because of an assumption that that person is spoiling civilization, that killer literally "defiles" the land, since it implies a view of the whole of humanity as secondary and superfluous to the land. According to the Torah's outlook, the land is secondary to people, who were created in the Divine image, and each individual constitutes an entire world. Thus people should always take precedence over the land.

Deuteronomy

Parashat Devarim

These are the words which Moshe spoke to all the Children of Israel. (Deut. 1:1)

Loyal advocate

"These are the words" - the words of morality and admonition that Moshe preached to the Children of Israel. Moshe only said these things when he was addressing "all the Children of Israel". When he addressed the Almighty, the Holy Blessed One, he did not mention Israel's wrongdoings. On the contrary, he would recount their praises at length, exaggerate their good qualities, overstate their rights and advocate only good for the whole of Israel.

The story is told of a certain preacher, who would make his way from city to city, preach his sermon and receive his remuneration. When he reached the city of Berdichev, he went to Rabbi Yitzhak Levi, who was known for his love of Israel, to obtain his permission to speak in the synagogue.

Rabbi Levi Yitzhak said to him: You have my permission, but with the proviso that you speak about the words of the Torah only and do not consider yourself to be a purveyor of ethics, specifying the wrongdoings, sins and crimes of Israel. The preacher accepted the terms and Rabbi Levi Yitzhak went to the synagogue himself to accord the preacher greater prestige, so that his audience would be larger and his income would grow accordingly.

The preacher started with the weekly portion and made various comments. He interspersed his words with the sayings of the sages and jumped from one matter to another, not stopping to consider the nature of his subject matter. Then he began to make critical comments about light and heavy mitzvot, about things done unintentionally and wantonly. He started to complain about Israel that they did not spend

319

enough time with matters of the Torah and in charitable deeds and found fault in the many who indulged in gossip and slander, and so it was that he enumerated all the sins of the congregation.

Thereupon, Rabbi Levi Yitzhak of Berdichev got up on his feet, raised his eyes towards Heaven, and exclaimed: "Master of the Universe! In Your great mercy, please do not believe this preacher. I give witness that Your people Israel are all beloved and that the congregation of Israel is holy. But this preacher is a poor man and his troubles are making him speak this way. The members of his household are hungry. His daughters are of marriageable age but, because of his sins, he is unable to marry them off. This is why he is bitter. You, Who feed and provide for all, grant him, I pray, a good living so that this preacher will never again speak for the prosecution against Your holy people Israel...."

Darchei noam

The Book of Deuteronomy was originally called 'Mishneh Torah' - a Copy of the Law – since it reiterates much of what had already been written in the four previous books. In this retelling of the Torah, Moshe attempted to teach the people about Torah and ethics, so that Israel could avoid the lengthy list of sins it had committed since shedding the yoke of slavery. Moshe chose to focus his retelling on anecdotes and stories, drawn from the tribes' wanderings in the desert. But, while relating tales of these events, Moshe wove into them ethical teachings as well as admonitions intended for the multitudes.

Rabbi Yisrael of Rozhin commented: This was how Moshe, Israel's faithful shepherd, chose to teach that a leader who seeks to teach his people about Torah and ethics, is advised to "wrap up" his message in stories and yarns, parables and fables which will attract their listeners' attention in an uncontrived fashion. In this way the hearts and minds of the multitude will be receptive to those parts of the Law and ethics which constitute the substance and point of the message that the speaker wishes to convey.

A friend to rebuke us

"The rebukes should have been uttered by Balaam, and the blessings by Moshe. But if Balaam had given the rebukes, Israel would have said: 'An enemy rebukes us. [So what?]' And if Moshe had blessed them, the nations of the world would have said: 'A friend blesses them. [So what?]' Therefore the Holy Blessed One declared: Let Moshe, who loves them, rebuke them, and let Balaam, who hates them, bless them, so that the genuineness of the blessings and the rebukes bestowed upon Israel will be made clear". (Deut. Rabbah 1:4)

Beyond the Jordan in the wilderness, in the Aravah ... and Hazerot. and Di-zahab. (Deut. 1:1)

Room for admonition

Rashi comments: "'And Hazerot' refers to the controversy of Korah. 'And Di-zahab' refers to their chastisement over the Golden Calf". But the Golden Calf incident preceded the controversy of Korah. Shouldn't Moshe have placed the dissension of Korah before the Golden Calf episode in his rebuke?

There are people who do not believe in anything sublime, nor in anything holy, and yet they are inclined to believe in nonsense and emptiness and all kinds of superstitions. They scoff at the God-fearing, but they themselves consult necromancers and sorcerers and those who mutter incantations An unsophisticated individual who has erred once and gone astray can be forgiven But it is difficult to forgive someone who is filled with a spirit of denial of the principles of Judaism and the revelations of the prophets and who believes in lies and falsehoods. So after the outbreak of the controversy of Koran, who was unwilling to believe in Moshe as God's prophet, the sin of the Golden Calf flared up anew, because then their disgrace was revealed; they disobeyed Moshe, the servant of Adonai, and rejected his prophecy, while they believed in a golden calf, to the point of saying: "This is your god, O Israel "

After he had smitten Sihon the king of the Amorites ... and Og the king of Bashan. (Deut. 1:4)

Deeds before words

The Sages asked: Why does the Torah specify the precise time when Moshe admonished his people? Is it of any importance that Moshe's address was given after his victories over the two kings to the east of the Jordan, and not before?

Two important lessons can be learned about proper leadership from this text: First, a leader who is devoted to the people will put deeds before words, just as Moshe struck a blow at Israel's foes before taking time to address his people with words of admonition and ethical teachings. Second, a faithful shepherd does not harass the flock in times of danger. First and foremost, the people's spiritual welfare and physical safety must be addressed. They must first be protected against external enemies, and only after the danger to the people's very existence has passed can the leader take the time to right defects at home....

How can 1 myself alone bear your cumbrance, and your burden, and your strife? (Deut. 1:12)

The power of faith

Rashi interpreted: "And your burden' - this teaches us that they were heretics".

Rabbi Nahman of Bratslav said in this connection: Heresy inflicts an enormous burden and profound suffering on an individual. In contrast, the believer enjoys sturdy, firm support, which lightens the burden of life, since for a believer everything is grounded on the solid, lasting foundation of faith, while the heretic is racked with doubts and constant introspection, which cause unceasing torment ...

I charged your judges at that time, saying: 'Hear the causes between your brethren, and judge righteously between a man and his brother, and the stranger that is with him'. (Deut. 1:16)

Every one is equal before the law

The command in this verse has become a great principle in Jewish justice: "Rabbi Hanina said: The court is warned not to hear the words of a litigant before the other litigant has arrived, and a litigant is warned not to put the case before the judge before the other litigant has arrived" (Sanhedrin 7b). Hearing one of the litigants in the absence of the opposing party can lead to favoritism and bias, as the judge might form an inaccurate impression of the case.

The text then goes on to say: "Do not give anyone special consideration when rendering judgment" (Deut. 1:17). The Greeks, who loved to create visual expressions of philosophical ideas, portrayed the goddess of justice with her eyes closed, to prevent her from seeing those who came before her. Both the Greek and the Israelite versions amount to the same thing: Do not judge by appearances. Sight can be more misleading than any other sense. Hearing is considerably less so. The voice stems from the soul, and it is more difficult to deceive by means of it. A judge who truly listens can penetrate more deeply into the soul of the person standing trial.

Judges are further commanded: "Listen to the great and small alike" (Deut. 1:17). The Sages explained this verse in the following way: "Resh Lakish said: Let a lawsuit involving a mere *prutah* be as important to you as one involving a hundred *maneh*" (Sanhedrin 8a).

An alternative interpretation is: "Do not say, this one is a poor man and the other is rich. Since it is a mitzvah to maintain the poor person, I will acquit the poor person and so the poor person will be maintained. Yet another way of putting it is: Do not say, Am I to discredit this rich person for a denarius? I will acquit now, and when they leaves the court. I will say to the rich person: 'Give the poor person that which you owe him'. (Rashi following Midrash Sifre)

Hear the causes between your brothers, and judge righteously between every man and his brother, and the stranger who is with him. You shall not respect persons in judgment; but you shall hear the small as well as the great. (Deut. 1:16-17)

Do not enforce your opinion

Rabbi Tzvi Hirsch Kalischer used to say: The instruction given here by Moshe our Teacher to the judges is worth repeating to the rabbis and lay leaders of the congregations of Israel: "Hear the causes between your brothers". Try to incline your ear, to hear and to listen to the sensitivities of the masses who are led by you. One must humor and be conciliatory to the opinions of the congregational members and desist from things which are unacceptable to the majority of the community. When the rabbis uphold the command to "hear the causes between your brothers" in the community, they also merit the upholding of the continuation of the verse: "and judge righteously between every man and his brother". The community can sense the sincerity of their leader's attitude and it evokes an atmosphere of relaxation and peace of mind in the local people and in their relationships. with each other. When love and camaraderie reign among members of the community, it becomes easy for the rabbi to give "righteous judgment" in the city.

A weighty matter

The story is told of two traders in flax who rented a ship together to transport their cargoes. Each placed his cargo in the ship in a separate place. In the course of the journey, one of the merchants had an evil thought and, in the dark of night, when the other merchant lay asleep, he got up and went to the cargo hold. There he transferred some of the merchandise from the other's cargo to his own.

When the ship anchored in the harbor, the thief weighed his cargo. To his astonishment and confusion, he found that, although he should have now had more flax that he had brought on board, in fact he had less! He immediately grasped that he had made a bitter mistake and, instead of transferring from his fellow's cargo to his, he had erred in the dark of the night and had transferred from his to his fellow's. What was he to do? If he disclosed the truth, he would be admitting that he was a thief. If he didn't, he would suffer great damage. After lengthy consideration, his materialistic tendencies overcame him and he went to the other merchant and told him the whole truth, exactly what he had done, that he had intended to steal from him but, to his regret, had in fact stolen from himself. He was, therefore, now asking the other merchant to return the merchandise to him.

The other merchant claimed that he did not believe him nor was he of the opinion that his fellow was capable of such a deed. It was true that the quantity of merchandise he had was larger than it should have been but this was not proof that the surplus weight had come from the other merchant. Maybe the landowner from whom he had purchased the flax had made a mistake? If so, it was his duty to return the surplus to him.

The two of them went to Koenigsberg to obtain a religious judgment from Rabbi Meir Loeb, the son of Yehiel Michael (and one of the great rabbis in Europe in the 19th Century, also known by his nick-name: The Malbim). They put their cases before him. The first one argued: Rabbi, I made a bad mistake and intended to steal from him but, in error, I stole from myself. The other argued: It is not so, Rabbi, do not believe him. I have known him for many years as a decent and honest merchant. Under no circumstances could he be capable to committing such a deed of dishonesty.

The Rabbi ruled that the first merchant should be required to take an oath: he had to swear on oath that he had intended to steal from his fellow, and only then would he receive back the merchandise that he had stolen by mistake from himself....

Keen Perception

Rabbi Aryeh Leib (known as 'Harif' - sharp-witted) says about this verse: An expert judge also has to have a keen eye and a sharp perception, able to put two and two together and make inferences so that litigants will not be able to deceive the judge with their sophisticated tricks. That being so, a judge may sometimes inappropriately rely on the faculty of sight: when a particular litigant blushed or went pale, the judge might assume this litigant is liable and the other litigant is innocent. The Torah, therefore, warns judges, both religious and secular: "You shall not respect persons in judgment" - you may not give a ruling based on body language or facial expressions of the litigants, but "Hear the causes between your brothers, and judge righteously between every man and his brother". You have to render judgment according to proven facts, without.

You shall not be afraid of any person. (Deut. 1:17)

Fearlessly

When Rabbi Leib of Kovno served as the rabbi in Smargon, there was a violent man in the town who, because of his wealth, was appointed as a lay leader over the community. He behaved arrogantly and caused fear to lay upon the entire town.

On one occasion, this man came as a litigant before the Rabbi. The case was difficult and the claim was large. The man was about to be found liable. The members of the household started to talk to the Rabbi, telling him to be lenient in his ruling and to find a way to mitigate the judgment so as to mollify the man, since he was violent and could do harm to the Rabbi.

For my part, I say to you - said the Rabbi - the Torah warns judges: "You shall not be afraid of any person". What sort of person is Scripture referring to? Would you say: a primary school teacher, the poor and downtrodden, who wouldn't touch a fly? No, Scripture refers only to a person such as this man who stands in trial before me, for he is rich and aggressive and has the ability to harm me.

As he was saying this, Rabbi Leib called for the litigants to be brought back in, and he said to the man: "Listen, please. I have found you liable according to the law...".

Adonai spoke to me, saying: You have wandered around this mountain long enough; turn northward. And command the people, saying: You are to pass through the border of your brothers the sons of Esau, who live in Seir; and they shall be afraid of you; take you good heed to yourselves therefore - do not contend with them. (Deut. 2:2-5)

You have been warned

Scripture explicitly states: "and they shall be afraid of you" yet "take you good heed to yourselves therefore". Why?

Our sages sensed this dichotomy and tried to uncover this mystery: Rabbi Yudan said: When Israel came to wage war with Esau, God showed to Moshe the mountain where the Patriarchs are buried. God said to him: 'Moshe, say to Israel, you cannot successfully attack him! Still outstanding and owing to him is the reward for the respect he paid to those who lie buried in this mountain.' Rabbi Simeon ben Gamliel said: No son has ever honored his parents as I have done, and yet I find that Esau honored his father even more than I. How was that? Rabbi Simeon ben Gamliel said: I used to wait on my father dressed in soiled clothes, but when I went outside into the street I would discard those clothes and put on attractive clothes instead. Esau did not do that. The same clothes in which he was dressed when attending on his father were his best. From this you may conclude that Esau was very careful with the honor of his father. (Deut. Rabbah 1)

Parashat Va'ethanan

I beseeched God at that time saying…. (Deut. 3:23)

Any time is appropriate

"At that time"- what time is that? Rabbi Yisrael of Salant used to say: From this we learn that people should not say: Now is not the proper time for prayer or Torah study, because right now, I'm tired from a hard day's work, I'm impatient and I have no strength, attention span or free time. However, when I have more time, I'll pray then. When I get around to it, I'll study. Rather, "at that time" means any time is the proper time for prayer, it is always appropriate to study Torah and do mitzvot. And if not now- when?

Please let me go over and I will see the good land. (Deut. 3:25)

I will be worthy and I will see

Why does it say " And I will see" It is obvious that if I go to the land then I will see it! Rather, as R. Menahem Mendel of Kotzk used to say: Moshe prayed that when he would come to the land , he should not err, and he should be able to see the good in the land 'The good land' and NOT as the spies saw it.

For what nation is there so great, that God is so close to them? (Deut. 4:7)

There is a God in the heavens

The story is told of a person who sent a messenger to the Hafetz Hayyim in order to ask for a blessing. The Hafetz Hayyim grinned sadly and said: Alas, one beggar sends another beggar to a third beggar to ask for a blessing. Isn't it absurd? Wouldn't it be better for him to just turn directly to our Savior, since he is so close, and it is so easy to reach him "For what nation is there that God is so close to them"

For what nation is there so great, that has statutes and judgments as this Torah? (Deut. 4:8)

Everyone will acknowledge this

There are types of laws in the Torah: Statutes, Judgments, and Teachings

Statutes are commandments that have no apparent internal logic, and are not understood by people - so the other nations ask: "what is the point of these laws?" Judgments are commandments that make sense, and if they weren't mentioned in the Torah, people would have eventually instituted them anyway. The nations look at these commandments and say: "The Torah is not teaching us anything new" as they also have these ethical and reasonable laws, even though they did not receive the Torah. Teachings are commandments that people would not think of by themselves and only now that they have been mentioned in the Torah can the nations contemplate them, only now can they begin to properly understand the logic in these teachings, and realize their depth and greatness.

It stands to reason, then, that from the Teachings, one can extrapolate that the Statutes and Judgments are also just, right and holy. This means that, undoubtedly, the Statutes have internal logic and the Judgments have a great holiness.

You must watch yourself and guard your soul diligently, lest you forget what your eyes have seen (Deut. 4:9)

Memory and forgetfulness

Rabbi Yisrael of Rodzin taught: In the "memoirs" section of our prayers recited on Rosh Hashanah, we say "For You remember all forgotten acts because nothing is forgotten by the Almighty". However, this seems like a self-contradiction because if God remembers our forgotten actions, that means that forgetfulness exists for God, and yet it goes on to say that "nothing is forgotten by the Almighty" which implies that forgetfulness does not exist for God. How can this apparent contradiction be explained? It must mean that whatever people forget God remembers and whatever people remember, God forgets. For example, a person who sins and then forgets to repent, God remembers this, and if that person then goes and does a Mitzvah, then God "forgets" it. This is what is meant by "For You remember all the forgotten acts of man", both the Mitzvot and the Aveirot.

The tale is told of a Hassid that complained to his Rebbe about his own tendency towards "forgetfulness". The Rebbe said to him "Did you ever forget to do something essential, like eating?" The Hassid answered "No". The Rebbe continued: "Because eating is a necessity for your life and well-being, you would never forget it. Thus, how can you forget Torah, which is also vital to your survival? As King David said: " I will never forget Your commandments, because they are the source of my life" (Ps. 119:93). For if they are the source of your life, how can you forget them?"

Body and soul

Rabbi Yisrael Lipkin of Salant, founder of the Lithuanian Mussar Movement, used to say: I've seen many people being extra careful regarding their physical well-being, and worrying about the souls of their friends. So, they criticize others when they feel that their fellow Jews are not observing the mitzvot properly. In addition, when their friends transgress a minor sin, they immediately rebuke them and do not hide their joy in seeing the downfall of their friends. I say that a true Hassid is exactly the opposite: A true Hassid is one who is especially careful with one's own soul and who worries about the physical well-being of fellow Jews. As a result, such a person is always careful when it comes to fear of God and the fulfillment of the mitzvot and is simultaneously giving as much financial aid to the poor of Israel, as is possible

The mountain burned with fire to the heart of heaven. (Deut. 4:11)

Burning love

Rabbi Menahem Mendel of Kotzk used to ask: Does heaven actually have a heart? And did the flames of Mount Sinai really reach "to the heart of heaven"?

The truth is that the fire on Mount Sinai was so intense and so exhilarating that the mortal heart of each of those present on that occasion turned into a "heart of heaven" - the heart became heaven.

But if from there you shall seek Adonai your God, you shall find him, if you seek him with all your heart and with all your soul. (Deut. 4:29)

From the depths of the heart

Why does this verse start in the plural ('you shall seek' is plural) but continue in the singular ('you shall find' is singular)?

Rabbi Dov Baer of Mezeritz quoted: Two people take to their bed suffering equally from the same disease, or two people are before a criminal court to be judged for the same offence; yet one gets better and the other does not, one escapes death and the other does not. Why does one get up and the other does not? Why does one escape death and the other not? Because one prayed and was answered, and the other prayed and was not answered. Why was one answered and the other not? One prayed whole heartedly and was therefore answered, the other did not pray whole heartedly and so was not answered (Rosh Hashanah 18a).

The rabbi continued: this is where Scripture is very careful to state: "But if from there you shall seek Adonai your God". It is possible that many of you will seek Adonai. Nonetheless: "you shall find him", you, in the singular, will have your request answered "if you seek him with all your heart and with all your soul", if your prayer is with your whole heart and soul, then you will merit having your prayer accepted on high.

Return to Adonai, your God. (Deut. 4:30)

Trying to achieve too much

Rabbi Hayyim of Sanz used to say: "When I was young, I wanted to help the whole world improve and get closer to God. After a while, I saw that I could not improve the entire world, so I decided to focus on helping my neighbors. This, too, was unrealistic, and I said to myself, at least I should try to help the members of my household, by implanting in their hearts the fear of God. Finally, I saw that I was trying to accomplish too much and that I would have to settle for the minimum and at least try to find a way to improve myself and find the path to repentance. But, with all of my transgressions, I did not even achieve that".

Know therefore this day, and consider it in your heart, that Adonai is God in heaven above, and upon the earth beneath; there is no other. (Deut. 4:39)

The Shekhinah in exile

Once, at the end of the Day of Atonement, after he had returned home from the synagogue services, Rabbi Simhah Bunam of Pasischa told his followers the following story:

A king's son rose up against his father and the king sent him into exile. Subsequently, the king felt compassionate toward his son and ordered that he be sought out. A long time elapsed before one of the messengers found the son of the king in a village tavern, dancing barefoot and wearing a torn shirt, among drunken peasants. The member of the royal court bowed down before him and said: "I have been sent by your father to ask you what you want. Whatever it may be, the king is ready to fulfill your request". The son of the king burst out crying and said: "If only I had some warm clothing and a pair of strong boots - that would suffice me!"

You see - continued Rabbi Simhah Bunam - we are so pitifully concerned about the small things of now that we forget that the Shekhinah itself is in exile....

Then Moshe set apart three cities on this side of the Jordan toward the rising sun; That the slayer, who killed his neighbor unintentionally, and did not hate him in times past, might flee there; and that by fleeing to one of these cities he might live: Bezer in the wilderness, in the plain country, of the Reubenites. (Deut. 4:41-43)

Gratitude

Rabbenu Bahya ben Asher commented: The first city of refuge, to which those committing unintentional manslaughter could flee so that those seeking blood vengeance could not harm them was in the tribal area of Reuben. Why was that so? Because Reuben, Yaakov's first born son, was the first to engage in the saving of lives, as it is written in the episode of the sale of Yosef: "Reuben heard it, and he saved him from their hands" (Gen. 37:21). Reuben came forward to save his brother Yosef from their other brothers who had wanted to kill him. For that reason, Moshe rewarded him for this rescue and determined that the first city of refuge, dedicated to saving Jewish lives, should be in Reuben's area.

I am Adonai your God. (Deut. 5:6)

The Torah was given to you personally

The sages of Israel drew attention to the fact that the Ten Commandments are in the singular, from start to finish. The Torah thus teaches us that each and every Jew must say: For my sake the Ten Commandments were given, and the obligation is imposed on me to observe what is written in them.

Honor your father and your mother, as Adonai your God has commanded you. (Deut. 5:16)

An independent mitzvah

Rashi commented: "they (the Children of Israel) were also commanded regarding honoring parents at Marah". Why did Rashi consider it important to note where, precisely, this commandment was given to the Children of Israel?

People usually try to explain this commandment of honoring one's parents as a natural human obligation, as an expression of gratitude and appreciation to their parents for having cared for them over a lengthy period, for having fed them and clothed them and educated them. The children are thus obligated to recompense them for all the kindnesses with which the parents showered them.

But the truth of the matter is that this is not the reason. The significance of this mitzvah has nothing to do with materialistic gratitude. People are required to honor their parents "as God commanded you at Marah". It was there, at Marah, that the needs of the Children of Israel began to be supplied miraculously. "Adonai showed [Moshe] a tree, which, when he threw it into the waters, made the waters sweet" (Ex. 15:25). Immediately after that, we read: "Behold, I will rain bread from heaven for you" (Ex. 16:4), and "Your garment did not grow old upon you" (Deut. 8:4). In other words, the children were not [materially] dependent on their parents at all and their parents did not have to toil to provide for their children.

So the point that Rashi makes is that it was under such circumstances that the commandment was given to honor one's parents. From this, one can deduce that the mitzvah in no way depends on whether the children received any material benefits from their parents or not.

Honoring your mother

There once was a Torah scholar who came on Aliyah to Israel together with his widowed mother. He intended to have her live with him and his family, in order to provide proper care for her. When this scholar came to the Hazon Ish in order to ask for his opinion, the Hazon Ish disagreed with this approach saying: "This is not the proper thing to do, because if you are constantly with your mother, then you may inadvertently offend her, and as a result, your reward will be outweighed by your punishment. The right way to honor you mother is for you to set her up in an apartment and provide for her needs. Find volunteers to help her, and even if you have to pay them for their trouble, she will still be better off and you will be properly fulfilling the commandment of honoring your mother"

Hear O Israel Adonai our God, Adonai is One. (Deut. 6:4)

God is King

Rabbi Yisrael Salanter used to say "A Jew who recites the Shema and accepts that God is the Master over the four directions and every place contained within must not forget to also place God as a Master over the self".

You shall love God with all your heart, your soul and your might. (Deut. 6:4)

Please do good for me and not bad

Rashi explains "with all your heart" to mean that your heart should not be wavering in your love of God. Rashi explains "with all your might" to mean that, for every measure allotted to you, good or bad, "one must bless the bad just as one blesses the good" (Berakhot, 60b).

Rabbi Yitzhak from Gur taught: Rashi interpreted "with all your soul" to mean "even if God takes your soul". So too, one should read "with all your heart" to mean even if God takes your heart. Even if you are not whole-heartedly content with something, even if you are full of doubt and in pain, then too, you should "love" God.

Parashat Ekev

Therefore it shall come to pass, if you pay heed to these judgments, and keep, and do them, that Adonai your God shall keep with you the covenant and the mercy which he swore to your ancestors. (Deut. 7:12)

A heavenly court

The story is told about Rabbi Avraham Yitzhak Kook that, once, while he was immersed in a Talmudic problem he was studying, he suddenly became aware of a hesitant knock on his study door. The door opened slightly and a small man, with touches of gray in the hair around his temples and beard, entered the room. He locked the door after him and remained standing in the doorway, with his back to the door, and his head bowed down as though afraid to look the Rabbi in the face.

"Come closer, my son", the Rabbi said to him, while trying with his gentle tones to give the man some self-confidence. The man moved closer to the Rabbi's desk slowly. "Your Honor", the visitor falteringly said in a low voice, "I have come to ask the Rabbi an important question".

"Ask, my son, ask", the Rabbi encouraged him.

"For the past twenty-five years, I have labored hard from morning to evening. I have hoed out weeds from fields earmarked for the planting of orchards. I have planted and even in de-stoned fields. I have dug out the foundations for the construction of houses in the Land of Israel. I have invested the best of my endeavors in manual labor and, despite all that, it is only with difficulty that I am making a living for my family. And so now I would like to ask: Am I allowed to leave the country and move to America and try there, where perhaps my luck will shine for me and I will be able to provide for my family with dignity?" the laborer concluded, and continued standing there, silent.

337

Rabbi Kook remained sitting, quietly thinking. After a few moments of silence, he suddenly rose from his chair and, pointing at the chair with his finger, instructed the man to sit. The visitor was overcome by nervousness and began to stammer: "Your Honor, 'let no stranger sit upon his seat!'[quoting the Bible] "

"Sit", the Rabbi again ordered him. With small, hesitant steps, the man walked around the desk until he came to the Rabbi's chair and sat himself upon it, all shaking and fearful. No sooner had he sat down, than his head fell upon the desk and a deep sleep came upon him. After a while, he awoke, all emotional.

"What's with you, sleepy one?" the Rabbi asked him. The laborer responded: I had a dream in which I passed away and my soul ascended on high. When I reached the gates of heaven, an angel was posted at the entrance and he directed me to the Heavenly Court where I stood before the One Who Dwells on High and the scales of justice. All of a sudden, carts harnessed to horses began to pass by, loaded with packages, some small, some medium and some large. And angels began unloading the packages and placing them on one of the pans of the scales. And the pan collapsed under the weight and was near the floor.

"What is the meaning of these packages?" I asked the angel who was posted over me. "These are your sins and your wrongdoings, O mortal man, that you sinned and erred during the days of your life on earth, and everything will come to the trial". I totally lost heart.

Then, other carts began to arrive, overloaded with clods of earth, stones, rocks and sand, and the angels were loading these onto the second pan of the scales which also began to go down, until it was almost level with the pan with the sins and wrongdoings. "What is the meaning of these packages of earth?" I asked the angel who was posted over me. "These are the stones, the rocks and the dirt that your hands labored so hard to remove from the soil of the Land of Israel and they will take the stand and speak to your credit about your portion in the upbuilding of the Land...". I stood there trembling and watched the pan of the scales bearing my good deeds as it slowly descended and pulled up the other pan, but then it suddenly stopped descending, with just a tiny bit more to go for it to outweigh the other pan.

You see, my son, the Rabbi answered him pleasantly, you have received an answer to your question from on high.

Be as meticulous with a minor mitzvah as with an important one

Rashi commented: "If you listen to the minor commandments which people trample in their wake...".

Rashi's interpretation does not, God forbid, endorse the evil person who holds both the easy and the complex. mitzvot in disdain. Rather, it refers to a person who indeed observes the Torah and mitzvot, but treats the simple Mitzvot lightly.

Midrash Tanhuma explains King David's concern, when he said: "Why should I fear in the days of evil, when the iniquity of my persecutors surrounds me?" (Ps. 49:6) as follows: "May the Name of the Holy One be praised for giving the Torah to Israel where there are 613 mitzvot, both minor and major. There are simple Mitzvot about which people are not meticulous, discarding them under their heels, as if they are insignificant". This is why King David feared the Day of Judgment saying, "King of the Universe, I am not afraid of the mitzvot in the Torah which are difficult. I fear the easy Mitzvot lest I overlook one of them or lest I observed it or not simply because it was easy". It was for this reason King David wrote: "Why should I fear in the days of evil?" (Ekev 1).

You shall keep them and do them. (Deut. 7:17)

Give to each person according to their deeds

The warning to observe the mitzvot is given in the plural: "you (all) shall keep and do...", but the promise of reward is phrased in the singular: "God will love (specifically) you and bless you". The caution and the command to observe the mitzvot were given equally to all, but not everyone will do and observe the mitzvot equally, nor are they equal in their willingness and enthusiasm, nor in their purity of motives. Therefore, the plural is used for the imperative to all, but the reward is not identical, for each shall receive according to the willingness and enthusiasm invested in the observance of that particular mitzvah.

A land of wheat and barley, and vines, fig trees and pomegranates, a land of olive trees and honey. (Deut. 8:8)

In praise of Eretz Israel

Even before Moshe our Teacher surveyed the Promised Land from the mountain summit, he praised it to the Children of Israel. He enumerated the seven species with which the land is blessed, and it is difficult to know what was stronger - Moshe's desire to endear the Land to the people, or his own love of the Land. He concluded as follows: "And you shall eat and be satisfied, and bless Adonai your God for the good land which God has given you" (Deut. 8:10).

Moshe opened with these words: "good land", without the definite article, and it was only after he had enumerated its great goodness that he closed with: "the good land", using the initial "heh". He mentioned the blessing of the harvest, beginning with the staple produce of wheat and barley, and continued with the rest of the seven species, concluding with honey. If all these are to be found in the Land, then the people who dwell there will not starve. They will not be dependent upon others, for the people will gain their bread from their land.

"So that you might gather in the corn, and the grape harvest, and your (olive) oil" (Deut. 11:14) - Eretz Israel should be plentiful in wheat, grapes and olive oil, so that other countries will shower her with an abundance of silver and gold" (Sifrei, Ekev). The Torah emphasizes that a country requires not only political independence, but economic self-sufficiency, which is why Moshe continued with: "Adonai will open to you the Divine goodness of plenty ... and you shall lend to many nations, but shall not borrow" (Deut. 28:12).

Yet no grain, grapes or olives are a sufficient guarantee of wealth and economic independence. At times, a country must sell its produce in order to purchase other goods which if requires. The text therefore continues: "you shall not lack any thing in it" (Deut. 8:9). To this phrase

Rabbi Shimon Bar Yohai attributed the following meaning: 'Tevel' [Land] means Eretz Israel. Why was it termed 'Tevel' ? Because it is 'metubelet' [seasoned] with all. Whereas, in the case of other countries, one will have something that another will not, and another will have something not available somewhere else, Eretz Israel lacks nothing. As it is said: "you shall not lack anything in it" (Sifrei Ekev 37).

People are born to toil

In order to produce all this goodness and plenty from the soil, a person must toil and labor. Nothing can be expected to fall from Heaven, no earth will bring forth crops. of its own accord, because the Heavens will not give of their blessings spontaneously. Instead, if we work the land, we are promised that it will give of its fruits. And people who toil and see the blessings of their labor are doubly blessed, because they had not sat idly by waiting for Heaven's blessing to come without making any effort of their own.

The Land in our hearts

"Rabbi Levi said: At the time when Avraham was wandering in Aram-Naharayim and in the land of Nahor, he observed them eating, drinking and acting recklessly. He said: I hope that I will not have a share in this land. When he reached the Ladder of Tyre (Ras el Naqura - the mountain pass from Lebanon into Israel), he saw people engaged in weeding in the weeding season, and hoeing in the cultivating season. Here he said: I hope I can have a share in this land. The Holy Blessed One responded: To your seed will I give this land" (Gen. Rabbah 39). If we have not always been privileged to dwell securely under our vines or fig trees, we have always lived with the hope of doing so. If we survived for generations without a land, we nevertheless drew strength from our aspirations to dwell and inhabit the land of our ancestors. We did not always have a terra firma beneath our feet; nor did our Land always bear our people upon it - but our people have always carried the Land in their heart.

Your silver and gold shall be increased. (Deut. 8:13)

Are you really rich?

The story is told of a rich man who boasted to the Hafetz Hayyim that the Holy Blessed One had granted him wealth and that he wanted for nothing. The Hafetz Hayyim replied: "It is befitting that you set aside at least one hour each day for the study of Torah". The former replied: "I have no time to spare". "If so", replied the Hafetz Hayyim, "then you are the most destitute of paupers. For if you do not have time, what is left you? There is no-one poorer than the person in need of time".

To serve God with all your heart and all your soul. (Deut. 11:13)

A lesson

"From everything we can learn to serve our Creator", so said Rabbi Avraham Yaakov of Sadigora to his disciples. "Everything has something to teach us. - Not only things which the Holy One has created, but also things which people have made – all have something to teach us".

"What can we learn" - asked one doubting disciple - "from the railway?"

"That in just one second, you could miss everything".

"What can we learn from the telegraph?"

"That each word is counted and significant".

"And from the telephone?"

"That what we say over here can be heard over there"

I will place grass in your fields for your cattle, that you may eat and be full. (Deut. 11:15)

Cruelty to animals

The sages deduced from this verse that one is forbidden to eat before feeding one's beasts (Berakhot 40a).

It was said about Rabbi Naphtali Tzvi Yehudah Berlin that he would not partake of a meal in his house until he had ascertained that his poultry had been fed. It once happened on Rosh Hahanah, after midday, that the Rabbi came home from the synagogue and did not want to sit down at the table until the poultry had been given their food. The chicken coup, however, was locked and the key could not be found. The Rabbi ordered that a non-Jew be brought to break the lock and neither he nor any member of his household tasted a single morsel until the non-Jew broke the lock and the chickens were given their food. Only then did he say Kiddush over the wine and they all sat down to the festive meal.

To love Adonai your God, to walk in all God's ways, and to cling to God devotedly. (Deut. 11:22)

The resurrection of the dead

Our Rabbis taught: It is possible to cling devotedly to God, and it is an "all-consuming fire". But the intention here is that you devote yourself to the Almighty's good qualities: insofar as God is merciful, you should also be merciful; insofar as God is gracious, you should also be gracious.

The Lubavitcher Rebbe, Rabbi Menahem Mendel Shneerson, taught: If only people would truly aspire to cling devotedly to the qualities of the Holy One, and walk in God's ways of Mercy and Grace - and that would be good. However, in our prayers, we say three times a day that God is: "the Reviver of the dead". How can we possibly resurrect the dead? The Rebbe then answered: There are people walking the street who are alive in every sense, but they have no joy of life, no happiness.

Worry gnaws at their hearts and gouges their minds, they walk stooped and mournfully, without the spirit of life springing within. Whenever you ask how they are, or show some interest in their situation and offer encouragement, you are - in all conceivable ways - "resurrecting the dead", you restore life and afford them some anticipation and hope. You therefore fulfill the commandment of clinging to God devotedly, and, through your actions, you become the Holy One's partner.

Single-minded devotion

The Baal Shem Tov said: Before a silversmith can bind two silver items together, each item must be cleaned and scraped thoroughly so that not a smidgen of dirt remain on it. This is because the dirt creates a separation and the binding will not be successful. Similarly, it is impossible to hold fast to Adonai unless all the dirt and every scrap of litter is removed from the heart. One of his students asked the Baal Shem Tov: What is the reason that a person who is devoted to the Creator and feels close to God may, nonetheless, sometimes feel an interruption and a remoteness?

The Baal Shem Tov answered: When a father wishes to teach his small daughter how to walk, he first stands her in front of him and holds out his arms close to her so that she will not fall. And the child walks between the arms of her father and gets nearer to him. As soon as she is close to him, the father moves back little by little and again opens out his arms. He does this time after time until his daughter can walk on her own...".

Parashat Re'eh

See, I set before you this day a blessing and a curse. (Deut. 11:26)

Free choice

The text does not read: "I shall set before you", but rather, "I set before you this day". Why? The Vilna Gaon suggested it was to teach us that each person, each day, is always granted this choice - to reject evil in favor of good; to return to the path of observance and renew life, as if reborn.

The Vilna Gaon added: It is written, "Behold, I set before you", in the plural, so why does it begin with "Behold" in the singular? The sense is that a person should not say: since many people follow one path, it must be good and straight, so I shall walk with them, too. This is precisely what people must not do: each person, being a human, must independently choose the good and straight path, in accordance with the Torah and Mesorah (Tradition). For we have already seen many who walked the path of the masses in error, going astray, and misleading others with them.

The story is told of the Baal Shem Tov, whose students asked him: How can we know that this path we walk is the true way of the Torah? He said to them: Shall I explain what it resembles through an allegory? It is like two people who both erred in their direction, and both became lost in the dense, entangled forest, so they walked along the paths and wandered through the forest trails for days on end without finding a way out. After some days, they met each other in the depths of the forest. The first said to the other: "My brother, perhaps. you know the right way which will guide a man out of this thick forest and lead him to his destination? The second replied: I do not know the right way, but I can tell you one thing. I, like you, am lost in the paths of the forest. Do not follow any of the paths which I have taken to date, and I shall not go in those which you have followed. Let us both seek a new path

345

and since "the Almighty is near to all those who call", perhaps God will guide us in the path we shall take.

Exclusive vision

Rabbi Menahem Mendel of Kotzk said: This verse starts with the word "see" in the singular and continues with "before you" in the plural. What is the meaning of this?

The Torah was given "before you" in the plural, to the whole of the Jewish People, but the "seeing" is in the singular because each person sees in the Torah something special. Each person has an individual insight into the Torah – something no one else can discern.

To the place which Adonai your God shall choose. (Deut. 12:5)

Materialism and spiritualism

An ancient legend relates that in ancient times two brothers had lived at the site on which the Temple was built. The older brother was alone, without family, while the younger brother had a wife and three children. Both brothers were poor farmers. They had just one field, which they had inherited from their father, and they divided the crop between them, in equal shares.

One night, after the harvest, the older brother was unable to sleep because of his concern for his younger brother. His brother had to care for a wife and children and the crop that year had not been great. How would his brother provide for his family? So he got up in the middle of the night, took some sheaves from his pile, placed them on his brother's pile and returned to sleep.

The younger brother also had difficulty sleeping. He was concerned for his older brother who was alone, without a family who could have cheered him up and made things easier for him in times of deprivation and poverty. Toward morning, the younger brother got up, took some of the sheaves from his pile and placed them on the pile of his older brother.

When morning come, the two brothers went to their piles and, surprisingly, they lacked nothing. They were nonplussed and, on the second and third nights, repeated what they had done on the first night. On one of the nights, as they were transferring the sheaves to each other, they met in the middle of the field, with the sheaves in their hands. They understood each other's intention and actions and fell on each other, hugging and kissing.

The older brother saw to the material needs of his younger brother who had children to care for. The younger brother saw to the spiritual needs of his lonely older brother. The Holy Blessed One saw what the brothers had done and the goodness of their hearts and blessed that place. Where there is concern for both spiritual and material needs - that is where heaven and earth touch. In later times, King Solomon built the Temple in the field that had belonged to the brothers.

If there arises among you a prophet, or a dreamer of dreams.... (Deut. 13:2)

The treasure is concealed in your own home

Rabbi Nahman of Bratzlav told the following story: A certain Jew who lived in Austria once saw in a dream that a valuable treasure was hidden in Vienna, under a bridge. He traveled there and stood on the bridge, wondering what to do. Were he to start searching in the daytime, people would see him and realize what he was up to.

Meanwhile, a soldier crossed the bridge, saw the Jew standing there, wondering. He asked him: What are you doing here and what are you looking for? The Jew decided to tell his closely guarded secret to the soldier and asked for his help in searching for the treasure. When it was found, they could divide it between them, half and half.

The soldier replied: You are mistaken. I also had a dream, and in it I saw that, in the house of a certain Jew in a particular town, there, in the courtyard of the house, is buried a valuable treasure. Should I then get up and journey there?

The man was taken aback, for the name of the Jew was his and the town was the town of his birth. The Jew immediately took a cart, harnessed to a pair of strong horses, and traveled as fast as he could to his home town. He went into the courtyard of his home, dug there and found the treasure.

When the Jew saw this, he said: The secret has now been revealed to me. The treasure was always hidden in my own home but I had to go on a long journey in order to discover it...

Bad influence

The Torah mentions three different pitfalls, three ways in which people may be inadvertently led away from Jewish observance.

The first pitfall is the false prophet. A certain person may be held by others to be a leader, or a far seeing politician. Such a person will utilize this unearned trust to dominate and influence people. Those who listen to such a person are thus diverted from the path of Judaism. This is the Torah's understanding of a false prophet, regarding whom the Torah said: "You shall not listen to the words of that prophet".

A second pitfall arises from our nearest and dearest - relatives, friends, brothers and sisters, - whose influence diverts a person from the straight path. In such a case, "if your brother and son of your mother or your son or your daughter or friend who is as one soul with you shall lead you astray", the Torah commands us as follows: "You shall not obey, and shall not listen to such a person".

Then there is the person who is swept up with the crowd and subject to the influence of the street, of fashion, and of public opinion. Whenever anyone says something or does something, such a person follows suit. This kind of pitfall is compared to that of the perverted city: "The people who were sons of wickedness went out and led the residents of their city astray". In this case it is imperative to go to war: "For you shall surely strike the residents of that city".

That Adonai your God may bless you in all the work of your hands, which you do. (Deut. 14:29)

The curse of idleness

One of humanity's purposes in this world is to work — in order to continue with what the Almighty began in Creation. In this manner people become the partner, so to speak, of the Holy One.

This task is indeed a blessing with which people have been gifted. The Torah portion speaks of it as follows: "That Adonai your God may bless you" - can you therefore sit by idly? The significance is "in every act of work by your hands that you do". A person who does something - is blessed. But if the person does nothing, no blessing will be forthcoming" (Tanna of Rabbi Eliyahu 14).

Moreover, people must understand that the blessing is not granted, other than through manual toil and through their own doing: "That a person might not say: I shall eat and drink and will see the good without troubling myself, and the Heavens will be merciful. Thereto it is written (Job 1:10): 'You have blessed the work of his hands' – a person must toil and work with his own two hands and the Holy Blessed One sends a blessing". (Tanhuma Vayetze)

Work is also an educational means of keeping people away from idleness, sloth and crime, which is why Rabbi Yehudah said: "Anyone who does not teach his son skills (a craft), it is as if he teaches him to go astray (to steal)" (Kiddushin 29a).

Rabbi Yehudah Ben Betira used to say: "One who has no trade to follow, what will he do? If he has a courtyard in ruins or a desolate field, he will go and occupy himself with it...". Rabbi Yossi said: "A man does hot die, other than from idleness" (Avot de Rabbi Natan 11).

You shall surely give to him. (Deut. 15:6)

Two acts of giving

A poor man came to Rabbi Mendele of Rimanov, poured out his bitterness to him, and told him of the desperate state in which he found himself. Rabbi Mendele gave him a fair donation. When the man was about to leave, the Rabbi called him back and gave him another coin. The rabbi's student asked why he gave the poor man two donations. Rabbi Mendele replied: The first time I gave him something because his words touched my heart deeply and I felt sorry for him - which means that this gift was given for my own sake, for my peace of mind, to calm my feelings and settle my conscience. The second time, however, I gave him a donation for the sake of the Mitzvah - the good deed. So it follows, he concluded, from the words of the commentators on the verse "and your heart shall not pain you" - that your heart shall not be unhappy, distressed or sad - and this act of giving is for your own sake, to ease your mind. The second time "you shall give him", it is for the person's sake, for the Mitzvah".

You shall surely give

One of the opponents of Rabbi Menahem Mendel of Kossov came to the Rabbi in his hour of need and asked him for help with money for his daughter's marriage. The Rabbi took all the cash he had at the time and gave it to him.

The Rabbi's wife asked in astonishment: "For the most essential needs of the home you have no money, yet for this man who opposes you and your way of life, you gave all your money?" Her husband responded with a smile: "Just a few minutes ago, someone else made the same claim with much greater skill".

-"Who was that?" - asked the Rebbitzen.

-"My evil inclination". - answered the Rabbi....

If there be among you a needy man, one of your brothers. (Deut. 15:7)

"And your brother shall dwell with you"

The story is told of a man who visited the home of Rabbi Aryeh Levin in Jerusalem and offered him a donation for the Yeshivah which carried his name. Rabbi Aryeh refused to accept the donation from him, saying: 'You are prohibited from giving a donation!' The man in question was astonished at this response and asked: 'Why? I am a man of means.' Rabbi Aryeh answered him: 'Because you have relatives and family members whose situation is hard-pressed and will be so as long as you do not assist them. I am therefore not allowed to accept your donation, for it was surely written: "You shall not turn away from those of your flesh" and "the poor of your city have priority"'. He held fast to his refusal. These words entered the heart of the donor and from then on this person assisted members of his family who were financially hard-up.

You shall surely give him, and your heart shall not be grieved when you give to him. (Deut. 15:10)

With willing spirit

Some give charity against their will out of embarrassment and others give charity to the poor fearing that the poor will resent them and curse them. There are also people who given charity because they cannot say "We don't have", for example, those who sit in a shop with coins lying in front of them, or because it is not their habit to lie and say "I don't have any".

None of these gives wholeheartedly. That is why Scripture says: "You shall surely give". [in Hebrew: "a giving you shall give]. That is why there are two givings - one in the heart and one in practice. "and your heart shall not be grieved when you give to him". In other words, you should give charity not just in practice; at the same time as actually giving, you should not regret doing so.

Parashat Shoftim

Judges and officers shall you appoint in all your gates. (Deut. 16:18)

Living up to one's principles

Rabbi Yaakov Yosef of Polonnoye used to say: Scripture says, "You shall appoint" for yourself. "First adorn yourself, and then adorn others" (Bava Metzia 107b). First of all, judge yourself. Then, to the same extent that you take measure of yourself, do likewise for others. Do not be lenient on yourself and stringent on others. Do not be forgiving and conciliatory towards yourself and punctiliously hair-splitting with others, demanding of them what you do not keep yourself.

You shall not take a bribe. (Deut. 16:19)

You have been warned

Rabbi Hayyim of Kosov commented on this verse: In Rabbeynu Bahya's book "Duties of the Heart", it is stated that it is the way of the evil inclination to give a person a bribe. How is that?

It tries to persuade a person that enough mitzvot have already been kept, much Torah has already been learned, and that it is allowed to do something not according to the Torah. About this, too, the Torah warned: "You shall not take a bribe".

Without fear

The Rabbi of Nickelsberg had a bag and a walking stick hanging on the wall of his study, (where people would often come to ask him to pass judgment on cases). These objects served as a warning to all who entered "Anybody who comes to me to present a case, (even people of influence or important people in the community), if you try to coerce me into judging you favorably, you should know that I judge impartially and fairly and I will not waiver judgment based on status. Whatever happens, justice will be served. If you are not satisfied, I am always ready to quit as Chief Rabbi. I will take my bag and walking stick and seek another dwelling place.

For a bribe blinds the eyes of the wise and perverts the words of the righteous. (Deut. 16:19)

Give your opinion on the matter

When one person says that another is "rich", this is not necessarily factual, because "rich" is a relative concept. It depends on how that person defines riches. If the person is poor, even middle class stature seems rich. However if a wealthy and famous person were to call another person "rich", then we could rely on this testimony.

This is also the case with wisdom. The testimony of one person that another is wise will not be accepted until we verify the knowledge level of the witness. For if the witness is a fool, then the witness does not know what wisdom is, and would even say that another fool is wise. However if the most learned person of the generation will testify, then we know that the person testified about is indeed wise. The Hafetz Hayyim says "Now imagine if God were to say that a particular person was wise, then we would know that there are no bounds to this person's wisdom. So, if the Torah states "A bribe blinds the eyes of the wise" it is clear that this pertains to even the most learned sage, because God is testifying to this person's wisdom, and states that bribery will even blind this person's eyes.

According to the sentence of the Torah which they shall teach you, and according to the judgment which they shall tell you, you shall do. (Deut. 17:11)

Without resentment

The question is asked: Why does Scripture emphasize here, by repeating the same idea in different words, that one must follow the instruction of judges? Isn't it obvious that one must do so?

It is commonplace that, when a rabbi rules a certain piece of meat non-kosher, the ruling is accepted without appeal and without a shade of resentment of the rabbi who so rules. On the other hand, in financial matters and in other disputes people have with each other - the litigant who is found liable will resent rabbi.

The reason for this is that, litigants are not as worried about the financial loss they incur as about the win of their rival. This is why the Torah here warns us, with a repetition: "According to the sentence of the Torah which they shall teach you" referring to the laws of kashrut and other categories of prohibition, "and according to the judgment which they shall tell you" referring to financial laws and other categories of dispute between people, "you shall do". Either way, you must accept the ruling without appeal and without resentment.

You shall set a king over you ... from among your brothers shall you set a king over you. (Deut. 17:15)

The Monarchy in Israel

Is the crowning of a king in Israel a matter of permission or obligation? Opinions are divided on this matter. Some sages viewed this as a mitzvah of the highest importance while others had an objection to the institution of the monarchy and spoke out against it.

In the Talmud, we find the opinion of Rabbi Jose, who said: "Three commandments were given to Israel when they entered the land: to appoint a king; to cut off the seed of Amalek; and to build themselves the chosen House" (Sanhedrin 20b).

In other words, Rabbi Jose places the mitzvah of appointing a king on the same level as the other two commandments from the Book of Deuteronomy, the observance of which is conditional on the settlement of the Children of Israel in the Land, and on their dwelling there securely, with rest from their enemies.

At first glance, it would appear surprising that the One who commanded Israel "nor shall you walk in their ordinances" (Lev. 18:3), is the one who now places in their mouths the request: "I will set a king over me, like all the nations that are around me" (Deut. 17:14). It is, however, possible to explain the formulation of Israel's request as follows: Had the nations around the Land of Israel not had kings and had they not had someone to unite them and incite them to war against us, we would not have asked for a king to be appointed over us. But, since all the nations around us have kings who are devising evil against us, it is essential that we, too, place a king over us who will head the nation and go to war against the enemy.

In the Midrash, another opinion is given, which is vehemently opposed to the appointment of a king. According to this opinion, the monarchy per se is to be viewed as something bad. And so we read: "The Holy Blessed One said to Israel: 'I had thought that you should be free from kingships' ... and that you should have no fear of kings; but you did not so desire". (Deut. Rabbah 5:8)

The Midrash further states that all the bad things that Israel suffered from the kings were as a punishment for having asked for a monarchy: "When kings arose over Israel, they began to enslave them. The Holy One exclaimed: Did you not forsake Me and seek kings for yourselves? Why do you ask for a king? By your lives, in the end you will learn to your cost what you will have to suffer from your kings in the future. (Deut. Rabbah 5:8-9)

His fear shall be upon you

The sages, of blessed memory, deduced: "If a king forgoes the honor due to him one may not avail himself of the permission, as it is said: "You shall set a king over you" - that his fear may be over you!" (Sotah 41b).

The late Chief Rabbi of Jerusalem, Tzvi Pesah Frank, commented: Since the people had appointed the king, it was in the nature of things that they would tend to deride him in the course of time, and say: We are the ones who made you king, and the royal crown on your head was placed there by our hands - therefore we are not obliged to accept your rule over us. Hence, the sages teach us: "That his fear may be over you!" Even if you chose the king and you crowned him king over you, willingly and on your own initiative, treat him with respect as befits a king in Israel!

He shall write for himself a copy of the Torah in a book. (Deut. 17:18)

Torah as a way of life

We learn in the Talmud: "How foolish are the people that stand in honor of the Sefer Torah, yet, do not stand for sages learned in Torah!" (Makkot). Rav Shmuel of Slonim explained: "What is a Sefer Torah? It is but letters of the Torah that were written by humans on a parchment made of animal hide. And if we stand up for the Law which consists of letters written on animal hide, how much more so should we stand for Torah Law that has been circumscribed on a the heart of a Jew who has read and studied the Torah".

When you go out to battle against your enemies, and see horses, and chariots, and a people more numerous than you, be not afraid of them; for Adonai your God is with you, who brought you out of the land of Egypt. (Deut. 20:1)

War and peace

We seemingly live in a period of neither war nor peace - in the world at large, in the relationships. between the great powers, and with the neighboring countries.

The Torah of Moshe believes this seeming situation is an illusion. The only ones interested in propagating this view are those who try to throw sand in our eyes and who want to take advantage of the time until an opportune moment to wage war presents itself. Our Torah determines quite clearly: "And if it will make no peace with you, but will make war against you – if it (the city) does not make peace with you, it will in the end make war against you" (Yalqut Shimoni, Shoftim 2).

The enemy, if it can, will choose war at a time convenient for it. There is nothing more dangerous at a time of war than a delusion about the nature of the enemy and its inclination. Our sages commented: "The Holy Blessed One said to Israel: Go to meet them as enemies. Just as they have no pity on you, do not pity them. Listen to what they are saying! "They have said: Come, and let us cut them off from being a nation; that the name of Israel may no longer be remembered" (Ps. 73:5). Go out against them, therefore, as enemies". (Tanhuma Shoftim 15)

Despite the clear message that Israel is facing an enemy, the Torah requires that peace be promoted before war. "When you come near a city to fight against it, first offer peace to it" (Deut. 20:10). Our rabbis said: "The greatness of peace can be gauged from the fact that even when dealing with war, upon which one enters with swords and spears, the Holy One nonetheless said: 'When you go to make war, do not begin (with war) but by proclaiming peace". (Deut. Rabbah 5:12)

And in another Midrash we read: "When you come near a city to fight against it, first offer peace to it" (Deut. 20:10). Rabbi levy said: Moshe did three things with which the Holy One concurred, namely: "... and one in the days of Sihon and Og". The Holy One said to Moshe: Go and challenge him in war, close off his water supply. But Moshe did not do so. Instead "sent messengers out of the wilderness of Kedemot to Sihon king of Heshbon with words of peace" (Deut. 2:27). Said the Holy One: Is that how I told you to fight him? You start by offering him peace?! On your life, you did the right thing, and I agree with what you did. Whenever faced with a war, start only with an offer of peace. (Tanhuma Shoftim 19)

Do not destroy its trees. (Deut. 20:19)

A real environmentalist

When Rabbi Avraham Yitzhak Kook was Chief Rabbi of Yafo, he heard that Baron de Rothchild had ordered that all the trees in a particular area were to be uprooted for a house to be built. The Chief Rabbi went to the settlement and when the workers came wielding the axes in their hands, ready to do the job, he stood in front of them and said "What is going on here? Are you planning on uprooting trees in the Land of Israel? This is not going to happen, as I will protect them with my own body, if I have to!" Rabbi Kook stood there an entire day and did not budge until he was assured that the plan to uproot the trees was cancelled.

The righteous Rav Arieh Levin wrote in his memoirs: I remember in the year 5665, I was privileged enough to immigrate to the Holy Land and settle in Yafo. There, I met the great Rabbi Avraham Yitzhak Kook z"l, and he greeted me warmly, as was his way with all. We were discussing Torah topics and after praying the afternoon service, the great Rabbi went to the field, as he often did, to sit and contemplate. I accompanied him. On the way, I picked a flower or a piece of grass. Although the Rabbi was shocked, he said to me, in a pleasant manner "Believe me that I never in my life unnecessarily picked a flower or piece of grass that could continue to grow and bloom. For there is no leaf on earth that is not told, from heaven, to grow. Every shoot of grass says something, even stone whispers secrets, every creation sings praise". These words that came from such a pure heart were forever engraved in my heart, and from then on I started to feel compassion for everything on earth.

Only the trees which you know to be non -fruit-bearing trees, may you cut down, and you shall lay siege on the city. (Deut. 20:20)

Waste not

In this Parashah, the Torah forbids us to cut down fruit bearing trees, even for the purpose of laying siege to a city in times of war. We know that even for the purpose of building a sanctuary for God we were told to use acacia trees and not fruit-bearing trees (Ex. 26:15). The Midrash comments: 'And you shall build the planks of the sanctuary from acacia trees' - Why acacia trees? God was teaching future generations proper behavior. So, if a person would want to build a house out of a fruit-bearing tree, we can say: 'Even God, who is possessor of all that you see, commanded us not to build the sanctuary from fruit-bearing trees, and you, how much more so, for your private house, should not use fruit-bearing trees'!" (Ex. Rabbah 35:1)

Parashat Ki Tetze

If someone has a stubborn and rebellious son, that does not listen to his/ other or his mother and though they chastise him, he still does not obey them. (Deut. 21:18)

His father did not reprimand him

Why did this boy grow up to be stubborn and rebellious? He became rebellious because, when he was a child, he did not listen to his father and mother. They did not raise him properly; rather they let him do all kinds of things he was not supposed to do. They let him do whatever he wanted to do, whatever his heart desired. They would say: He's a baby; he's a child and he's doing childish things, he's a boy and he's acting his age let him be; when he matures, he'll behave better. But since they let him do whatever he wanted, he stumbled onto the wrong path and became a stubborn and rebellious son. This problem sounds all too familiar. It is "The generation Gap" between parents and children, a problem very much still around these days.

The generation Gap

Our Sages refused to accept the fact that such youths are entirely responsible for their actions. A generation of stubborn and rebellious youth is a direct result of the society in which they were raised. Thus, when our Sages delved deeper into the text that deals with the rebellious child, they created criteria with which to judge each situation. Based on these rules, the parents could publicly accuse the youth of being a "rebellious child" and request the maximum possible punishment. Rabbi Yehudah said: If the mother and father were not compatible, then the child is not considered a 'rebellious child'; If either of them was one-armed, deaf, dumb or blind then the child is not considered a 'rebellious child' according to the Torah's definition (Sanhedrin 8:4). In the Babylonian Talmud, the list of restrictions barring us from accusing a youth of being rebellious is even longer: If the mother was not equal to the father, either in voice, looks, or height, then we can not accuse the youth of being a 'rebellious child' (Sanhedrin 71a). All these restrictions render it impossible to impose the death penalty on a rebellious youth under any foreseeable circumstances.

We cannot blame a rebellious child if the parents are "one-armed"- that is, if they act as if they are helpless, and do not lift a finger to improve the situation and the environment in which the child grows up. We cannot blame a rebellious child if the parents are "blind" or "dumb"- if they turn a blind eye, or don't speak up when the child misbehaves. Finally, we cannot blame a rebellious child if the parents are "deaf- meaning they do not listen when their child is "crying for help", if they ignore the fact that the child needed more love, more protection or more attention. You can only blame a rebellious child if the parents get along and if they are of the same "voice, looks and height" – if they are on the same wavelength. Parents must share and outlook in life and agree on how to raise the child, without letting society influence them and without giving in to what is easy for them.

You shall not watch your brother's ox or his sheep go astray, and hide your-self from them; you shall surely restore them to your brother. (Deut. 22:1)

It's all relative

The sages explained: Sometimes you may hide yourself, and sometimes not. How could this be? For example, if the finder of the lost article was a priest, and the lost article was in a cemetery [which is out of bounds for a priest]; or if the finder was an old person, and it was undignified to lead the animal home (or the lost article was a sack or large box and it is unbecoming for an important personage to carry them through the public domain); or if the finder's own work and time was more valuable than that of the owner of the lost article - therefore it is said: "And you shall hide yourself" (Baba Metsia 30a).

The story is told that Rabbi Eliyahu Hayyim Meisel was once in a neighboring town on a legal matter. When the case was over, he asked to be taken to visit a certain widow in the town who was a relative of his. They said to him: Our Rabbi, is it dignified for a Torah scholar to drag himself to visit this sorry widow in her home? Let the Rabbi send his servant to summon his relative to come to him.

The rabbi replied: It says in the Torah "you may not hide yourself". The sages, of blessed memory, remarked that "Sometimes you may hide yourself, for example if the finder was an old person, and it is not dignified". But, with respect to relatives, it is said: "That you hide not yourself from your own flesh" (Is 48:7). We do not find in the case of relatives that it is said anywhere "and hide yourself from them", and the sages, of blessed memory, did not say of relatives: "Sometimes you may hide yourself...". Consequently, even an old person and a rabbi "for whom it may not be dignified" is not allowed to hide from relatives. And if this is the case for any relative, how much more is it so for a relative who is a poor widow....

... with every lost thing of your brother's, which he has lost, and you have found, shall you do likewise; you may not hide yourself. (Deut. 22:3)

Seeing eye

Why did the Torah not use here the imperative form, as with all the other commandments? Why does it use "may"?

A person without integrity who finds a lost article, could say: It is beneath my dignity to deal with restoration of the lost article to its owner. I will pretend that I have not seen it. Be it known, therefore, that "you may not hide yourself". Even if you hide yourself from other people, you may not hide yourself from the Holy One before Whom all mysteries stand revealed.

The Hafetz Hayyim was once traveling by cart, to distribute copies of his book to whoever was interested. He passed near an attractive park, full of fruit trees. The driver overcome by desire, stopped the cart and got off to pick some fruit, which was visually desirable and good to taste. When the rabbi saw what was happening, he immediately called out aloud: "You can be seen! You can be seen!" The driver was scared and returned to his seat. Having done so, and after he had calmed down, he looked around and saw no one, so he asked the rabbi: "Why did you shout like that? There is no-one in the whole vicinity!" "You are mistaken", replied the rabbi, "there is One who sees…"

As a sign and as an example

We learn in the Jerusalem Talmud: Rabbi Shmuel Bar Susarty went to Rome. The Queen of Rome had lost some jewels and he found them The Queen had put out an edict that the person who finds them and returns them within thirty days will get such and such a reward; but if they return them only after thirty days, they will be beheaded. Rabbi Shmuel did not return them within thirty days. After the thirty days he went to the palace to return the jewels. "Were you in town?" asked the Queen. "Yes" said Rabbi Shmuel. "Did you not hear the edict?" asked the Queen. "I heard the edict", said Rabbi Shmuel. "So why didn't you return the jewels within the thirty days?" asked the Queen. Rabbi Shmuel replied "Because I did not want you to think that I was returning them out of fear for you, the Queen. Rather, I was returning them out of fear of God! Then the Queen exclaimed, "Blessed be the God of the Jews"! (Bava Metzia 5:5)

You shall not see your brother's donkey or ox fallen down by the way and hide yourself from them; you shall surely help him to lift them up again. (Deut. 22:4)

Causing pain to an animal

This statement is referring to the law of loading: It is a positive commandment to help others reload their packages onto their animal. In Parashat Mishpatim it states: "If you shall see the donkey of your enemy succumbing to his load … you shall help him to unload the animal"(Ex. 23:5); This is the law of unloading: It is commandment to help others unload their packages from their animal.

Our Sages of blessed memory differentiated between these two commandments: It is a commandment in the Torah to unload the animal for free, but not to load the animal for free. The reason for this is because with unloading you cause pain to the animal (the more you wait to unload the animal's back, the more pain it suffers), but this is not so with loading (Bava Metzia 2:10). The Rambam rules that one who reloads packages that fell off an animal may request payment, whereas one who unloads an animal, must do so for free.

If a bird's nest chances to be before you in the way ... and the mother bird is sitting on her young ... you shall not take the mother with the young: you shall send away the mother, but the young you may take for yourself. (Deut. 22:6-7)

Do not take advantage of the situation

Rabbi Yosef Hayyim Sonnenfeld of Jerusalem used to explain the Mitzvah of sending away the mother bird as follows: Is it possible that a person could trap a bird, although it is quick and can fly away? No! But in this situation, when a mother bird sees that her fledglings are in danger- she does not move- she sits on them to protect them and can then be trapped together with her young. In this way, the hunter is taking advantage of the bird's motherly instincts and the fact that she tries to save her young. Therefore, the Torah says, "You shall send away the mother", because you have no right to take advantage of the fact that the mother bird has pity on her fledglings, in order to trap her.

... that it may be well with you, and that you may prolong your days. (Deut. 22:7)

You must focus your thoughts

How does the Torah promise us that we will be rewarded if we do this act of sending away the mother bird? Doesn't the Mishnah in Avot tell us that we should be "As slaves who serve their master not for the sake of a reward"? There is a story told of Rabbi Hayyim, the Rabbi of Karsena, one of the students of the Baal Shem Tov. Once Rabbi Hayyim went to the circus in order to watch the tightrope walker walk across the rope that was stretched between two poles over either side of the river. Other Jews in attendance wondered: "Why is this holy man of Israel here to watch the tightrope walker?" Rabbi Hayyim answered them: I looked into the face of the tightrope walker as he walked across the rope, with the deep raging river under him. Then I thought to myself, 'this man is focusing all his thoughts on this walk. He knows that he faces the danger of falling if for one moment he thinks about anything else while he is crossing this rope. He must not even focus on the cash prize that awaits him if he manages to do this wonderful feat'. At that moment I learned from him the importance of focusing on the subject at hand. A Jew engaged in fulfilling a mitzvah, must stay completely focused and not let the mind wander, not even to the reward that awaits at the completion of this very mitzvah. Otherwise, such a Jew is in danger of falling.

You shall not plow with an ox and an ass together. (Deut. 22:10)

Cruelty to animals

It is related that Rabbi Gershon Hanikh of Radzhin arrived incognito at a certain township. He went into the beit midrash and saw there a band of beggars talking vociferously amongst themselves.

- What is all this noise about? asked Rabbi Gershon Hanikh.

- The richest man in town, members of the band told him, is marrying off his daughter and he has locked the doors of his house to poor people.

- Come with me - Rabbi Gershon Hanikh said to them. And he went to the house of the rich man and knocked on the door.

- We are receiving no visitors today - came the answer from within.

- I have a question I wish to put to the rabbi who is with you, he said.

They let him in because if a Jew wishes to ask a halakhic question, he is not to be prevented.

- Rabbi, he said, I have a question to ask. Why did the Torah say: "You shall not plow with an ox and an ass together"?

- We do not know - the rabbi pushed him away - the reasons for the mitzvot. It is a decree from the Almighty.

- But I, Rabbi Gershon Hanikh said, do know the reason for this mitzvah. Oxen chew the cud while asses do not. An ass, seeing an ox chewing the cud, would think that the ox is eating food while he, the ass, is not eating any food and he would be upset. The Torah thus had pity on the ass and said: "You shall not plow with an ox and an ass together". We can make an inference from minor to major, continued Rabbi Gershon: If the Torah had pity on the ass that he should not see his fellow eating and be upset, how much more is this the case with human beings that it is not right that some people should sit and feast, eating and drinking, while these others, the poor people, from the outside, do not taste any food or drink, and they are upset....

Let him write her a bill of divorcement, and give it in her hand, and send her out of his house. (Deut. 24:1)

For that the Rabbi danced

A close associate of Rabbi Meir Simhah HaKohen of Dvinsk once went round to the Rabbi's home and saw an amazing sight. The Rabbi was dancing in a circle with a husband, wife and their son. The Rabbi - who was the leader of his generation - was holding the husband with one hand and the son with the other, and the husband and the son were holding the hands of the wife.

The visitor was overcome by astonishment at this sight and was totally amazed. When the dance ended and everyone had sat down, Rabbi Meir Simhah told him what had happened.

The husband and the wife had come to him the previous day to obtain a divorce. The husband presented his complaints and the wife also put forward her complaints. The Rabbi then asked them: "Do you have any children?"

"Yes, we have one son", they replied. But who will their son live with after they are divorced? With his father or with his mother? The Rabbi pondered aloud and then immediately said to them: Come to me tomorrow with the boy. The next day, they came back to him with their son. Rabbi Meir Simhah took the boy, sat him on his lap and began to cry. The brilliant rabbi said to him: "My boy, from now on you remain a living orphan, without a father and without a mother".

The boy began to cry and then his mother broke out in bitter weeping. And, with everyone else crying, the father also began to sob. At that moment, they both resolved not to get divorced and then they all began to dance from sheer joy....

Parashat Ki Tavo

It shall be, when you come in to the land which Adonai your God gives you for an inheritance, and possess it, and live in it. (Deut. 26:1)

There is no such thing as a free inheritance

If, at the beginning of the portion, Scripture has already stated: "which Adonai your God gives you for an inheritance" then it is for you and is yours. Why, then, does the verse continue: "and possess it, and live in it"?

Scripture is here telling us that the Land of Israel is acquired by two means: one is God's promise and the other is the sweat of the brow and the labor of the hands. One is not worthy of inheriting and living in the Land if one does not make an effort to live there and gives one's soul to do so. Adonai gave us an inheritance but that, in and of itself, is insufficient; we also have actively to inherit it and live in it.

There shall come upon you all these blessings, and overtake you.... (Deut. 26:2)

The blessing of God will catch up to you

It would seem that the real order of this verse should have been, "All these blessings will overtake you and come upon you". Is it possible that after the blessings have come upon you, they still have to overtake you?

Rabbi Tzvi Yehudah Berlin of Volozhin explained: It is people's nature to go run after their luck, they fervently search for it in every place, and they fail to understand that if they stop running, and just stand still, then their luck will catch up to them. The Torah promises us in this verse that, even if you stray very far away, God's blessings will run after you "and overtake you", they will catch up to you wherever you are.

... and say to him: I proclaim this day to Adonai your God.... (Deut. 26:3)

Gratitude

Rashi comments: "and say to him" - "that you are not ungrateful".

The Mishnah states: "And all the craftsmen [in Jerusalem] used to rise up before them [those who brought the first fruits] and greet them" (Bikurim 3:3). As a rule, a hired worker was not allowed to greet people because all workers were hired out for a daily wage to an employer and it is viewed as a form of time stealing. In the case of those who bring the first fruits to Jerusalem, however, the sages permitted laborers to ask them after their welfare, because of the fondness for the mitzvah of bringing the first fruits. What is so special about this mitzvah?

The Torah went out of its way to emphasize the importance of the mitzvah of bringing the first fruits to Jerusalem and, because of it, permitted laborers to stop work because, with the bringing of the first fruits, a person gives recognition to the good things that the Holy Blessed One has provided, with bountiful blessing from the land. The Halakhah thus determines that even a person who has only one stalk of wheat has to bring first fruits so as to express thereby gratitude and thanks to the One who granted all things good.

The Egyptians dealt ill with us. (Deut. 26:6)

They made us evil

Why does it say "And the Egyptians dealt ill with us " and not "The Egyptians were evil to us"? Rather, says the Holy Alshikh, 'And they dealt ill with us' means they made us evil. The back-breaking work that they made us do during all those years of servitude, made us change in our attitude towards our fellow Jews, and we became evil and cruel towards one another....

You shall rejoice in every good thing which Adonai your God has given to you. (Deut. 26:11)

"Let us not be in need of the gifts of men nor of their loans" (Grace after Meals)

Rabbi Moshe Leib of Sassov said: When can you "rejoice in every good thing"? When Adonai is the one who gives to you of the fruits of your endeavors and you are not in need of gifts from other people. One measure of peace of mind from Adonai is better than ten measures from other people.

The Egyptians dealt ill with us. (Deut. 26:6)

They made us evil

Why does it say "And the Egyptians dealt ill with us " and not "The Egyptians were evil to us"? Rather, says the Holy Alshich, 'And they dealt ill with us' means they made us evil. The back-breaking work that they made us do during all those years of servitude, made us change in our attitude towards our fellow Jews, and we became evil and cruel towards one another...

All these blessings shall come on you, and will catch up with you. (Deut. 28:2)

The blessings of heaven will catch up with you

Commenting on the use of two verbs - "shall come upon" and "will catch up with" - Ibn Ezra writes: "And they shall come" - they will come automatically and "will catch up with you" - without effort on your part. Rabbi Ovadia Sforno, one of the great rabbis of Italy in the first half of the 16th Century, expands this idea in his commentary: "'And all these blessings shall come on you' - even though you make no effort to obtain them. And that will happen when you make your Torah study a permanent feature in your life and your craft a temporary feature, therefore the blessings will catch up with you without any effort on your par.

…you shall be above only, and you shall not be beneath. (Deut. 28:13)

A force that is pulling you from above

Rabbi Azriel Hildesheimer said: We see in nature that a stone that falls down, drops very quickly. However, if a stone is thrown up, it rises very slowly. We see the opposite with fire. It rises very quickly, yet it goes down very slowly. Just like a stone, by nature, is drawn downwards, so too fire by nature is drawn upwards. The rule is that every object goes quicker in the direction of its origin, whereas it goes slower in the opposite direction of its origin. The soul of a pious Jew is always being drawn heavenward, because that is where it is rooted, and going down is against its nature. However, the soul of a sinner is drawn towards the earth and going upwards is against its nature. Thus the Torah says "and you shall be above only" you shall rise up quickly, because it is your nature to reach for the heavens, "and you shall not be beneath", you should not go slowly up, as an object which is naturally drawn towards the earth.

Your heaven that is over your head shall be bronze. (Deut. 28:23)

The most difficult of all

Rabbi Menahem Mendel of Kotzk said: This is the harshest of the curses in the admonition, because a person is prevented from penetrating that barrier and going on to what is beyond it….

...because you did not serve Adonai, your God with joyfulness. (Deut. 28:47)

Serve God with happiness

Just because the Jews did not serve God with happiness, did they deserve such a curse?

Rather, as Rabbi Simhah Bunim of Pashischa said, not only did they not serve God, but they were happy and lighthearted that they managed to avoid doing as God commanded.

Rabbi Simhah Bunim added: 'The Torah says "The people who seek God will be happy in their hearts" (Ps. 105:3). It is only natural that a person who is searching for something, should feel frustrated by the endless searching. When does such a person achieve true happiness? Only when the object of the search is finally found. This is not so with a person who seeks God. The search for God itself brings such a person joy and happiness: 'The people who seek God will be happy in their hearts'.

Rabbi Yehiel Meir of Gustinin said: "Notice how the Torah only stated the sin of 'Sadness' as a sin which brings about the punishments and curses in this passage of rebuke, whereas none of the other possible sins have punishments attached to them. This is to teach us that sadness is a very grave sin".

You have seen all that Adonai did before your eyes. (Deut. 29:1)

"... and renew a constant spirit inside me" (Ps. 41:12)

Moshe reminds Israel: "You have seen". Despite the fact that everyone saw and no-one can deny it, forgetfulness has lot of power. There is here a great teaching for all time: A person can see great things with, wonderful things the like of which have not been revealed before, but still not see.

It is true that Adonai gives a person eyes to see with, and ears to hear with, and a heart to perceive with - said Rabbi Elimelekh Bar Shaul,

Chief Rabbi of the city of Rehovot - but it is the person, him or herself, who has to do the seeing, who has to do the hearing and who has to do the perceiving.

Adonai shows us wonders, but a person has to open the eyes wide in order to see the gamut of wonderful disclosures; just opening one's eyes is insufficient to catch the full splendor. A person's heart must be wholly open in order to understand and appreciate what the eyes see and what the ears hear.

Parashat Nitzavim

You stand this day all of you before Adonai your God ... from the hewer of your wood to the drawer of your water. (Deut. 29:9-10)

All the tribes of Israel stand together

Moshe explains that "You" is referring to the entire group, here at present - the whole nation. It was not selected individuals with whom the covenant was made; not with 'messengers'; not with 'holy people'; not with 'prophets', not with a cult. Rather, the covenant was made with the whole nation without differentiating between gender, age or status - from the leaders to the water carriers. This is something that does not exist in the history of any other nation or religion.

Everyone is equal

The Holy Rabbi Alshikh adds: Usually Moshe would initially address the leaders of the Jewish people, but in this case, from the start, Moshe was directly addressing all the people, as it says: "And Moshe called unto all of Israel and he said unto them" (Deut. 29:1), he did not address the leaders by themselves.

Thus Moshe said "You are standing this day all of you" - and there is no difference between the people and the leaders, for you are standing "before Adonai, your God" - you are standing before the Holy Blessed One, and we do not know how to differentiate between one who is more or less important in God's eyes. It is very possible that someone we hold to be a leader, on a very high level, is less important than someone we consider as a simple person. In Heaven there is a totally different calculation and it is possible that the truth is that "the higher ones are lowly (in status) and the lowly ones are higher (in status)". "Your leaders, your chieftains, your elders and your law enforcers" - all these titles are only from your point of view, as a person who is viewing them from outside. But as far as God is concerned, these things are totally different. Thus, at the time when you are all "standing before Adonai, your God", you are all equal.

The leaders of Israel should also draw a lesson

Is this then the order of seniority and the work order? Should not Scripture have said: "From your leaders to the hewer of your wood"?

An axe is lifted high above the person hewing with it, but does that mean that the axe will brag to the hewer: "I am bigger than you; I am at the top!"? That is certainly not so. Were it not for the hewer, the axe would not be lifted up at all.

A bucket is lowered down into a well in the hands of the person drawing water with it. Does that mean that the drawer of the water will brag to the bucket that it, the bucket, is lower and inferior?. Certainly not! Were it not for the drawer who lowers it, it would not descend.

The same applies to the leaders. They should not boast that they have gained their position of leadership through their own merit for they are leaders because God raised them up as the elected representatives of the people; and the leaders should not see even one Jew as being lower or inferior to them, as though it depended on them whether each Jew shall be up or down. It is up to the leaders to raise those who are led, to stand them up and to stabilize them at a high and sublime moral and spiritual level. That is why Scripture says: "from the hewer of your wood to the drawer of your water" - that the leaders may keep their charges in mind.

Who can assess the heart of a Jew?

R' Monya Mossinzohn, who was known as a great trader in precious stones and diamonds and was also extremely rich, once stayed at the court of the Rebbe, Shmuel of Lebovitz.

One day, as R' Monya was sitting with a group of Hassidim beside the Rebbe, the conversation turned to the difficult situation of the Jewish communities in Russia. In the course of the conversation, the Rebbe spoke in praise of the simple folk in the various Jewish villages who labored from morning to evening hard at work in order to make a living for themselves and the members of their households and did not have need of charity from strangers.

R' Monya interrupted the conversation and said: "I am surprised at what the Rebbe is saying, making a whole business about the simple folk". Rabbi Samuel answered him pleasantly: "These people have many good qualities". "I don't see these qualities!" commented R' Monya, with a dismissive gesture of his hand.

The Rebbe did not respond to this remark, the following day, asked him if he had brought any diamonds with him on his visit. I have some fabulous diamonds with me - exclaimed R' Monya with some joy and immediately began to set out on the Rebbe's table some attractive and glittering stones. Later, he pointed to a particularly radiant stone, which stood out in the long line of diamonds, and exclaimed in admiration: "This stone is truly fantastic!".

"I do not see anything special about this stone", the Rebbe remarked with a smile. "Rebbe", R' Monya cried, "one has to be a connoisseur in order to appraise the value of diamonds correctly".

The Rebbe answered him: "A simple Jew is also something quite fantastic, but one has to be a connoisseur in order to become aware of this also...".

You shall enter into the covenant of Adonai, your God, and into His oath – which Adonai, your God, makes with you this day. (Deut. 29:ll)

Love that will never dissipate

Why was it necessary to make a covenant with Israel before they entered the Land - wasn't the covenant from Horev enough? Rabbi Shneur Zaiman from Liadi said: A covenant that is made between a couple in love is not only for the present, when their love and friendship is fresh, rather it is important for the future, because as time goes on their love is weakened, therefore they make this covenant that their friendship should endure, even when the reasons for love have dissipated. Thus, during Moshe'ss lifetime, when there were constant miracles, and supernatural phenomena was commonplace, there was a fear that when the Jews would enter the Land and then have to raise crops. naturally by sowing, planting and harvesting, their love for God would weaken. Therefore, in order to insure that the Jewish people would not waiver in their love for God, a covenant was established. Even when they will be busy working for their livelihood and all the miracles will be hidden in nature, or when a shadow will darken the land so too will the people of Israel be able to rekindle their love for God, and never separate from their Creator.

The hidden things belong to Adonai our God; but those things which are revealed belong to us and to our children forever, that we may do all the words of this Torah. (Deut. 29:28)

Hidden Tzaddik

Rabbi Menahem Mendel of Kotzk said: I prefer the people who sin in public and keep the commandments in private, to those who uphold the commandments in public yet sin in private. He added that people often define the term "hidden tzaddikim" as those who fulfill the commandments in private, and hide their righteousness from public view. The truth is that "hidden" refers to those who do not even realize, themselves, that they are righteous. It is hidden from them. They even know that they are tzaddikim.

One never knows the reward

Rabbi Avraham Binyamin Wolf Sofer used to say: Our sages taught that the Torah did not disclose the reasons for the mitzvot and their reward so that a person would not miss performing a mitzvah whose reward is little and would only keep those whose reward is great. There are just two mitzvot whose reward the Torah did reveal to us: the most demanding - honoring one's parents - and the least demanding - not to take the mother bird with her eggs. In both cases, the Torah promised: "that it may be well with you, and that you may prolong your days".

From this we may deduce that all the mitzvot are equal in terms of the reward for performing them and should all be kept in equal manner.

This, then, is the plain meaning of the verse: "The hidden things belong to Adonai our God". Adonai has hidden from us the reward for performing the mitzvot in general but has revealed to us the reward of two mitzvot - "those things which are revealed belong to us and to our children". One "belongs to us", namely not taking the mother bird with the eggs, and one "belongs to our children", namely honoring parents, and this is so as to "do all the words of this Torah", that is to say, that we should observe all the mitzvot and not chose for ourselves just those mitzvot whose reward is greater.

Adonai your God will turn [ve-shav] your captivity, and have compassion upon you, and will return [ve-shav] and gather you from all the nations. (Deut. 30:3)

Double prophecy

Why is the word ve-shav (return) repeated twice in this verse?

Rabbi Meir Simhah HaKohen of Dvinsk explained: Because there are two sorts of exiles and two sorts of deportees. "And Adonai your God will turn your captivity" is stated about those who live in exile, who feel the sorrow of the exile, and who yearn for the Land of Israel. God will bring them back first. The continuation of the verse: "and have compassion upon you, and will return and gather you from all the nations" refers to those members of the Jewish People who have settled into exile and are comfortable with it. The yearning for the Land of Israel no longer exists within them. But Adonai will gather them, too, and bring them back to our Land.

This is the meaning of the double prophecies: One has first to awaken the Children of Israel so that they will yearn for redemption but, even when they do feel the need for redemption, they have to be re-awoken so that they will actually return to our Land.

It is not in heaven, that you should say: Who shall go up for us to heaven, and bring it to us, that we may hear it, and do it. (Deut. 30:12)

The Torah was given to us

When a dispute broke out between Rabbi Eliezer and the sages regarding impurity and purity, we find in the Talmud that: On that day Rabbi Eliezer brought forward every imaginable argument, but the scholars of the beit midrash did not accept them. He said to them: 'If the halakhah agrees with me, let this carob-tree prove it!' Thereupon the carob-tree was torn a hundred cubits out of its place. They said to him: 'No proof can be adduced from a carob-tree'. Again he said to them: 'If the halakhah agrees with me, let this aqueduct prove it!' Whereupon the stream of water flowed backwards. They said to him: 'No proof can be brought from a stream of water'. Again he urged: 'If the halakhah agrees with me, let the walls of the schoolhouse prove it,' whereupon the walls inclined to fall. But Rabbi Yehoshua rebuked them, saying: 'When scholars are engaged in a halakhic dispute, it is not for you to interfere!' Hence they did not fall, in honor of Rabbi Yehoshua, nor did they resume the upright position, in honor of Rabbi Eliezer; and they are still standing thus inclined. Again he said to them: 'If the halakhah agrees with me, let it be proved from Heaven!' Whereupon a Heavenly Voice proclaimed: 'Why do you dispute with Rabbi Eliezer, seeing that the halakhah agrees with him in all matters!' But Rabbi Yehoshua stood up and exclaimed: 'It is not in the heavens!' What did he mean by this? - Said Rabbi Yirmiahu: Since the Torah had already been given at Mount Sinai, we pay no attention to a Heavenly Voice, because You have long since written in the Torah at Mount Sinai: "After the majority must one incline" (Ex. 23:2).

Rabbi Eliezer is unable to persuade the sages of Israel that he is right by using logical arguments or precedents of halakhah. Being totally confident in the correctness of his arguments, he appealed for divine help and tried to prove to the sages of Israel that he was right by virtue of evidence from on high, by way of miraculous events. But his colleagues remained unconvinced. We learn from this that even the Holy Blessed One cannot intervene in negotiations over the Halakhah and decide the issue because the Torah is no longer God's. It has been given to humanity and the obligation is imposed upon those who study it to teach it and to interpret it.

Where is the Torah found?

The people of Israel said to Moshe "You have said to us that 'it is not in heaven and neither is it beyond the ocean' – so where is it?" Moshe said to them "It is very close to you - 'it is in your mouths and in your hearts, to fulfill' - it is very near to you". (Deut. Rabbah 8)

It happens very often that people think that keeping the Torah and Mitzvot are beyond their capabilities - beyond their reach. Thus the concise answer comes to teach us "it is in a very close place". A person might think that the greatness in Divine attributes is that they are impossible to achieve. Such a person looks heavenwards longingly towards things that seem beyond all grasp, thinking: 'I wish I could go up to the sky and bring down these Divine attributes'. But this is not the case. We learn that the greatness in these Divine attributes is in the fact that they **are** in fact attainable for a person willing to have an open heart with which to receive them.

I have set before you, the blessing and the curse; therefore choose life, that you may live, you and your seed. (Deut. 30:19)

Raison d'etre

Moshe tries time and again to convince the people that the only way to live is to accept the Mitzvot, as God has commanded them in the Torah. He gives a full report on the blessings that are promised to the Jewish people if they keep the Mitzvot and the curses that will befall them if they do not adhere to the commandments. He brings as witnesses heaven and earth before the Jewish people, as he retells all the details of the conditions for life and death, and he continues to beseech them "choose life, so that you and your seed may live". "To live", means to grow, to respond, to realize. "To be dead" means to stop growing, to become lifeless, like a rock. Many people in the world do not meet this challenge to either have a meaningful life or to die, thus they walk around like "living corpses" - their bodies are alive, but their souls are dead. The choice to live is an imperative condition for love and freedom.

"This man", said Rabbi Nahum from Chernobyl about an acquaintance of his, "has been dead for five years already, only no one has bothered to inform him...".

Parashat Vayelekh

Moshe went and spoke these words to all of Israel. (Deut. 31:1)

Do not fear, my servant Yaakov

Biblical commentators have expressed surprise at the special opening of this portion and ask: "Where did Moshe go?" According to Ibn Ezra, Moshe went, on his one hundred and twentieth birthday, to each and every tribe to say goodbye to them and to tell them that he was soon to be departing this world. Among other things, Moshe told the tribes that they had nothing to worry about with respect to the future because the God of Israel would go before them on the way to the land promised to them. For it is written: "Adonai your God, he will go over before you, and he will destroy these nations from before you, and you shall possess them" (Deut. 31:3).

He said to them, I am one hundred and twenty years old this day; I can no more go out and come in. (Deut. 31:2)

With this, my job is completed

Rashi comments on this verse: "This teaches us that the traditions and well-springs of wisdom were stopped up for him". Rabbi Yaakov Yosef of Polnoye said on this matter: "The righteous never stand still in one place but are forever going from one level to another. They leave one level and go up to a higher level. That is why Moshe, just before his death, says: "I can no longer go forth from the level on which I am standing today and 'come in' and go up to the next higher level. Hence my death is nigh and my end approaches, apart from which the well-springs of wisdom have been stopped up from me".

Rabbi Avraham Mordechai Alter of Gur added: Before his death, Moshe Our Teacher attained the very highest levels that a normal person could never reach. He reached the wellsprings of wisdom which are closed off from simple flesh and blood. That is why he said: "1 can no more go out and come in" - I can no longer be your leader, whose job it is to remove from materialism and take to spirituality, because there is no longer any contact between me and you. A leader can only be an influence so long as ties are maintained to the people, but a leader who is excessively raised above the people, is unable to do anything for them.

Yehoshua will go over before you, as Adonai has said. (Deut. 31:3)

Generation to generation

God makes it clear to Moshe that he will not enter the Land and that the leadership will go to his heir. Moshe accepts the judgment after having appealed to God with many agonizing pleas and he begins to prepare his people for the unavoidable change. With this in mind. he delivers a long farewell speech, which constitutes the bulk of the Book of Deuteronomy

In order to assure continuity and a quiet transfer of the leadership, and to prevent power struggles, Moshe follows God's advice and selects Yehoshua as his heir. He presents Yehoshua to the priests and before the whole people and lays his two hands upon him (Num. 27:15-23). The difficult moment of actual departure and the transfer of authority, however, had not yet come

How will Moshe feel and act at that moment? How will the Children of Israel react? After forty years under Moshe's leadership, after having shared so many unforgettable moments with him, of joy and uplifting, of trials and tribulations, will they now be able to accept his relatively young assistant as their new leader? And Yehoshua himself, who, for many years, had been accustomed to being number two or even three (after the high priest), will he be able to emerge from his place behind the scenes and step forward to the center of the stage to stand at the head of the people? Will he be able to take upon himself the full authority at this decisive moment in the life of his people as they are about to reach their destination? Was his heart not full of foreboding in view of the tremendous responsibility inherent in acceptance of the leadership, on which the fate of the future of his people would be dependent? Should he fail, then all the achievements of the Jewish People to that point – the exodus from Egypt, the Divine Revelation on Mount Sinai, the experiences of the people in the Wilderness - all would be lost.

It is one thing to understand in theory the meaning of fulfilling the role of the outstanding and admired leader. The actual challenge entails something altogether different, something larger than understanding, the actual bearing of the burden.

Moshe called to Yehoshua and said to him in the sight of all of Israel: 'Be strong and of good courage; for you will go with this people to the land which Adonai swore to their ancestors to give them, and you shall cause them to inherit it'. (Deut. 31:7)

Leadership ability

Rashi writes here (based on Sanhedrin 8a): Moshe said to Yehoshua: "You will go with this people", as one of them. The elders of the generation will be with you and everything is to be done according to their opinion and their advice. Later, however, the Holy Blessed One, said to Yehoshua: "You shall bring the Children of Israel into the Land ..." (Deut. 31:23). You shall bring them, even against their will. It all depends on you! How could Moshe Our Teacher, when speaking to Yehoshua, have changed the words of the language used by the Almighty? How could Moshe have said, "You will go" when the Holy Blessed One said "You shall bring"? Rabbi Elhanan Wasserman answered this with the following explanation: Both are the words of the living God - both are correct. There is truth and justice in both versions quoted in the Torah. On the one hand, it is clear that the leader of the generation has to listen to the opinion and counsel of the elders and sages. However, the leader, having heard the opinions of the advisers, must then show leadership ability and decide on a course of action. If the leader does not do that, then chaos will reign in the land and "every man will do that which is right in his own eyes".

Behaved forcefully

Rabbi Meir Simhah of Dvinsk said: With respect to a king of Israel, the Torah commands: "That his heart be not lifted up above his brothers" (Deut. 17:20) because he has to relate to everyone in Israel lovingly and in a kindly fashion and avoid arrogance. When fulfilling his state functions in public, however, he has to behave forcefully and in a high-handed fashion because even "if a king renounces his honor, his honor is nonetheless not renounced" (Ketubot 17a).

Moshe, when he instructs Yehoshua his student, who is about to receive from him the scepter of leadership, says likewise: "In the presence of all Israel, be strong and courageous". When you are facing the masses, do not indulge in the niceties of humility and modesty, do not show any weakness and faint-heartedness in your conduct. Deal with people audaciously, without any concessions, and then the masses will treat you with honor and respect and will obey you without hesitation.

Adonai said to Moshe: Behold, your days approach that you must die; call Yehoshua, and present yourselves in the Tent of Meeting, that I may give him a charge. (Deut. 31:14)

It is better for me to die than to live

When the pillar of cloud departed, Moshe approached Yehoshua and asked him: 'What was revealed to you?' Yehoshua replied: 'When the word was revealed to you, did I know what God spoke with you?' At that moment Moshe bitterly exclaimed: "Better it is to die a hundred times than to experience envy, even once!" (Deut. Rabbah 9:9)

This is magnificent. Why, in all truth, did Yehoshua not want to reveal to Moshe what God had said to him? The Vilna Gaon replied to that: That is exactly what God, blessed be His name, told Yehoshua to say to Moshe. Moshe had wanted to remain alive as Yehoshua's student. God, therefore, told Yehoshua to say these things to Moshe so that he would feel how difficult it would be to turn from teacher to student. He would then agree willingly to die because 'Better it is to die a hundred times than to experience envy, even once!'

Rabbi Meir Yehiel of Ostrovtza used to say: How did Moshe Our Teacher, the most humble of men, come to be envious? Furthermore, what is the connection between envy and a student, for we have learned: "Of everyone a man is envious, except his son and disciple" (Sanhedrin 105b)? The truth is that the heavenly beings ran to ease Moshe's sorrow and to relieve his pain that he was about to die and so they put into him a small drop of envy. Moshe called out 'My entire life, I have tried to kill the indecent qualities within me and to subdue the evil inclinations and, finally, close to my death, I feel the bad quality of envy. It is better for me to die than to live. A hundred deaths rather than envy once'.

Is it not because our God is no longer among us, that these evils have befallen us? (Deut. 31:17)

"I will be with him in trouble" (Ps. 91:15)

If they confess and say: "Is it not because our God is no longer among us, that these evils have befallen us?" why, then, should they be punished, as is stated in the next verse: "And I will surely hide My face on that day"?

Rabbi Simhah Bunam of Pasischa said: "The very suggestion that "God is no longer among us" is considered a sin because Israel has to believe that, even in times of the most grievous trouble, Adonai is among us, as it says: "I will be with him in trouble". Since they did not so believe they really are fit to be punished. They bring into question God's being among them and so God hides the Divine face from them.

I will surely hide My face on that day. (Deut. 31:18)

Divine Providence

Only the strong, those who are strong in spirit, who discern the ways of the Holy Blessed One, can see the guiding hand of Divine Providence directing things from above, even through a screen of "face hiding" [i.e., divine anger].

When a person is not able to discern and does not sense that the Divine Presence displeased, no attempt can be made at changing the problematic behavior. Thinking that one is righteous and that one's deeds are becoming – there is no incentive to consider making amends. It is only when one discerns and senses the Divine displeasure that there incentive exists for praying and attempting to draw close to God.

This is the intention of the verse: "And I will surely hide My face on that day". In other words, Adonai will conceal the actual anger so that the people will not know of the Divine displeasure. People will think of themselves as doers of good deeds and for will be punished precisely for this misconception. The concealment, the displeasure is not total and the catastrophe is not that great, but will be followed by yearnings and cravings for revelation of the Divine Presence which will break through all the barriers separating Israel and their Creator in Heaven. There can be no greater repentance than this.

The sorrow of the Shekhinah

The story is told about Rabbi Dov Baer of Mezeritz who was walking in the street with his associates and saw a small girl hiding behind a wide tree-trunk, crying bitterly. He said to her: Baby, why are you crying? The child sobbingly replied: We were playing hide-and-seek. When my turn to hide came, I hid myself but my friends are not looking for me and are not finding me.

When the rabbi heard the girl's response, tears formed in his eyes and he cried with her. His associates were surprised and astonished: Why was the rabbi crying over children's play?

Rabbi Dov Baer explained to them: From the answer of this baby, I hear the sound of the crying of the Shekhinah, as it were, weeping and saying: I concealed My face and no-one wants Me and no-one seeks Me. In vain do I hide and expect them to come and look for Me; they have abandoned me and have forgotten my hiding. That is why I weep ...

Now, write for yourselves this song. (Deut. 31:19)

Going through the motions

Rabbi Avraham Binyamin Wolf Sofer commented: From this verse, our sages, of blessed memory, deduced that every Jew is commanded to personally write a Torah scroll, as we have learned in the Talmud: Even if a person's parents have left a Sefer Torah, it is proper that the person should personally write one, as it is written: "And now, write for yourselves this song". (Sanhedrin 21b)

This teaching of the sages says Rabbi Sofer, is to teach us not to take the Torah for granted. Each and every one of us has to accept it anew as though we ourselves stood on Mount Sinai. The commandment is, therefore, that everyone should personally write a Torah scroll rather than make do in this respect with the legacy of one's parents.

For I know their Inclination and what they do, even today. (Deut. 31:21)

Pursue the inclination

Rabbi Pinhas of Koretz came to the school-house one day and saw his students deep in conversation. They were startled at his arrival. He asked them: "What were you talking about?" "Rabbi", they said, "we were discussing our concern that the evil inclination was pursuing us". "Do not be concerned", he replied, "you have not yet reached a high enough level for the evil inclination to be pursuing you. For the time being, you are pursuing it ...".

Reproach the evil inclination

The Hafetz Hayyim was in dire straits in his younger days. Things were so bad that he and his wife fed themselves with leftovers from the bakery. For only a small amount of money, the Rabbanit would buy from the baker bread that had been baked insufficiently or excessively. And they would eat this bread throughout the week. Once, on a Friday, the Hafetz Hayyim came home and found his wife weeping. When he asked her for the reason, she replied, "Until now, the baker gave us the leftovers on credit, but now he refuses to give any more because he is demanding settlement of the accumulated debt and we have nothing with which to pay. I was unable to bring even a slice of bread home!" The Hafetz Hayyim banged the table with the palm of his hand and said in a tone of reproof: "You, the evil inclination, you will not win over me and you will not prevent me from studying Torah!"

Parashat Ha'azinu

Give ear, O heavens, and I will speak; and hear, O earth, the words of my mouth. (Deut. 32:1)

The quality of justice and the quality of mercy

"Give ear, O heavens, and I will speak" is harsh language, "and hear, O earth, the words of my mouth" is softer speech. However, one should not wonder at that. What can this be likened to? To rain and dew. Just as some plants can survive with dew alone, others need rain. Grass is happy with showers but weeds need light rain. So, too, it is with people. Soft language is sufficient for some but others have to be spoken to harshly. Everything is for the good of each, according to their level.

Learning a lesson

Rabbi Menahem Mendel of Kotzk said: Why do we say about a God-fearing person that the "fear of Heaven" is in him? Moreover, we have learned in the Mishnah: "Let the fear of Heaven be upon you" (Pirke Avot 1:3). Would it not have been more seemly to say "the fear of God"?

We find in the Heavens the greatest respect for the word of God, for our sages said that, although the Heavens were created on the first day, they were still unstable, shaky. It was only on the second day, when God said: "Let there be a firmament!" that the Heavens froze in their place and became firm. People are the same. When they hears a loud shout, they becomes frozen to the spot and their whole body hardens out of fear. (Hagigah 12)

It thus follows that the fact that the Heavens have existed [as they are] from the time of Creation until now and are not trembling is by virtue of that fear and respect of the initial Divine call: "Let there be a firmament!"

That is why the expression "fear of Heaven" is used. A person has to learn from the Heavens how to be respectful toward the word of Adonai, to serve the Creator throughout life untiringly, standing firm the whole time. This is also the straightforward meaning of the verse: "Give ear, O heavens" Listen and attend to the word of Adonai just as the Heavens listened and paid attention — a heavenly listening ...

My doctrine shall drop as the rain, my speech shall distil us the dew. (Deut. 32:2)

For the sake of Heaven

Rabbi Elimelekh of Lizensk commented on Moshe's opening words: "Just as the rain and the dew descend on the earth not for their own benefit, but for the sake of the world, so also my words are being spoken not for self-enjoyment or some personal benefit but only for the sake of Heaven and for the good of my people Israel".

Rabbi Simhah Bunam of Pasischa used to say: The words of the Holy Torah are like rain descending upon the earth. The effect of rain on plant life is not immediately discernible when it falls, and it is only after a time that it is expressed and the soil is watered. The words of the Torah work in a similar manner on those who hear them. As they are being heard, their indispensable impact is not immediately discernible but they have a positive effect on those who study them in the long run.

For all God's ways are justice; a God of truth and without iniquity, just and right is God. (Deut. 32:4)

"Righteousness shall go before him" (Ps. 75:14)

Rabbi Yisrael Meir HaKohen of Radin used to say: One of the foundations of belief in God is that "all of God's ways are justice". Even though we are often astonished at the deeds of the Creator and do not comprehend God's ways, we must believe and not doubt that all Divine acts are accompanied by righteousness and justice. In this respect, we are likened to a sick child who is given very bitter medications. At the time, the child must think that the physician and parents are being heartless. The truth, however, is that the parents want to do their best for their sick child and, in order to effect a cure, they have to enforce things which cause physical and mental suffering.

Of the Rock that fathered you, you are unmindful, and have forgotten the God who formed you. (Deut. 32:18)

Thanklessness

Rabbi Menahem Mendel of Kotzk said: The Holy Blessed One imprinted in you the character and quality of "unmindfulness", of forgetfulness, for your own good, so that you will forget the troubles and the injuries that happen to you, and you will be able to continue and survive in this life. However, the result is that "you have forgotten the God who formed you", you use this character trait to forget your Creator.

The Magid of Dubno created a parable about this: A person who owed money went to consult a friend of his as to what to do about the creditors who were pressing him for payment and not leaving him alone. His friend advised him that, when they came to him, he should make out as though he were insane and start dancing and whistling and, in the end, they would give up and leave him alone. So it was. The advice worked well.

The friend with the advice, however, had forgotten that the man also owed him an amount of money and he came to ask him for its repayment. However, when the debtor saw him coming and heard what he wanted, he pretended to be insane, dancing and whistling.

His friend lost his temper: Don't you have any shame - he yelled - I am the one who gave you this advice so that you could protect yourself against other creditors and in the end you are using my advice against me? Do you really think that you can convince me that you are mad?

The moral is: The verse "Of the Rock that fathered you are unmindful" should be understood as "The Rock who fathered in you the ability to forget". God has implanted in you the special faculty of being able to forget, to divert your attention from the troubles and miseries you have known. But, in the end, "you have forgotten the God who formed you"; you have used that same faculty of forgetfulness to forget God. Do not think, for even a moment, that this would work!

I will hide My face from them, I will see what their end shall be. (Deut. 32:20)

Pre-empting the blow

A certain woman came to Rabbi Pinhas HaLevi Horowitz, of Frankfurt to complain about her husband who was giving away all his wealth to charity. She was still speaking when a certain poor man came to complain about his rich brother who was not supporting him. Rabbi Pinhas summoned them to him. The husband of the woman argued: Since he cannot know when his time is up, when he will die and leave his estate to others, and lest he die the following day, he was, therefore, disbursing his property to charity, as it is written: "Righteousness shall go before him" (Ps. 75:14). The stingy rich man who had not supported his brother argued, on the other hand, that since he did not know how long he would live and he might even live for a hundred and twenty years, he was obliged to be responsible and keep his money for himself.

Rabbi Pinhas responded: May Adonai preserve each of you from what he fears. The squanderer who fears that he might die tomorrow - may Adonai preserve him that he live a long life. The stingy one who fears a long life, may Adonai preserve him from longevity.

"Looking through the lattice" (Song of Songs 2:9)

Is not everything revealed and known before God, Who reads the generations ahead of time, Who observes and looks to the end of all the generations? What, then, is the meaning of the words: "I will see what their end shall be"?

Rabbi Shmuel of Sochaczew likened the matter to a father whose son had gone bad. The father hid his face from him in his anger and left him on his own, to his own fate. But from the place of his concealment, the father looked through the leaves of the lattice and watched over his son. So long as his son moved and failed, fell and got up, fell and got up again, the father did not show himself. But the moment the son was standing on the verge of an abyss and, had he fallen, would have had no chance of rising again, his father immediately disclosed himself, warned him and saved him from the danger.

And so it is that, even at a time of concealment, the Holy Blessed One does not remove the Divine providence from the people. Even when "I will hide My face from them", then, too, "I will see what their end shall be", as they stand and immediately the Divine Providence appears over the People of Israel to save them from all distress and trouble.

For they are a very perverse generation. (Deut. 32:20)

Changing their tune

You may ask certain people why they are not seen in the synagogue, and they will reply that, unfortunately, they does not have enough time as they are very troubled with business affairs. When you approach the same people and ask them for a charitable donation, they puts on a sorrowful expression and tells you how difficult times are, business is on strike and they have nowhere from which to take money for a donation.

You enter their home on a fast day and find them eating and you ask: Is this possible? Why are they not fasting? They tells you that they finds it difficult to fast for earlier generations grew weak and died ... but, when the door opens and a poor person comes in to ask for alms, they immediately forgets the "weakness of earlier generations". They turn to the poor angrily, accusing them of being lazy and being unwilling to work.

This, then, is the meaning of the verse: "for they are a very perverse generation" for people change their tune as it suits them for the moment!

He will make expiation for the land of his people. (Deut. 32:43)

Holy Land

We read in Midrash: Rabbi Yohanan explained that the verse 'Better is a dry morsel, and quietness with it' (Prov. 17:1) refers to the Land of Israel, for even should one who eats only bread and salt every day, but live in the Land of Israel, one is assured a place in the world to come. Rabbi Yohanan said: Anyone who walks in the Land of Israel, even for just one hour, and dies therein is assured a place in the world to come, as it is said: "and will make expiation for the land of his people" (Prov. 17).

Moshe came and spoke all the words of this poem in the ears of the people. (Deut. 32:44)

Lesson from the past

In this portion contains the whole history of the Jewish People - from the beginning of its existence as a people and on into the future.

Moshe our Teacher formulates his words in poetic language, but this poem encapsulates all the events of the past and of the future. In the same way as the whole of the Land of Israel was folded under Yaakov's body during the dream of the ladder, so are all the chronicles of the Jewish People condensed into this poem.

In the Song of the Sea, which was sung as Israel departed from Egypt, it is written: "And Israel saw" (Ex. 14:31), for this song was an expression of the wonderful sight they beheld. What they saw then, however, was a one-time sight, never to be repeated. But, in our portion here, it is said: "Moshe spoke in the ears of all the congregation of Israel the words of this poem, until they were ended". This was not a one-time wonder.

Hence our sages, of blessed memory, said about Haazinu: "This is a great poem for it contains something of the present and something of the past, something of the future and something of the world to come" (Sifrei, Haazinu).

Moshe our Teacher admonishes the Children of Israel before his death. He starts by saying: "Remember the days of old" (Deut. 32:7). The events of former generations have to be recalled, so that we may know that we have a glorious past, unlike that of any other nation. And this past was shown in the moral integrity and deeds of loving kindness and mercy of our ancestors in their inter-personal relationships. Do not think that history starts with you or with your parents. No! It begins with "the days of old", with your ancestors, with the simple and guileless behavior of our forbearers who lived an exemplary life of purity.

But remembering alone is insufficient. One also has to give some thought to the matter and understand the past. One has to understand the events; one has to come to grips. with their causes and with their unfolding. From a deep penetration into the nature of the events, we can learn how to conduct ourselves in the future. The glorious past of the Jewish People can provide a lesson for the generations yet to come.

But, if you do not understand the events, then "ask your father, and he will tell you" (Deut. 32:7). If your parents, too, do not understand, then ask "your elders, and they will tell you" (ibid). The instructions here are quite clear. If you are having difficulty understanding the problems of the world, if you are making mistakes in the pathways of life - then turn to ancient sources, go into them in depth and you will find there a solution for all your problems.

Parashat Vezot Habrakha

This is the blessing, with which Moshe the man of God blessed the people of Israel before his death. (Deut. 33:1)

The last blessing

The last act Moshe did before his death was to bless his people. The blessing comes in the form of a long poem, parts of which are directed at the whole people, with other parts addressed to each tribe in its own right. Many titles and names were given to Moshe during his long life. Now, close to the hour of his death, he is called for the first - and also the last - time "the man of God". He is so called not only to emphasize his relationship with God but also to underscore his remaining "a man", even now. More than ever in the past, Moshe is close to God. He is about to leave the earthly world and go to the eternal world but he, nevertheless, does not concentrate on himself alone and he does not muse about his own life in preparation for his meeting with his Maker. Even at such a moment, his heart is given over to the Children of Israel, to bless them. Moshe is permeated throughout with the spirit of God yet he remains a man to his final breath.

Another point: After all the trouble and tribulations Moshe suffered from the Children of Israel for all of the forty years in the Wilderness, and after they were the cause of his having to die in the Wilderness and not enter the Land of Israel, his ideal, nevertheless, was to stand up and bless them. Such a person, who is forbearing and who blesses his people Israel, despite everything, is fit to be called "man of God".

The top step

Rashi comments: "Before his death" means very close to the time of his death. As proof, he adds the saying: "For, if not now, when?"

Rabbi Yitzhak of Vorka was once asked: What was Rashi's intention here and why was he saying something that had not been stated in the Torah? He then replied: nowhere in the whole of the Torah except for here is Moshe termed "man of God". Because of his love for Israel, Moshe should already have blessed them but he always felt in his heart that he had to attain a higher level so as to give his blessing greater force and so he delayed giving them his blessing. But now, having attained the level of "man of God", which is the level of the angels who are permanent and unchanging, not like mortals, he knew that he was very close to the time of his death, and he so blessed Israel "For, if not now, when?"

Indeed, You showed affection for [other] People. (Deut. 33:3)

True love

Rabbi Yosef Zechariah Stern used to say: There is a great difference between affection and love. The Holy Blessed One has affection for other People. But the Torah says in connection with Israel: "Who has chosen God's People, Israel, with love" and "Who loves the People Israel".

A person can have affection for a friend, but, since there is no such thing as a righteous person in the land who does good without sinning, hence the affection is only for the friend's good qualities - not for the friend's shortcomings. When one loves another person, however, it is with all of this person's shortcomings. That is why we say: "And you shall love Adonai your God" (Deut. 6:5), since a person is required to bless the bad just as he blesses the good, hence one has to love the Holy One . And so, too, is it written in the Torah: "And you shall love your neighbor as yourself" (Lev. 19:18). A Jew is bidden to love others with love equal to self love. People have many shortcomings, yet they love themselves. Therefore Scripture says "as yourself". And just as you love yourself, with all your shortcomings, so shall you love others with all their shortcomings.

Moshe commanded us a Torah. (Deut. 33:4)

Eternal Torah

Rabbi Yehoshua Leib Diskin used to say: It is customary among the nations that the rulers enact laws as they see fit. When the ruler changes in a particular country, the existing laws there also change, in accordance with the will of the new rulers. This is not the case with the Torah of Moshe. Its laws and commandments are an eternal inheritance, existing and remaining in the format which was given to us at Sinai, as it is said: "Moshe commanded us Torah, the inheritance of the congregation of Yaakov".

The sages of Israel have already noted that there is a substantive difference between an inheritance in the sense of legacy and an inheritance in the sense of heritage. In the case of a legacy, the inheritors may do as they see fit and they does not have to account to anyone. With heritage, on the other hand, the inheritors are obliged to adhere to it throughout their life and to pass it on to their children.

That is why the following verse is: "And he was king in Yeshurun, when the heads of the people and the tribes of Israel were gathered together". This points to three types of governments. A royal one ("And he was king in Yeshurun"), a governing conducted by a council of elders and heads of the people ("when the heads of the people ... were gathered together") and a republican government, a sort of popular rule of all the citizens in the country ("the tribes of Israel ... together"). We learn from the proximity of these verses here that the laws of the Torah are unchanging - whatever form of government there may exist in the land.

Yearning is also a matter of pain

Rabbi Yitzhak of Gur recounted the following tale: A rich man, an outstanding scholar, sought a husband for his daughter. He traveled to a particular yeshivah and asked the head of the yeshivah to select for him a young prodigy. The head of the yeshivah presented him with three outstanding students so that he could test them and examine their characters. The wealthy scholar asked them a difficult question and said that whoever first solved it would be the husband of his daughter and he would meet all their financial needs.

The three young men struggled with the problem, toiled at great length but were unable to solve it. Two of them realized that they were wasting their time, and withdrew from the contest. The third young man, however, pleaded with the father of the bride to settle the issue for him.

The learned father asked him: Why are you concerned about the solution? You did not manage to solve the problem and so, either way, will not have my daughter as a wife. But the young man continued pleading with him and said: It is true. I did not find the solution on my own. I have lost out and am not fit to marry your daughter. But what am I supposed to do? I am dying to hear some teaching from you, and the problem which you posed is troubling me. I would like to resolve this matter of halakhah. Please do not deny me this. When the wealthy man saw that the young man's soul yearned for Torah in all honesty, he gave him the answer to the problem and also gave him his daughter in marriage.

When the heads of the people and the tribes of Israel were gathered together.... (Deut. 33:5)

His joy is my joy

Rabbi Naftali of Ropshitz used to tell of a great lesson he once learned in a conversation he had had with a simple Jew, a porter by profession. The man was extremely joyous on Simhaht Torah. Rabbi Naftali asked him: What is this joyousness? What connection do you have to this happy occasion? How much Torah have you studied this year that you are so joyous on Simhaht Torah? The Jew answered him straightforwardly and naively: Rabbi, if my brother is celebrating a happy occasion, is his happiness not also mine and should I not be happy with him? Even if I have not myself learned any Torah, I am happy at the joyousness of my brother, the rabbi, who was worthy and studied Torah.

And it is related that a certain person who celebrated excessively on Simhaht Torah was asked: What is the cause of this joy of yours? The rabbi studied and you are joyous? The man replied: On the Eve of Yom Kippur I confess using the words of the "Al het", which contain the verse: "For the sin we have committed before You in the taking of a bribe" although my Creator knows that I have no connection with such a sin and have never been faulted for it. But I have to confess this sin out of a sense of the communal responsibility of all Israel for it is possible that someone has committed it. And if there is communal responsibility for sins, how much more so is there for the study of the Torah and so I rejoice for the Torah learning of my fellow....

The beloved of Adonai shall dwell securely by God; Adonai protects him all the day long. (Deut. 33:12)

That I may dwell in the house of Adonai all the days of my life

Rabbi Avraham Yitzhak Kook said: Our books of ethics teach us that a person should not be excessively friendly with someone else because, where the friendship is too close, they end up hating each other. Therefore, King Solomon also warns us: "Let your foot be seldom in your neighbor's house; lest he become weary of you, and hate you" (Prov. 25:17).

But there is one Friend upon whose friendship it is possible to rely, and with whom one can be friendly at all times, and that is God.

Naftali, satisfied with favor, and full with the blessing of Adonai. (Deut. 33:22)

A double blessing

In each generation, one finds many poor people who are happy with their lot and are welcoming to others; in contradistinction, there are many rich people who are never satisfied with what they have. King Solomon, the wisest of men, already noted: "He who loves silver shall not be satisfied with silver" (Eccles 5:9). This is the reason why Moshe blesses Naftali with a double blessing: that the members of the tribe should be satisfied with what they have and should also feel satisfied at what they have achieved in life and should merit the blessing of Adonai and not know poverty and need in their life.

There has not arisen since in Israel a prophet like Moshe, whom Adonai knew face to face. (Deut. 34:10)

Be yourself

After thirty days of mourning (which is, incidentally, the origin of the thirty day mourning period still observed in the Jewish tradition), Yehoshua appears as the next leader to perform the tasks facing the people - the conquest and settlement of the Land.

The Torah testifies about the new leader that he "was full of the spirit of wisdom" (Deut. 34:9) and ready for the position and the great responsibility it entailed. His wisdom is expressed primarily in the immediately following verse: "And there has not arisen since in Israel a prophet like Moshe...". In his wisdom, Yehoshua understood that, Although he had inherited the position of Moshe, he would never be like Moshe, that he would never succeed in being similar to him.

But the great miracle lies in the fact that the Children of Israel accepted the authority of Yehoshua "and the Children of Israel listened to him". There were, of course, some who grumbled that, by comparison with Moshe, Yehoshua was a much smaller personality and that, if one makes a comparison between them, one is like the sun and the other is like the moon. Nevertheless: "and the Children of Israel listened to him". They understood that Moshe was no longer with them and that the comparison of current leaders with the giants of the past is neither fair nor realistic.

Moshe's death

We are approaching the end of the Five Books of the Torah and, with them. the dramatic death of Moshe, the leader. When Yehoshua, his student, is appointed in his stead, Moshe transfers the leadership of the people to him, and says to him: This people that I am entrusting to you, they are still young kids, they are still babies. Do not be too strict with them with what they do, just as their Master has not been strict with them (Sifrei, Nitzavim).

And Moshe adds: "Be strong and of a good courage; for you must go with this people to the land; and you shall cause them to inherit it" (Deut. 31:7). And then the time comes for Moshe our Teacher to depart this life: "They came and said to him [to Moshe]: The time has come for you to leave the world. He said to them [to the Children of Israel]: I have made things difficult for you over the Torah and the commandments, but now, forgive me. And they said to him: Our Teacher. Our Master, you are forgiven. And the Children of Israel stood around him and said: Moshe, Our Teacher, we have much angered you and have caused you much trouble, forgive us. He said to them: You are forgiven. But I have a request of you. When you enter the Land, remember me and my bones and say: "Poor [Moshe] Ben Amram who ran before us like a horse and whose bones fell in the wilderness".. (Tanhuma, Va-et-hanan 6)

SIMCHA RAZ

Simcha Raz is an Israeli author and educator. He has an M.A. in public administration from the Hebrew University and rabbinic ordination from Merkaz HaRav Kook Yeshivah in Jerusalem. He is the author of many popular books on Aggadic and Hasidic themes, several of which have appeared in English translation, including *A Tzadik in Our Time* (1972), *The Sayings of Menahem Mendel of Kotzk* (1995) and *Hasidic Wisdom: Sayings From The Jewish Sages*, translated by Dov Peretz Elkins and Jonathan Elkins (1997). His articles frequently appear in the Israeli press, and he hosts literary programs in the electronic media in Israel. He has received several literary prizes, and he was awarded the Israel Minister of Religious Affairs' Jewish Heritage Prize in recognition of his efforts in teaching Hebrew language and literature in Israel and throughout the Jewish world, most recently in the Commonwealth of Independent States. He lives in Jerusalem with his wife, Colleeen. They are the parents of two children.

z222.07 Raz
    Raz,Simcha
      The Torah's seventy faces

z222.07
  Raz   Raz,Simcha
          The Torah's seventy faces

Printed in the United States
34019LVS00003B/145